P9-CJF-221
03829165

Considering *Maus*

OKANAGAN COLLEGE
LIBRARY
BRITISH COLUMBIA

Considering *Maus*

Approaches to Art Spiegelman's "Survivor's Tale" of the Holocaust

EDITED BY DEBORAH R. GEIS

UNIVERSITY OF ALABAMA PRESS

Tuscaloosa

Copyright © 2003

The University of Alabama Press
Tuscaloosa, Alabama 35487-0380
All rights reserved
Manufactured in the United States of America
Typeface: Goudy and Goudy Sans

First published 2003
Paperback edition published 2007

∞

The paper on which this book is printed meets the minimum requirements of
American National Standard for Information Science—Permanence of Paper for
Printed Library Materials, ANSI Z39.48-1984.

The Library of Congress has cataloged the hardcover edition as follows:

Considering Maus: approaches to Art Spiegelman's "Survivor's tale" of the
Holocaust / edited by Deborah R. Geis
p. cm.
ISBN 0-8173-1376-1 (cloth : alk. paper)
1. Spiegelman, Art. Maus. 2. Spiegelman, Art—Criticism and interpretation.
3. Holocaust, Jewish (1939–1945)—In literature. 4. Holocaust, Jewish (1939–1945)—
Poland—Biography—Comic books, strips, etc. I. Geis, Deborah R., 1960–
D810.J4C665 2003
741.5´973—dc21

2003005507

ISBN-13 978-0-8173-5435-0 (pbk. : alk. paper)
ISBN-10 0-8173-5435-2 (pbk. : alk. paper)

The editor dedicates this collection to
the memory of her father, Norman W. Geis,
for his bravery in World War II
and in all things thereafter.

Contents

Acknowledgments

I am grateful beyond words to the many people who have stood behind this book from its inception and who have helped to guide it to completion. I thank the staff at the University of Alabama Press for their support and assistance, and Jonathan Lawrence for his skillful copyediting. For their support and encouragement on earlier versions of the manuscript, I thank Ann Lowry, Marianne Hirsch, Stan Garner, David Mikics, and several anonymous readers who wrote thoughtful comments. For the professional inspiration of their own work in related areas, thanks to Scott McCloud, Ellen Schiff, and James Young. The secretarial support at the various institutions where I have taught during the time I spent working on this book has been invaluable, and I especially thank Gerry Beckerman and Evelyn Diaz at Queens College, CUNY, Sue Elkevizth at Oberlin College, and Bobbi Kelley at DePauw University. I am grateful to the Faculty Development Fund at DePauw for providing additional support in the later stages of this project, and to my new colleagues at DePauw, especially those who have shared their enthusiasm for Maus, for inspiring further conversations. Thanks to the many students whose contributions to our discussions of Maus in various classes over the years have shaped this volume in myriad ways. Of course, I offer tremendous gratitude to the writers who contributed to this volume, all of whom have been models of patience, dedication, and talent.

My heartfelt thanks, as always, to my family (Dorothy Geis, Nancy and

Mark Bardgett, Sarah and Brian Moore, and Shirley Geis) for their love and support, as well as to David J. Weiss, Kathleen Moore, Anthony Barone, Karen Vrotsos, Janet Pennisi, Tracy Cornelius, Beth Baldwin, Joyce Ann, Maura Abrahamson, Claudia Petersen, Steven F. Kruger, and Regina Wilmes. The greatest debt that I owe on this project, for his unwavering enthusiasm and innumerable instances of help and support (and for making the world funny again), is to James S. Bennett.

Several of the essays in this volume initially appeared elsewhere, and grateful acknowledgment is made to their editors and publishers for permission to reprint them. Hamida Bosmajian's "The Orphaned Voice in Art Spiegelman's *Maus*" was first published in *Literature and Psychology* 44 (1998): 1–21. Michael Levine's "Necessary Stains: Art Spiegelman's *Maus* and the Bleeding of History" first appeared in *American Imago* 59.3 (2002): 317–41, © The Johns Hopkins University Press, reprinted with permission of the Johns Hopkins University Press, and in *The Belated Witness: Literature, Testimony, and the Question of Holocaust Survival*, copyright by the Board of Trustees of the Leland Stanford Jr. University, forthcoming with Stanford University Press, used with the permission of the Stanford University Press. Nancy Miller's "Cartoons of the Self: Portrait of the Artist as a Young Murderer—Art Spiegelman's *Maus*" was originally published in M/E/A/N/I/N/G 12 (1992): 43–54, © M/E/A/N/I/N/G. Alan Rosen's "The Language of Survival: English as Metaphor in Art Spiegelman's *Maus*" first appeared in *Prooftexts* 15.3 (1995): 249–62, reprinted by permission of Indiana University Press. Michael Rothberg's "'We Were Talking Jewish': Art Spiegelman's *Maus* as 'Holocaust' Production" originally appeared in *Contemporary Literature* 35.4 © 1994, reprinted by permission of the University of Wisconsin Press. Arlene Fish Wilner's "'Happy, Happy Ever After: Story and History in Art Spiegelman's *Maus*" was first published in *Journal of Narrative Technique* 27.2 (1997): 171–89.

Considering *Maus*

Introduction

Deborah R. Geis

Art Spiegelman's two-volume "comic book" *Maus: A Survivor's Tale* is not exactly a comic book, nor is it exactly a novel, a biography (or autobiography), or a work of oral history—and yet it is all of these things. *Maus* is a "graphic novel" insofar as Spiegelman uses pictures as well as words—in more or less the serial comic format—to tell his story, but the story itself is an imaginative rendering of years of his father's real-life oral narratives of the Holocaust, mixed in with the artist's own anguished, ironic personal musings. Like that of many other postmodern "comix" artists,[1] Spiegelman's subject matter is far from comical—and yet the two parts of *Maus* are undeniably filled with rueful, subversive moments of laughter. Ultimately, perhaps, it is the inability to fit *Maus* into a clearly specified genre that makes the work so compelling and unforgettable.[2]

The framework of the two parts of *Maus* (*Maus I: My Father Bleeds History* and *Maus II: And Here My Troubles Began*) is deceptively simple, beginning with the casting of the characters as animal figures: Jews are drawn as mice, Nazis as cats, Poles as pigs, and a few others appear as well. In choosing mice to represent the Jews, Spiegelman plays upon the Nazi propaganda image of the Jews as vermin, combined ironically with the iconic all-American cartoon figure of Mickey Mouse.[3] Indeed, in one moment of *Maus I*, Vladek, the father, tells his cartoonist son Artie that maybe if he's lucky he'll become as successful as "the big shot cartoonist . . . Walt Disney!" (I:133).[4] And in other moments Spiegelman plays with the boundaries of his own chosen metaphor, such as when Vladek the mouse must put on the mask of a pig to pretend he is Polish (I:64 is the first time); when Vladek tries to protect his first wife, Anja, from the rats while they are in hiding by telling her that they are only mice (I:147); when Artie portrays himself at the drawing board with a human face covered by a mouse mask (II:41); and when, in a narrative aside, he asks whether including the stray dogs and cats at his psychiatrist's place "completely louse[s] up [his] metaphor" (II:43).

This cast of animal characters is situated within the intensely self-reflexive, disturbingly comic frame narrative of the strained relationship between Artie and Vladek. Like other postmodern writers and artists, Spiegelman does not deliver a straight chronological narrative; rather, he shows the story that Vladek tells his son about the past developing by fits and starts, interrupted by digressions in the present that reflect both humorously and painfully on how the past has shaped Vladek's behavior in the present (as when he throws out Artie's coat and attempts to give him a new one, or when we see him counting out his pills or attempting to return a half-eaten box of cereal to the grocery store), and by sidetracks and ellipses in the narrative of the past. The act of telling, too, is complicated in postmodernist fashion both by Art/Artie's frequent portrayal of the act (and difficulty) of creating the project of *Maus* (e.g., he draws himself at his drafting board, surrounded by mouse corpses that simultaneously represent the carnage of the Holocaust and his own guilty role as the maker and destroyer of the characters in his own work) and—as several authors in this volume discuss—by employing a variety of nonlinear "tricks" to violate the borders, frames, and sequencing of the comic book frame itself. As Scott McCloud explains in *Understanding Comics*, the comic book format uses a series of sequential panels, read straight across and adhering to certain narrative conventions—as well as key departures from linearity and sequentiality—in order to tell a story within a limited amount of space (5–9, 70–72). Spiegelman, like many other comix artists (e.g., Kim Deitch, Daniel Clowes, Howard Cruse, David Sandlin, Mark Beyer, Ben Katchor, to name only a small sampling of his contemporaries), deploys what is in some ways a cinematic style to play against the linear/sequential: he changes motion from horizontal to vertical; he changes the sizes of frames; he uses close-ups and other "filmic" techniques; he frequently allows material to cross out of the borders/"gutters" and to permeate adjoining frames. In a *Comics Journal* interview with Gary Groth, Spiegelman says, "I'm *literally* giving a form to my father's words and narrative, and that form for me has to do with panel size, panel rhythms, and visual structures of the page, so that a page is a very specific and significant unit, it's not just a stream of panels one after another" ("Spiegelman Interview" 103, 105).

As a work of the postmodern era, Maus is caught up in the problems of representation unique to second-generation Holocaust literature. Theodor Adorno's famous assertion that there could be no more poetry after the Holocaust suggests that horror in its deepest manifestation cannot risk being sanitized and framed as "art." If the Holocaust somehow stands outside the realm of narration, though, one must ask what is to prevent it from becoming mystified or depoliticized. Since to tell the story of the Holocaust is to call forth an area of representation that is ultimately unspeakable or untellable because no form of narrative can hope to portray it, second-generation Holocaust writers have frequently shown the problematics of representation within their work as part of what they also see as an ethical response to the past; they engage in what Jean-François Lyotard refers to as the act of making the "unrepresentable" into the process of representation (81). In other words, the difficulty of telling becomes part of the fabric of the work (in the case of Maus, part of its narrative structure as well as its visual design). As Sidra DeKoven Ezrahi has said of recent Holocaust writing, "Precisely when it is most confined to the unimaginable facts of violence and horror, the creative literature that has developed is the least consistent with traditional moral and artistic conventions" (3). In addition to Spiegelman's work here, one might think of the creations of others as diverse as performance artist Leeny Sack (The Survivor and the Translator), novelist David Grossman (See Under: Love), filmmaker Agnieszka Holland (Europa Europa), and playwright Donald Margulies (The Model Apartment). The act of Holocaust testimony or "witnessing" itself marks a shift from the "documentary" or "realist" mode of representation to the postmodern sense that historical narratives are always fragmented, partial, and subjective—particularly, as we see in Maus, when these narratives are retold and mediated by the second-generation tellers whose own testimony is caught up in both the "responsibility" they feel in telling these stories and their own inability to do so. Sack's subtitle for The Survivor and the Translator, for instance, is "A solo theatre work about not having experienced the Holocaust, by a daughter of concentration camp survivors" (123; emphasis mine).

Critical reactions to Steven Spielberg's Schindler's List have made the problem of reproducing the Holocaust for mass consumption all the more emphatic: does Spielberg's film preserve the memory of the Holocaust in a way that will educate the post-survivor generations of filmgoers (those for whom it would otherwise be no more than a blurrily remembered page in their history textbooks), or does it sanitize and codify the Shoah in Holly-wood terms so that a kind of catharsis results from the closing reunion, where (as in *Jurassic Park*) the ultimate sense is that the audience members have vicariously been "saved" and can go home safely without having to worry about the threat, whether of Nazis or Velociraptors?[5] The second volume of *Maus* ends with a reunion of sorts—that of Vladek and Anja in the internal narrative—but as several commentators discuss, the way in which Spiegel-man frames this reunion leaves the effect far from cathartic.

Indeed, one striking characteristic of second-generation/postmodern Holo-caust literature is its resistance to catharsis. Post-Brechtian political theory has shown us that the Aristotelian notion of catharsis ultimately blunts the audience's ability to act and react in response to the sense that the protago-nists have met their "destinies" as surrogates for the spectators. This is why the mode of traditional tragedy ill suits literature of the Holocaust: the vic-tims (as we see clearly in the case of Vladek) did not "choose" their suffering, nor were they ennobled by it. As Lawrence Langer puts it, "the courage and intelligence of an Oedipus may have pacified that offstage threat we call the Sphinx; but at Auschwitz the devouring beast held center stage, and no hu-man resource seemed able to solve the riddle of its insatiable hunger" (*Ver-sions of Survival* 10).

At the center of the shock and horror that some might experience over the idea of a Holocaust *comic book* is the association of the Holocaust with the idea of the "comic," an association that seems to violate the very idea of what Terrence Des Pres has referred to as Holocaust "etiquette." The comic book itself has a long history of non-comic associations, some of which David Mikics details in his essay in this volume. The specific category of the oxymoronic "Holocaust comic," though, is also an attempt to resist the aes-theticizing impulses that Adorno addresses by forcing the contemplation of the events into a transgressive realm or medium, by calling for the unfamil-iar, the unsettling. In a sense, this goes back to the strategies invoked by the previous generation, the survivors of the concentration camps themselves. Joseph Czarnecki, a Polish photojournalist who visited Auschwitz, said that among the relics of incarcerated artists he found drawings of "elegant bath-room mirrors that mocked the camp's stark reality" (Lipman 161).

Another central critique of *Maus* has been the invocation of metaphor as its artistic strategy: what does it mean to depict Vladek's story through cartoon animal imagery? For second-generation artists like Spiegelman who are struggling with the "place" that the Holocaust can have in a postmodern world where history itself has been shorn into fragments, metaphor becomes an agent for the continual remaking of meaning—or, to paraphrase Norma Rosen, a continual process of re-membering (Ozick, "Roundtable Discussion" 282). As James Young says, "to leave Auschwitz outside of metaphor would be to leave it outside of language altogether: it was known, understood, and responded to metaphorically at the time by its victims; it has been organized, expressed, and interpreted metaphorically by its writers; and it is now being remembered, commented upon, and given historical meaning metaphorically by scholars and poets of the next generation" (*Writing and Rewriting* 91). *Maus*, as the essays in this book make clear, grapples with the "unimaginable" by defying conventions of both literary representation and Holocaust "etiquette." Spiegelman tells Groth, "What happened in *Maus* was the absolute shock of an oxymoron: the Holocaust is absolutely the last place one would look for something to be made in the form of comics, which one associates with essentially trivial, simplified matter. So those two particular things came together and ignited an explosion that I was able to harness" ("Spiegelman Interview" 76). The narrative voices of *Maus* are thus problematic and paradoxical, as is evident in Spiegelman's parodic multiple frames, in the overdetermined "Jewishness" of Vladek's testimony, and in the simultaneously self-mocking and guilty legacy of Artie as the survivor's child (and thus another sort of "survivor" himself). Above all, *Maus* foregrounds the complications of Holocaust storytelling itself; Spiegelman enacts what Hayden White describes as "mak[ing] the difficulty of discovering and telling the whole truth about even a small part of [the Holocaust] as much a part of the story as the events whose meaning it is seeking to discover" ("Historical Emplotment" 41).

Spiegelman's resulting project, the two volumes of *Maus* (parts of which originally appeared serially in the alternative comic book *Raw*—coedited with his wife, Françoise Mouly—and a prototype of which appeared in a 1972 comic entitled *Funny Aminals*), has, like his *New Yorker* covers, proven to be both successful and controversial.[6] Despite trepidation on the part of some more traditional Holocaust commentators who have argued that Spiegelman's choice of the comic book form inevitably trivializes the events and reduces the characters to stereotypes, *Maus* has also been canonized in the popular, scholarly, and alternative presses and has been published in translated editions all over the world; it has been the subject of a special exhibit at the Museum of Modern Art in New York and of a documentary for public television,[7] as well as the recipient of a special Pulitzer Prize in 1992, among other awards. And with Voyager's release on CD-ROM of *The Complete Maus* in 1994 (discussed in the final essay in this volume), Vladek's taped testimony, Spiegelman's notes and drafts, and other archival materials relating to the project became available both to scholars and the general public.

Inevitably, the amazing success of *Maus* took its toll on Spiegelman, and he even satirizes the resulting frenzy in *Maus II* when he shows Artie, swarmed by marketers, agents, and interviewers, reduced to a crying infant as he is besieged by offers: "MAUS—you've read the book—now buy the VEST!" (II:42). In a 1996 cartoon entitled "Mein Kampf" that was published in the Sunday *New York Times Magazine*, he draws himself being chased by a giant mouse and says, "I still prowl the murky caverns of my memory, but now I feel like there's a 5,000 pound mouse breathing down my neck!" (36). Of course, there is always a self-regarding ironic distance even in such moments, but it is clear that Spiegelman—like any artist who creates a career-defining epic work relatively early in his or her lifetime of creative endeavor (one thinks, e.g., of Tony Kushner and *Angels in America*)—has given himself what he refers to as "a hard act to follow" (36).

What distinguishes *Maus* as a subject of academic study—and what will, I think, make it a lasting part of the emerging canon of postmodernist Holocaust literature—is partly the extent to which Spiegelman has managed to say so much with so seemingly little. A "comic book" or "graphic novel" is a deceptively simple genre and framework for a complex, emotionally charged, and historically resonant narrative (Spiegelman later characterized "comic" as a "misleading word" that "often keeps the medium of my choice from getting any respect").[8] One might add to this the extent to which, in an almost unprecedented manner, *Maus* has generated interest across a variety of disciplines, ranging from historiography to oral history, postmodernist studies to Jewish studies (to name only a few of the academic ones). Although *Maus* has been the subject of considerable critical interest since it first began appearing in *Raw*, inspiring scholarly responses from, among others, the late Holocaust scholar Terrence Des Pres, cultural critic Miles Orvell, feminist autobiography expert Nancy K. Miller (reprinted in this volume), and comix specialist Joseph Witek,[9] the present volume marks the first critical book to bring together a collection of essays exclusively on the subject of *Maus:* its reception, its narrative structure, its controversial status as both "comic book" and Holocaust document. It is my hope that this volume will allow access to the tremendous diversity of voices speaking on *Maus* from across the disciplines, gathered here to mark an opportunity for interested readers to hear these voices speaking with (and sometimes even against) one another.

Although it is inevitable that there will be some overlap among the topics of the individual essays, the three sections of this book are designed to allow readers to focus on some critical "considerations" that particular essays have in common. The first of these, "Mice and Metaphors, Photographs and Comix: *Maus* as (Auto)biography," pays particular attention to the narrative and visual "tools" that Spiegelman uses, especially the countercultural narrative devices of underground comics, the casting of the characters as animals, and the use of photographs within the cartoon medium. *Maus* may be a biographical portrait of Vladek (or an autobiographical portrait insofar as he speaks his testimony in the first person), but it is also a type of autobiography of Art Spiegelman, and the artist's difficulties with his family and his subject matter are an integral part of the work. The three essays that explore this facet of Spiegelman's project emphasize Art/Artie's complicated and troubling role as a "survivor of survivors" and a self-reflexive commentator on his own creations.

David Mikics's essay, "Underground Comics and Survival Tales: *Maus* in Context," situates Spiegelman's work in the tradition of Judaic storytelling as well as the (counter)tradition of such underground "comix" artists as R. Crumb and Jack Jackson. Mikics argues that Spiegelman, like Crumb and Jackson, plays against the conventions of the mainstream Marvel Comics–style superhero genre; ultimately, though, *Maus* reveals a different approach to the act of self-disclosure and the depiction of violence than can be seen in these two artists' "satirical thematics of excess." In the context of Spiegelman's own career, Mikics sees Spiegelman's post-*Maus* illustrations for Joseph Moncure March's *The Wild Party* as a further movement away from the "neurotic immediacy" of his early underground work into an even more distanced realm of "artifice": "if *Maus* is about working through, *The Wild Party* is about playing out."

The effect of being a second-generation survivor-translator can be traumatic and deeply felt, as Hamida Bosmajian shows in her essay, "The Or-phaned Voice in Art Spiegelman's *Maus*." She emphasizes that the "Hell Planet" on which Art/Artie finds himself is connected to his feelings of guilt and abandonment as an "orphaned" child of Holocaust survivors. Using psychoanalytic theory as well as a close visual scrutiny of Spiegelman's tech-niques (and his earlier drafts and commentary on the creation of *Maus*), Bosmajian argues that underlying the apparent focus on *Vladek's* narrative is a complex set of narratives depicting Art/Artie's repressed pain that he—like other children of survivors—has been forced to consider "insignificant in re-lation to the disastrous history of Auschwitz."

Nancy K. Miller's essay, "Cartoons of the Self: Portrait of the Artist as a Young Murderer—Art Spiegelman's *Maus*," focuses on the autobiographical gestures that Spiegelman makes in *Maus* by his use of a technique Miller sees as common to female autobiography: the "construction of identity through alterity." In this case, of course, the "other" is Vladek, and Miller shows how the father/son relationship in *Maus* not only shapes Art's development as an artist but also raises questions about the risks he takes in creating a less-than-flattering portrayal of Vladek. Moreover, Miller is concerned with the erasure of the maternal that comes as the result of Anja's (and her diaries') disap-pearance: "through the father's murder of the mother's texts, the son seeks to regain his own monstrosity: the fatal unseemliness of surviving the vic-tims, but not without violence of his own."

The second section of the book, "Blood Legacies: *Maus* and Holocaust Testimony," brings together the two kinds of survivorship evoked in the pre-vious section to raise larger questions about where *Maus* fits (or resists fitting) in the genre of literature/testimony on the Shoah and how this, in turn, re-flects the difficulty of finding adequate verbal and visual languages to repre-sent the Holocaust in contemporary culture (especially in the medium of the comic book).

In "Necessary Stains: Art Spiegelman's *Maus* and the Bleeding of His-tory," Michael G. Levine discusses the implications of Art's status as a trans-lator of his father's tale, as a "talebearing survivor" himself. Levine takes on *Maus*'s visual tropes—such as bleeding, smoking, and the conflated safety de-posit box/coffin images—and subjects them to psychoanalytic scrutiny, argu-ing that the narratological functions of these images (e.g., the "bleeding" of frames, the "smoke screen" as structural principle) suggest ways in which the "body" of *Maus*'s text enacts Art's own processes of trauma, survival, and "translation," or bearing witness.

Whereas most of the (auto)biographical considerations of *Maus* have tended to focus on Art's suffering at the hands of his father, in "'Happy, Happy Ever After': Story and History in Art Spiegelman's *Maus*," Arlene Fish Wilner takes a different perspective, informed by her interest in Jewish ethical theory. After an initial consideration of the problems of using metaphor in Holocaust representation, Wilner turns to the portrayals of Mandelbaum (Vladek's friend in Auschwitz) and of Vladek himself to discuss Spiegelman's approach to the meeting of story (narrative) and history (that which, in the shadow of the Holocaust, resists totalizing representations but must nevertheless be told). Vladek's testimony, according to Wilner, is informed by the "tension between the coherence of a narrative informed by a personal victory that seems at least in part to have been earned and the knowledge that this victory is only to have survived as a moral human being—with never-healing psychic wounds—unimaginable and meaningless suffering."

Alan C. Rosen provides a different, speech-oriented approach to the issue of Holocaust testimony in "The Language of Survival: English as Metaphor in Art Spiegelman's *Maus*." Rosen focuses in this essay on how both Vladek's "fractured English" and Spiegelman's rendering of it problematize the extent to which English is a "fit" language to convey Holocaust experience. As Vladek's use of English at several points in his narrative conveys its connection with secrecy and authority, English itself serves as a site of "fantasies of mastery and transformation." Yet this deployment of English as "the competent language of survival" is complicated by Art's representation of Vladek's English in the frame narrative of *Maus* as the "incompetent language of the survivor," which ultimately becomes a reflection of "the foreignness of the Holocaust itself."

The final section of this book, "Kitsch, 'Commerz,' and Cybermice: Marketing *Maus*," opens our examination to broader social, cultural, and technological perspectives.[10] With *Maus*'s enormous critical success and Spiegelman's professed resistance to its exploitation, one might well ask what possibilities and predicaments are created as new generations of readers and scholars contemplate the work.

In "'We Were Talking Jewish': Art Spiegelman's *Maus* as 'Holocaust' Production," Michael P. Rothberg takes a perspective informed by the discipline of cultural studies to explore the significance of *Maus*'s widespread popularity in relation to the "marketing" of the Shoah (in, e.g., the film *Schindler's List*). Rothberg suggests that the late 1960s mark a turning point in Jewish identification with the Holocaust, one linked to upheaval in Israel and throughout world politics (including the events of May 1968). Strikingly, it is also the time of Spiegelman's mother's suicide. Spiegelman's paradoxical (and self-consciously ironic) entrapment between resistance to and participation in the commodification of the Holocaust, Rothberg suggests, marks him as a product of his generation as *Maus* reveals the narrator-artist-son caught within the tangled threads of assimilationism, rebellion, and tradition.

This volume closes with a look at contemporary technology by way of the "cyber*Maus*" in an essay by John C. Anderson and Bradley Katz entitled "Read Only Memory: *Maus* and Its Marginalia on CD-ROM." Spiegelman's work was in some ways given a new life (though, as Anderson and Katz argue, it should not be seen as having been reconceived entirely) with the appearance of *The Complete Maus* in 1994. The access that the CD-ROM provides *Maus* scholars and fans to audio transcripts, family documents, drafts, and so forth allows for a crucial resource. Anderson and Katz suggest, though, that this access raises new questions about what constitutes the "complete" text and about how the various production decisions that went into the making of the CD-ROM affect the issues of narrativity, memory, Holocaust documentation, and Anja's absent voice that are already present in *Maus*. Though valuable, they argue, the CD-ROM "by definition is incapable of completing the gestures in *Maus* that indicate how incomplete Spiegelman's project must remain."

As this concluding essay acknowledges, even a "complete" *Maus* foregrounds the feeling of incompleteness or insufficiency that seems to accompany any attempt to render Holocaust experience. Yet, Spiegelman's very awareness of these limitations allowed him to pursue the work, playing (sometimes with mordant humor) with the difficulty of re-presenting his parents' experience (and his own). And I hope it is a tribute to Spiegelman's work to suggest that despite all of the rich words these writers offer on *Maus*, this volume, too, can never really be complete—for the emotional, aesthetic, and intellectual power of *Maus* is of such resonance that there will always be more to say.

Notes

1. "Comix" is a term that originates with the underground comics artists of the 1960s; as DeHaven explains, it refers in part to the "co-mix, or blend, of images and words" (16).

2. As several writers in this volume discuss in different contexts, Spiegelman

requested that the *New York Times* move *Maus* from its fiction to its nonfiction bestseller list.

3. This connection is made explicit by the epigraph to *Maus I*, which cites a Hitler speech saying that the Jews are less than human, as well as the epigraph to *Maus II*, which quotes a German newspaper article condemning Mickey Mouse and denouncing Jewish "vermin." The connection with Mickey Mouse is complicated by historical accounts of Walt Disney's own anti-Semitism; see Leonard Mosley, *Disney's World* (New York: Stein and Day, 1985), cited in Gilman, *The Jew's Body* 26.

4. Parenthetical references here (and throughout this volume) will indicate *Maus I* as "I" and *Maus II* as "II," followed by page number.

5. For a variety of critical perspectives on *Schindler's List*, see Loshitzky.

6. The editor of *Funny Aminals* was Terry Zwigoff, later director of the film *Crumb* (1995). For a comparison between *Maus* and the proto-*Maus* in *Funny Aminals*, see Witek 103–6. For a critique of Spiegelman's infamous 14 February 1993 *New Yorker* cover depicting a Hasidic man and a black woman kissing, see the footnote in Michael Rothberg's essay in this volume, or see Williams 91–93. For Spiegelman's own (very frank) comments on his work for the *New Yorker*, see Groth, "Spiegelman, Part II" 112–23.

7. *Serious Comics: Art Spiegelman* (1994); broadcast on WNET (PBS). I thank Maureen Baum for referring me to this program.

8. See Spiegelman's essay on *Plastic Man* creator Jack Cole for further discussion of the problem of the current status of comics in high/low culture ("Comix 101" 77). He adds (surely with some awareness of the pun on "Art"), "Comic books must reposition themselves—possibly as Art—in order to survive as anything more than part of the feeder system for Hollywood. Otherwise, like vaudeville, they will vanish" (78). DeHaven also discusses this phenomenon (9, 16).

9. See Des Pres; Orvell; N. K. Miller, "Cartoons of the Self" (also in this volume); Witek 96–120.

10. In a page from his sketchbook reprinted in Groth's "Art Spiegelman Interview," Spiegelman plays upon the definition of "Commerz":

1. Abbr. com., comm. The buying and selling of goods, especially on a large scale. 2. Intellectual exchange or social intercourse. 3. Sexual intercourse . . . (Old French, from LATIN commercium: com (collective) + merz (stem merc-), merchandise.

To find a comix (Abbr. com.) free of commerce, an ART that can sustain and also sustain the ARTIST (to make a "living"). Fuck it. Fuck me. I'm fucked: fuckemISM. (109)

I
Mice and Metaphors, Photographs and Comix

Maus as (Auto)biography

1
Underground Comics and Survival Tales

Maus in Context

David Mikics

This essay places Art Spiegelman's *Maus* both within the arc of his own career, as a midpoint between *Breakdowns* (1977) and *The Wild Party* (1994), and in relation to the traditions of underground comics, where he began his work. I will try to define the way in which *Maus* draws on, and diverges from, underground comics' use of factual history, of autobiographical reflection, and of satire. Finally, I will examine one instance in which Spiegelman inflects *Maus* with a self-consciously Judaic theme, the blessing of the son by the father, in order to mark its difference both from the chaotic world of underground artists like R. Crumb and Jack Jackson and from the often prefabricated assertions of heroic destiny in mainstream comics. In comics all characters wear the mask, and the comics medium therefore emerges as perfectly suited to the story of Spiegelman's father, Vladek, with Vladek's reliance on disguise and Odyssean trickery. But Spiegelman's choice of the comics as the way to tell the "survivor's tale" also responds to the valuing within Jewish tradition of survival through interpretive agility.

Spiegelman's revision of a motif from Jewish tradition, namely, Jacob's deception of his father, Isaac, positions Vladek in both the parental and the filial·role. In this account I want to consider Vladek broadly as a hero along the lines of Jacob. Vladek is a trickster not just in order to survive under the Nazis but in order to flourish, as is shown in his seduction of Artie's mother, Anja, and his affiliation with her wealthy in-laws. Vladek, like Jacob, struggles with the angel of death and is spared, and he is much preoccupied with gaining the blessing, being marked for survival by paternal and priestly hands.[1] Before and during his experience in Auschwitz, Vladek survives through Jacob-like cleverness; but, at the very beginning of Maus, he is tricked by his son, who falsely promises Vladek that he won't include the story of his courting of Anja in Maus. In this way, Spiegelman announces from the start that this narrative is the seizing, as well as the honoring, of an inheritance: Artie takes Vladek's story from him with a Vladek-style deception. I will argue, though, that Vladek finally sees his survival as having been given the blessing rather than stealing it as Jacob did, a surrender of responsibility that responds to the enormity of the Shoah, which makes survival finally a matter of accident rather than heroic achievement.

When the first volume of Maus appeared in 1986,[2] its success, culminating in a Pulitzer Prize for both volumes in 1992, was seen as something of a coming-of-age for comics (which were already being rechristened "graphic novels").[3] Comics, both mainstream and underground, have frequently signified male adolescence, and Spiegelman's grasp of a subject matter unrivaled in its sobering, adult status, the Shoah, indicated his own passage beyond the flamboyant, unguided youthfulness of his earlier work, collected in Breakdowns (1977).[4] Instead of the arrested development and eternal questing of the comic book superhero, Spiegelman in Maus presents a recognition of temporality relatively uncharacteristic of comics, an encounter with history.

Maus is a coming-of-age for its medium and its author, but it is also a meditation on the stylistic choices that narrative comics have always confronted. The superhero tradition, involving heroic battles with larger-than-life forces, was confronted in the 1960s by the ferocious satirical energy of the underground. What came out of this meeting in the 1980s was an emphasis on the everyday that was already developing within both the superhero and the underground strains. But the new flourishing of autobiographical detail in comics at times ran the risk of banality, the avoidance of historically significant subject matter in favor of a sad or whimsical maturity (in the work of remarkable comics artists like Harvey Pekar, Julie Doucet, and Daniel Clowes). Spiegelman's Maus, by confronting a subject matter of unprecedented significance, for the first time lent high ambition to a familiar subgenre of comics, the comics of everyday life.

The last three decades of the twentieth century saw, in American comics, a backlash against the superheroic that led, all too often, to a tepid and aimless, if sometimes charming, low mimetic realism. Diana Schutz's introductory remarks to Terry Moore's diverting *Strangers in Paradise* suggest the typical "humanizing" agenda of such comics: "This looked to be a comic book about real humans—girls, even—with nary a spandex-clad super-type in sight!" (Moore n.p.).

One might not surmise from Schutz's statement, though, that from the early 1960s on the superhero strain in comics increasingly accommodated a realm of the personal and unheroic. Since the golden age of comics in the 1940s, the medium has depended on an energizing separation, but also interference, between the magical careers of superheroes and the mundane intimacy of the everyday. Superheroes like Batman and Superman, rather like former president Bill Clinton, appeal to us as characters burdened by a contemporary version of the medieval theory of the king's two bodies, a split between the larger-than-life office of a heroic savior and the everyday weakness of someone like us.

Beginning in the early 1960s, Marvel comics bounced back from the medium's commercial slump in the 1950s by integrating these dimensions, by humanizing its superheroes. Marvel heroes such as the Fantastic Four enjoyed an unprecedented integration of intimacy and superpowers. The Four's Stretch and Sue, as married superheroes, provided a parental framework, with Sue's brother Johnny (the Human Torch) as privileged elder son and their sidekick Ben Grimm (the Thing) as gargantuan, scene-stealing infant (see Daniels 86). In the Fantastic Four, afflicted by their consciousness of their implausible, mutant natures, we see a twilight-of-the-gods motif in which freakish outcasts are burdened rather than blessed by their superpowers. Such weakness is the price of eroding the barrier between the heroic and the intimate that remains in Batman and Superman but which melts away with the Fantastic Four and, even more definitively, with Peter Parker, the Spider-Man, Marvel's other great success story in the 1960s. The two major revivals of the superhero genre in the 1980s, Frank Miller's *Batman, the Dark Knight Returns* (1986) and Alan Moore and Dave Gibbons's *Watchmen* (1987), both rely on the pervasive sense of superheroism as a potentially shameful or lunatic manifestation of personality.[5]

In the Marvel comics of the early and mid-1960s, we see a marriage of heroism and everyday intimacy intended to "save" the superhero genre. In the explosion of underground comics that, as the 1960s went on, began to rival the superhero mode, a newly ruthless social satire appeared. Instead of exploring a personal realm lived soap-opera style à la Spider-Man, underground comics revealed the hero—who was often the artist's self-portrait, as in the exemplary cases of Crumb and Justin Green—to be a troubled, self-doubting outsider. By the late 1960s, underground comics reflected the alarming fragmentation of personality under the pressure of America's vast cultural crisis. The narrative germ of *Maus*, "Prisoner on the Hell Planet," which concerns the young, hippieish Artie's mental breakdown after his mother's suicide (he chants from *The Tibetan Book of the Dead*), hints that Spiegelman has chosen the underground, with its focus on the chaotic, traumatic encounter with parental and social authority, rather than the mainstream superheroic as his avenue to a comic book about the Shoah.

Other choices were possible. There have been attempts to tell the story of the Holocaust within the superhero genre, notably the two-volume work of Patrick Cothias and Paul Gillon derived from Martin Gray's Holocaust testimony, *Au nom de tous les miens*.[6] But in Cothias and Gillon the heroism resembles an all-too-familiar superhero fantasy: young Gray, blond and blue-eyed, disguises himself as an Aryan and courageously outwits the Nazis.[7] In *Maus* a different kind of trickster is depicted, one whose dignity in the midst of horrors enables him to survive in a disenchanted world starkly opposed to the quest-romance scenarios of the superhero genre.[8]

Part of the appeal of American underground comics in the late 1960s was their suspicion of superhero grandeur. As I have been suggesting, this suspicion has its beginning within the superhero genre itself. The underground, though, went further, moving beyond the tempered heroism of a comic like the Fantastic Four, with its sensitive portrayal of the superhero as a socially marginalized freak, to an exploding of conventional pieties and an invention of new ways to convey psychic distortion and suffering. The acknowledged master of the American underground tradition is, of course, R. Crumb. Crumb's beginnings in the 1960s were influenced by Harvey Kurtzman's work at *Mad* magazine, but Crumb saw satire as excruciation rather than *Mad*-style mockery. Northrop Frye describes Kafka's *Strafkolonie* (*In the Penal Colony*) as occupying the sixth phase of satire, in which, like Dante's pilgrim, we see Satan sprawled upside down, whereas tragedy sees him right side up.[9] Exactly such hellish extremism characterizes Crumb's oeuvre. Spiegelman, while drawing on the confessional energies and deep reservoirs of psychic pain that Crumb introduced into underground comics, will shun Crumb's savage, satirical manner. Sequences like those depicting a shrunken Artie in his studio and psychiatrist's office clearly demonstrate Spiegelman's characteristic use of distorted size to convey his autobiographical hero's jagged state of mind (II:43, 45). Though sometimes bottom-heavy and gargantuan, more often Crumb's miniaturized self, panicked and spindly, resembled Tenniel's Alice shoved through a countercultural looking glass.

For all its bluntness, Crumb's LSD-twisted style in the late 1960s developed an oblique, racy fragmentariness that carried over into Spiegelman's early work. Spiegelman himself describes the comics in *Breakdowns* as placing "obstacles" before the reader (see Juno 8). With *Maus*, Spiegelman moves from inventively shattering stories to successfully conveying his father's testimony, even as he approaches this survivor's tale by recognizing the difficulty of telling it.

The crucial issue of Spiegelman's career is the interference and connection between historical concern and autobiographical interiority. This issue, as I have suggested, can best be understood through the work of his predecessors in underground comics, especially Crumb. I now want to focus on another of Spiegelman's underground precursors, Jack Jackson. Jackson's historical comics, both fictional and nonfictional—for example, his tripartite saga of his invented American Indian hero Yoyo Pintada, *The Good Life, The Savage Within*, and *Possum on a Stick*—implicate the reader in the horrifying crimes of his demonic, Juvenalian characters. Spiegelman, though he is influenced by Jackson's painstaking research and fearless desire for the truth, achieves much greater distance from violence in his work. Jackson indulges an EC comics–derived adolescent fascination with gore. For him, as Joseph Witek observes, "politics and gore are inseparable" (53). By contrast, Spiegelman presents the violence of the Holocaust in a more detached way. The exceptions—the rumor Vladek hears about children having their brains dashed against a wall by the Nazis; the mass burning of Hungarian Jews at Auschwitz—stand out as exceptions (I:108, II:72). They would not be exceptional in the comics of Jackson or Crumb, which rely on a satirical thematics of excess.[10] Spiegelman's restraint clarifies the necessary reticence of a narrative that gives the scheme or blueprint of destruction rather than the naked and defiled bodies that are its result. Spiegelman has always employed clever, explanatory breakdown devices, the son's analogy to Vladek's trickiness. The Dick Tracy panels in *Breakdowns* become the explanatory diagrams of the hideout, of Vladek's shoemaking in *Maus*, of the crematoria at Auschwitz (I:110, II:60, 70). In *Maus* such deflecting of horror through design also serves to point up the central role of interpretation in Vladek's experience, from the priest who reads his tattooed number as propitious to Anja's gypsy fortuneteller (II:28, 133). In this disastrous world, paradoxically, the omens are favorable. As I will argue, the receiving of the blessing that Artie, like Vladek before him, achieves is *Maus*'s final evidence of interpretive luck.

Spiegelman in *Maus* develops a visual discretion, an economy and clarity of line, that contrasts with the densely hatched, superdetailed grotesquery of Jackson's work. In Crumb's oeuvre, as Scott McCloud puts it, "the curves of innocence are betrayed by the neurotic quill-lines of modern adulthood, and left painfully out of place" (126). Both Jackson and Crumb depict insane worlds, and their visual styles testify by way of fractured, hysterical overstatement to the shock that defines underground comics as a form: the collision within the self between the adolescent naïveté of mainstream comics and the horrors of a pitiless adult universe. In Spiegelman's mice, by contrast, innocence survives, only to be crushed by *die Katzen*: the confrontation that is internal in Jackson and Crumb remains external in Spiegelman.

Spiegelman's satire is far more decorous or tactful than that of the underground comics tradition that spawned him. Satire in Crumb and Jackson plays up the grotesque in a near-traumatic fashion, though it also fends off trauma by the outrageous use of horror-movie-style gross-out. In his saga of *Pintado*, for example, Jackson dwells on the mutilation of their female victims by the U.S. cavalry, and he summarizes the brutality of the American West with a tableau featuring a horrific, delighted skeleton, the body of historical death. In Crumb, a typically virtuosic rendition of adolescent distress is ornamented by a persecution-and-revenge fantasy that culminates in a gloriously excessive panel showing the narrator chopping up a nun, envoy of the oppressive superego that haunts the Catholic male teenager. Crumb accompanies his outrageous gesture of self-liberation with a memorable cry directed at his moralizing critics: "Eat nun's brains, you bastards!"

In Spiegelman's work, by contrast, satire provides a frightening, but also comforting, impersonality. Reducing Jews to mice and Germans to cats is frightening because it echoes the Nazis' own reduction of their victims to nonhuman status: *Maus I* uses as its epigraph Hitler's remark that "the Jews are undoubtedly a race, but they are not human." But in Spiegelman's hands this reduction veers off into the gentleness of beast fable, the "funny animals" convention instantly and universally identified with the comics medium. Spiegelman's use of theriomorphic characters functions as a shield, enabling the presentation of a history that would otherwise be intolerable in its horror and would devolve into a raw account of personal nightmare.

There is a sense in which *Maus* was always the center, even the starting point of Spiegelman's career. Vladek's practice of remembering through telling stories, prompted by his son, gives birth to Art's art. *Breakdowns* is subtitled "From *Maus* to Now," and it includes Spiegelman's first shaky attempt to tell a piece of Vladek's story. This brief proto-*Maus* achieves significance as a sign of the artist's early failure to convey his father's experience. As a mere inadequate snapshot of a horrific past, its fragmentariness suggests the breakdown in narrative technique that characterizes many Holocaust testimonials, which constantly bear witness to the difficulty of finding an answerable language for such unimaginably extreme experience. The existential extremism of "Prisoner on the Hell Planet," the early comic drawn in expressionistic-woodcut style included in both *Breakdowns* and *Maus*, functions as an instance of unbearably intense memory that cannot do justice to history as Vladek's story, when fully unfolded in *Maus*, can.

The nomination of Vladek for survival, first by his rabbi grandfather, who comes to him in a dream, and then by the priest in Auschwitz, signifies a design that would make Vladek's history make sense. The grandfather, with furry locks, phylactery, and enormous hands, tells Vladek, who is tossing and turning in bed, "Don't worry, my child . . . you will come out of this place—free! . . . on the day of Parshas Truma" (I:57). Unlike Vladek's father, who starves and sickens his son in order to enable him to escape the Polish draft in 1922, and is shown shaking him awake (I:46), the grandfather brings a promise of freedom rather than a contorted and laborious effort to avoid the inevitable. The vision of the grandfather and the appearance of the priest in Auschwitz are crucial moments of illumination in Vladek's history: in both he is saved by elder, male religious figures who bless him with fatherly assurance.[11]

The narrative's emphasis on such nomination from above or beyond does not, of course, negate Vladek's own ingenuity, the linguistic and artisanal skills, and the adeptness at disguise that contribute to his survival. Near the end of *Maus I*, Vladek wears a pig mask, using his excellent Polish to impersonate a Pole. The Pole hails Vladek with "Heil Hitler," a salutation that ironically ensures Vladek's own continued health (I:149). Even more than the mouse and the cat, the pig is a resonant animal in *Maus*. It is interesting to note that not only did the Nazis sometimes use the image of the pig for the Poles, just as they referred to Jews as vermin, but that Jewish prohibition of pork has traditionally been explained in anti-Semitic lore by identifying Jews, too, as pigs, who are reluctant to eat their own kin. Moreover, Rashi, the great eleventh-century commentator on the Hebrew Bible, associates the pig with the tribe of Esau, cheated by the brother, Jacob, who impersonates him.[12] Nazi doctrine privileged Poles over Jews, but the Poles' purpose, like that of pigs in pork-loving Germany, was to feed the Reich. Vladek the mock Pole engineers his own luck, as if literalizing a popular German expression, *er hat einen Schwein* ("he has a pig," i.e., a stroke of good luck).

Spiegelman's later work, an illustrated version of Joseph Moncure March's tale of the Roaring Twenties, *The Wild Party* (1994), moves even further into satirical impersonality and even further away from the punishing interiority that characterized his underground beginnings. In *The Wild Party*, human life becomes a cold, stylized dance of figures, guided by the masks they rigidly wear. Here Spiegelman develops, by acting out the predictable futures implied by the rigidifying, the fluidity of *Maus II*'s celebratory panel announcing "The War is Over" (II:105). The party takes on a stiff, hysterical cast in Spiegelman's rendition of March's herky-jerky plot, calling to mind Bergson's theory of comedy as mechanical, compelled action. Often in *Maus* Spiegelman evokes the sense of life's events as a controlling design that places us within it, and *The Wild Party* projects such a design relentlessly, everywhere the artist turns. An example from *Maus* is the panel of Vladek and Anja traveling along a swastika-shaped crossroads; another is the frequent use of cantilevered, latticed windows or framing devices like that of the Jews who see a swastika flag from their railroad car (I:125, 32).[13] As I have mentioned, *Maus* uses diagrams and maps to manage the horrors it depicts and to invoke Vladek's survival as a careful negotiation of Auschwitz, the familiar hell on earth about which, Vladek says, "We knew everything" (I:157).

The Wild Party is not a mere jeux d'esprit or desperately needed break after the huge labor of presenting Vladek's story. Instead, Spiegelman here as in *Maus* draws on the potential of satirical distance to elicit a detached readerly identification, in contrast to the neurotic immediacy that characterized "Prisoner on the Hell Planet" and other early work. But if *Maus* is about working through, *The Wild Party* is about playing out. The stakes are, obviously, far lower than in Vladek's story: now released from the enormous burden of historical responsibility, and free as well from compulsive autobiographical angst, Spiegelman in *The Wild Party* enters a world of pure artifice. By offering such liberty, *The Wild Party* makes us look back to Vladek's age of innocence, before the Nazis, as a Valentino-style sheik of the dance floor (I:9).

The panel near the end of *Maus I* depicting the gates of Auschwitz's hell reminds one of Primo Levi's comment in *The Drowned and the Saved* that

Auschwitz was a literalization or realization of Dante's *Inferno* (I:157). As readers waited for the second volume of *Maus*, they wondered how Spiegelman could possibly convey such a panorama of misery. The answer lies in part with the artist's agile, selective attention to Vladek's own maneuvering for survival. But the story reminds us, as well, that Vladek's luck is finally not the product of his own cleverness but the intervention of something else, whether one wants to call it God, fate, or chance. In the final panels of *Maus II*, Artie sits on his father's bed, his tape recorder still at the ready, as Vladek announces, "So . . . let's stop, please, your tape recorder.. . . I'm tired from talking, Richieu, and it's enough stories for now." As Artie stands up, the camera pulls back, and father and son recede into space; we then cut to the tombstone of Vladek and Anja, with Artie's signature beneath it. The signature, the son's blessing on his father, analogizes the years he has spent on *Maus* to the lifespans of his parents: the signature reads, like a memorial inscription, "Art Spiegelman 1978–1991." The analogy implies that this story is what counts, and what consecrates, Artie's life—a self-blessing, then, and a promise of rest.[14]

On this final page of *Maus*, Vladek, moving away from his audience into both sleep and death, anoints Artie by calling him Richieu, the name of the favored sibling with whom Artie has tried unsuccessfully to compete. Like Jacob, Artie has received the blessing destined for Richieu, but as in Vladek's case, rather than stealing it, it is unexpectedly given to him. Moreover, Artie, though a younger brother, is more an Esau than a Jacob, an unfavored son condemned to rival unsuccessfully Richieu's sad eternal, youthful promise (II:14). Artie is ignorant of Judaism and he has denied his father, calling him a "murderer" (I:159). But only through Artie's faithful attention to Vladek's religion, alongside his own Beckett-influenced nihilism, can Vladek be truly named by his son (for the Beckett, see II:45). As I have suggested, this attention takes the form of his use of an age-old religious motif, the giving of the blessing.

At the end of *Maus II*, Vladek's history, as well as his relationship with Artie, stills and resolves itself like a photograph—like the photograph we see of Richieu, to whom *Maus II* is dedicated, along with Art's own daughter, Nadja. As Richieu is a memory, so Artie too is receding into memory for Vladek, and vice versa. Vladek's phrase "that's enough stories for now" conjures innocence by implying the scenario of a parent putting a child to sleep at bedtime, with stories used as diversion rather than, as in *Maus*, as revelation. But something has been revealed that rarely appears in comics: the afterlife of a religious idea, the father's nomination of his son to history and to the future.

Notes

1. Sarna writes of the "unrelieved series of trials and tribulations" that distinguish Jacob's experience from those of Abraham and Isaac (183).

2. Between 1980 and 1985 *Maus* appeared in installments in the influential "graphix magazine" *Raw*, edited by Spiegelman and his wife, Françoise Mouly, but it always seemed to stand apart from the ascetic Euro-experimentalism and florid American underground pranks that set *Raw*'s tone. For more on *Raw*, see Spiegelman and Mouly's interview in Groth and Fiore, eds., *The New Comics*:

3. Will Eisner's *A Contract with God* was the first self-proclaimed graphic novel. For a discussion of the graphic novel, see Eisner's *Comics and Sequential Art*.

4. Adulthood, of course, entails in the case of *Maus* incorporation into academic discussions like the present one. Harvey writes that Spiegelman's artistic "choices give the work as a whole the kind of ambiguity that qualifies it for interminable analysis and discussion (making it eminently suitable for college literature courses)" (239). Spiegelman himself has bristled at the popularity of using *Maus* to present Jewish culture or experience in the college curriculum.

5. Sabin considers *Batman* and *Watchmen* along with *Maus* as the "Big Three" of comics' "new wave" (176).

6. *Au nom de tous les miens* was issued in German as *Der Schrei nach Leben*. Interestingly in the context of *Maus*'s beast fable, young Gray, growing up in Poland during the Nazi era, identifies with a neighborhood *Kater* (tomcat), sometimes an image of the Jew.

7. For an acute critique of Cothias and Gillon and a praise of Spiegelman, see Ole Frahm and Michael Hein, "Hilflose Täter: Was Auschwitz in einigen Comic-Geschichten verloren hat," in Kaps 90–106. See also, in the same volume, Kai-Steffen Schwarz, "Vom Aufmucken und Verstummen der Kritiker: Die Diskussion um Art Spiegelmans *Maus*," 107–14. The first attempt in comics to deal with the Holocaust was Bernard Krigstein's often-cited *Master Race* (1955), the subject of an article by Spiegelman, "An Examination of *Master Race*," in *Squa Trout* no. 6 (1975): 41–47.

8. For a reflection on the idea of heroism in the context of the Holocaust, see Deborah Dwork and Robert Jan van Pelt, "Reclaiming Auschwitz," in Hartman, *Holocaust Remembrance* 241–42.

9. See Northrop Frye, *The Anatomy of Criticism*.

10. The American underground excels in fierce satire; European comics, like

those of Tardi and Moebius, excel in the creation of fabulous and chilling other worlds (occasionally the two modes are combined, as in Max Andersson's brilliant *Pixy*). The Japanese comics scene is the most diverse and difficult to summarize of all; for Spiegelman's interest in one Japanese comics hero, Keiji Nakazawa's *Barefoot Gen*, see his introduction to *Barefoot Gen: Out of the Ashes*.

11. Mandelbaum's joyful remark in Auschwitz, "It's a miracle, Vladek. God sent shoes through you" (II:34), is presented less definitively.

12. See the review of Claudine Fabre-Vassas, *The Singular Beast: Jews, Christians, and the Pig* by Elliott Horowitz in the *New Republic*.

13. See also the panel showing Vladek's in-laws still living a life of luxury, but behind latticed windows resembling the bars of a prison, like those that will later appear in the final picture of Vladek's father-in-law (I:74, 115). The frontispieces for chapter 7 of *Maus I*, "The Mousetrap," chapter 4 of *Maus II* (II:101), "Saved," and other chapters invoke similarly determining behind-the-scenes patterns (I:129).

14. For a persuasive reading of this ending, see also Hamida Bosmajian's essay in this volume.

2

The Orphaned Voice in Art Spiegelman's *Maus*

Hamida Bosmajian

Art Spiegelman's two-volume narrative *Maus* is a Holocaust survivor's tale as told to a son who wants to record his father's story in a book with the hope that this effort will lead to acknowledgment by his father. In the course of the father's, Vladek Spiegelman's, narrative, Artie Spiegelman reveals through words and behavior what it means to be a survivor's child. This double autobiography of a son's relation to his father and the father's survival in one of history's most horrendous nightmares is depicted through the unconventional genre of the "comix," a comic book that is literally a graphic autobiography. Here Spiegelman pushes the well-established conventions of Holocaust narratives to the limit by incarnating the Nazi use of the rodent metaphor in all his Jewish characters. In *Maus* the faces of the Jews are those of mice, the Germans are the cats who hunt them, and the Poles—as victimizers, victims, or bystanders—are pigs. Nevertheless, the animal imaging, a deadly serious business in history and *Maus*, intensifies rather than detracts from the horror of the Holocaust and the familial tensions in the Spiegelman family.

In his post-*Maus* reflections, or "mouse droppings," Spiegelman declared in *Tikkun*: "*Maus* preserves a certain crystalline ambiguity that doesn't try to simplify the complexities of interpersonal relationships and disastrous history . . . and yet it comes across as an easy-to-take tale" ("Saying Goodbye" 44–45). With "crystalline ambiguity," the author-artist offers here an oxymoron that privileges, preserves, and makes clear an ambiguity that maintains the chaos of human relationships and history in the ordered structure of the text. Frame narrator Artie's relation to his parents is ambiguous because disastrous history has a disastrous effect on relationships between parent and child. Artie will retell his father's story, but throughout his telling of the frame narrative he avoids the direct articulation of his own pain because he must, from the epigraphic episode on, consider his pain and deprivations insignificant in relation to the disastrous history of Auschwitz. As a result, his own maturation is necessarily thwarted.

An "easy-to-take tale" is a story whose conventions are so predictable and simplify the content to such an extent that the reader or listener neglects to become conscious of the blanks and gaps in the telling. Such reductive simplicity can serve as a defense against horror. It is, therefore, not surprising that the testimonial narratives of Holocaust survivors often exhibit a predictable narrative line from which the teller will not stray in successive tellings. Spiegelman's *Maus*, however much it presents itself as an "easy-to-take tale," is hard to take. Our perceptions of the comic book and the iconic Disney mouse provide this graphic narrative with a protective veneer of childishness if not triviality until the reader is shocked into the awareness that what appeared to be simplistic is actually a "crystalline ambiguity." Moreover, the element of infantilism or childishness is an essential quality in the projection of the narrator.

The narrator Artie Spiegelman in *Maus* is indeed different from Art Spiegelman. Nevertheless, autobiography, familial contexts, and the history of the Holocaust are interwoven so intimately with the fictionalizing structures that it is at times difficult to maintain the difference between Artie and Art. In my discussion, I will therefore refer to either Artie or Art when the distance between narrator and author is difficult to discern. Spiegelman's readiness to talk publicly about his creative process and his childhood have also lessened that distance. Artie is, however, a lesser Art Spiegelman, an orphaned voice and self that seems more lost than his author.

What motivates Artie to ask his father about life in Poland, especially during the war and the Holocaust? As an only child who lives in the shadow of his dead older brother, Richieu, Artie has been shaped by his parents' unspoken history. The content of that history has seeped through hints and gaps, as the epigraph to *Maus I* reveals. Before Artie was born there was disastrous history that the survivors internalized and displaced into ordinary time, where it contributed to Artie's psychological breakdown and his mother's suicide. Through his father's narrative, Artie learns that his mother has written a journal whose intended reader was to be Artie. First, however, Artie turns tentatively and hesitantly to his father: "I still want to draw that book about you . . . the one I used to talk to you about . . . about your life in Poland, and the war." Vladek is reluctant and advises Artie to occupy himself with work that brings money, but then he relents with an "if you want" to the childlike request for a story about "the olden days" (I:12).

Stories of survivors are generally classified as testimonies; Vladek's narrative has also been defined as such (Hirsch 12). In his discussion of the literary origins of testimony, James Young points out that the traditional definition of testimony is "intricately tied into the legal process of establishing evidence in order to achieve justice" and is founded in the rabbinical law of Leviticus 5:1: "And he is a witness whether he has seen or known of it; if he does not utter it, then he shall bear his iniquity" (*Writing and Rewriting* 18). Vladek, however, does not "go public" with his narrative; Artie does, but he is not a rabbi, a judge, or a therapist, nor is he the community—he is the child of a survivor of iniquity, and as a child he has, in this context, no authority.

During the Holocaust a child had to grow up fast for the sake of survival. The child had to be able to use duplicity consciously or to "pass" as older than he or she was in order to be defined as "workable" in Auschwitz. "The destruction of childhood," writes Naomi Sokoloff, "the need to grow up prematurely, and the clouding of boundaries between childhood and maturity are themes that surface in Holocaust literature for adults and for juvenile audiences, as well as in the writing of children authors . . . to convey a childhood which—shaped by violence—was not a childhood" (259–60). At age fifteen, Elie Wiesel, for example, is able to "pass" as adult in Auschwitz and develops with his father a relationship that truly has shared adulthood in the nightmare of history (*Night*). Such a relationship is not possible between Artie and Vladek; Artie has neither the authority of the law nor the authority of experience. We can also argue that Vladek's private testimony to his unauthorized child does not fulfill the rabbinical law in Leviticus. Artie, who frequently strikes childlike listener poses that depreciate authority, cannot "do justice" to his father's narrative, cannot incorporate the testimony in the public record. Instead, Artie/Art is consigned to be a *Spiegelmann*, a mirror man, whose mimesis of his father's history insists, as Hirsch points out in her discussion of the photographs in *Maus*, on accuracy (the tape recorder) but abandons representation through the animal fable (12).

Nevertheless, Spiegelman comments that he "felt [he] was taking a deposition" (CD-ROM, *Maus II* 159) as Vladek spoke into the tape recorder. If a deposition is a testifying under oath that is recorded for eventual use in court, such use and judgment are here indefinitely deferred. It is personal history that determines the relationship between Artie and Vladek. In *Funny Aminals*, Spiegelman depicted a cozy Father Mouse telling his son Mickey bedtime stories of Auschwitz; the adult, then, knows what would get the parent to talk *to* him (not *with* him). The artist admitted to an interviewer that "a reader might get the impression that the conversations in the narrative were just one small part, a facet of my relationship with my father. In fact, however, they were my relationship with my father. I was doing them *to have a relationship with my father*. Outside of them we were still continually at loggerheads" (Weschler 64–65). The narrator-interrogator has discovered what will make his father respond to him and is thus able to create the illusion of a father-son conversation. By definition, then, Artie is in *Maus* not the ideal listener Dori Laub describes: "Being a witness is, in fact, a process that includes the listener. For a testimonial to take place, there needs to be a bonding, the intimate and total presence of the *other*—in the position of one who hears. Testimonies are not monologues; they cannot take place in solitude. The witnesses are talking to *somebody*: to somebody they have been waiting for a long time" (Felman and Laub 70–71). Bedtime stories provide intimate moments between parent and child, but the child must be able to understand the story. Artie/Art's yearning for a relationship that such stories preclude provokes a repeated narration of events and experiences that are anything but bedtime stories. The confusion of genres and storytelling situations contributes to Artie's withholding, in the text at least, the empathetic reaching out of the listener to the witness who gives testimony. This does not mean that Artie is not deeply moved by what his father tells him; he is, but he will not reveal his feelings to his father. They remain at odds; moreover, Artie feels that his memories and emotions, then and now, may well be irrelevant compared to those of his father.

The artist, however, gives Vladek's story existence. *Maus* is an autobiography that embeds as the master narrative Vladek's story of surviving the Holocaust. The father's master narrative is so intense and dominant that we forget what Mieke Bal calls "the fabula of the primary narrative" (143), namely, Artie's struggle for acknowledgment of his trauma as a child of Holocaust survivors. Vladek and his story marginalize Artie into insignificance. Artie Spiegelman, the narrator and the second self of the author, is not only the child of Holocaust survivors but also a substitute for his dead older brother, Richieu. Vladek never acknowledges that it may have been difficult for Artie to be a child of survivors. By appropriating his father's story within the frame of his own story, Artie writes and draws Vladek's ordeal into permanent existence, but he himself is at the end psychologically and literally unacknowledged and orphaned.

As Helen Epstein has shown, a parent who is a survivor of the Holocaust is frequently incapable of connecting with his or her children because of unresolved grief over lost ones, because of survivor guilt, and because of a psychological block or lack of affect (Epstein 92). Children of survivors feel at times as if they did not exist for their parents, for the controlling event—the master narrative, uttered or unuttered—all but consumes the parent. As an adult, Artie frequently depicts himself in infantile attitudes and postures; petulance, anger, sulkiness, self-pity, and ingratiating gestures signal the need for the acknowledgment he failed and fails to receive. Even the request to . hear about his parents' experiences in the Holocaust is a horror version of a child's wish to hear a story about the "olden days." His placement of the story in the "infantile" and subversive genre of a comic book in the underground comix tradition points to unresolved childhood issues of Artie/Art. He wants to hear his parents' story so that he can understand what orphaned him, but he is not granted such an understanding. The penultimate panel of Maus II makes it clear that Vladek told "survival in Auschwitz" as a bedtime story to the nonexistent brother: "I'm tired from talking, Richieu, and it's enough stories for now . . . " (II:136). Artie is the odd child out.

Within the frame of the son as listener and the father as talker is nested another story, Artie Spiegelman's "Prisoner on the Hell Planet: A Case History." Here Artie comes close to revealing his own center of horror, triggered by his mother's suicide. Structurally, the Maus books are akin to nested narratives such as Frankenstein or The Heart of Darkness that drive toward the center of some essential horror which, nevertheless, remains unarticulated. The two centers are Vladek's eyewitness experience at Auschwitz (Maus II) and Artie's mother's suicide and his reaction to it (Maus I). As he says to his wife, Françoise: "I can't even make sense out of my relationship with my father . . . how am I supposed to make any sense out of Auschwitz? Out of the Holocaust?" (II:14). The telling of stories is, of course, a primary means of ordering the disorder of experience; it provides a surface sensibleness that may be perceived as meaningful. Artie, however, will never make any sense or meaning of it all, no matter how often he articulates the horror verbally and graphically; he can only shape an imitation, an illusion of meaning through the telling of the tale. Art Spiegelman did this primarily through his choice of arranging his father's narrative in chronological order rather than leaving it in the associative and episodic order in which it was originally told (CD-ROM, "Interviewing Vladek").

The sequence of the text of Vladek's story follows the convention of Holocaust narratives, based, as they are, on the historical pattern of events (Bosmajian 28–35). However, by repeatedly highlighting his resourcefulness and survival skills, Vladek emerges, if not as a hero, then as a man of a highly developed practical intelligence who authenticates his narrative with blueprints and maps for the enlightenment and instruction of his listener(s). He has come to believe that he survived *because* of these skills. But Vladek does not ever tell how he *felt* during and after the Holocaust; he denies feeling, and that may have been one of his crucial failings in his relation with Anja. It is, therefore, significant that Artie asks his therapist, Pavel, who is also a survivor, "I can't begin to imagine what Auschwitz felt like." Pavel replies: "What it felt like? Hmm, how can I explain? Boo!" (II:46). Wide-eyed and startled, Artie levitates in the analyst's chair, where he has shrunk to the stature of a little kid with a mouse mask. The therapist's "Auschwitz as *Kinderschreck* [bogeyman]" communicates to the narrator that the camp demanded of the victim an intensely conscious alertness at all times: a poised state of perpetual terror. As nano-narrative, however, the scare expletive is also insufficient.

The subtitles of *Maus I* (*A Survivor's Tale: My Father Bleeds History*) and *Maus II* (*A Survivor's Tale: And Here My Troubles Began*) show the complicated relationship among history, Vladek's narrative, and Artie as the listener-son. Vladek bleeds history not only in the sense of a possibly therapeutic bloodletting of his experiences but also in the continuous seepage of repressed and displaced memories that affected Artie every day of his childhood. We might add here that in comic book parlance "to bleed" means to extend a drawing beyond the confines of lines that frame a panel. The blood of memory of the experience in traumatic history cannot be contained, and its seepage is contagious. The father's wound is internal and unhealed. The subtitle to *Maus II* can signify the continuation of the story after *Maus I* where Vladek and Anja arrive at the gate of Auschwitz as well as the troubles that pursued Vladek ever since. For Artie, too, the troubles began with Auschwitz. The seepage of those experiences will be a continual subtext in his life that affects him during summer retreats and beyond. No stories can cure the unhealed wounds in father and son. At best the teller can say, "it's enough stories for now . . . ," implying repeated tellings over the ground of deprivation that defines the heartless center of the Holocaust. In *Maus* this is graphically projected by Vladek's sitting on his exercycle and telling his story while accelerating his heartbeat.

Though Vladek's is the master narrative in Artie's life and work, other stories are also possible, and these may provide counter-memories to Vladek's official tale. Mala, Vladek's second wife, is also a survivor, and so is Pavel. But the most significant story for Artie would be that of Anja, his mother. When Vladek admits to burning Anja's journals, her counter-memory becomes a blank filled by Vladek's memory. Thus closure is always provisional for Artie. One psychoanalyst of narrative, Roy Schafer, has argued:

> We have only versions of the true and the real. Narratively unmediated, definitive access to truth and reality cannot be demonstrated. In this respect, therefore, there can be no absolute foundation on which any observer or thinker stands; each must choose his or her narrative or version. Further, each narrative presupposes or establishes a context, and the sentences of any one account attain full significance only within their context and through more or less systematic and consistent use of language appropriate to the purpose. (xv)

When Artie insists on seeing his mother's narrative, which would, by the very fact that it is written, have greater authority than his father's oral discourse, Vladek, who collects and hoards things out of necessity and habit, admits that he burned the diaries when he had a "bad day"; "After Anja had died I had to make order with everything . . . these papers had too many memories. So I burned them" (I:159). Vladek denies Anja self-definition as he shapes his memory of her. After she kills herself, he annihilates her written word and thus commits the "murder" of which Artie accuses him. Spiegelman recognized that the fact that Vladek "destroyed that journal of hers . . . meant that the story forcibly became increasingly *his* story" (Weschler 65). The "burning of the text" creates a blank that provides Artie with a ground on which to project the possibilities of answers that may have assuaged his own guilt feelings. Artie tries occasionally to deconstruct the reliability of Vladek's narrative. For example, when Vladek says that Richieu was a big baby weighing three kilos at birth, Artie questions, "If you were married in February, and Richieu was born in October, was he premature?" Vladek hesitatingly answers "Yes, a little" and immediately swerves to Artie's birth: "But you—after the war, when you were born—it was *very* premature. The doctors thought you wouldn't live" (I:30). Since Vladek at this point has already told the story about Anja's friendship with a young Communist, the question of paternity insinuates itself and could be supported by the events of Vladek's courtship of Anja. Graphics, too, can provide a commentary that counters Vladek's story. For instance, Richieu, idolized by his parents, is depicted by Artie as an obnoxious brat at the dinner table, where he overturns his dinner plate while the adults are discussing the increasingly difficult economic situation (I:75).

As a survivor, Vladek is a man of many skillful ways but not a sadder or a wiser man. We must, however, keep in mind that it is Artie who edits his father's words, and occasionally his drawings of Vladek give us glimpses of a man profoundly overcome by grief. Artie tells us a story about his father telling about himself. Fixed in image and print, Vladek owes his existence to Artie, but Artie remains the outsider. There is no moment of genuine communication between father and son. Vladek neither acknowledges Artie in such a way that Artie could forgive him nor—and that is too much to hope for—asks forgiveness of his son. Even in the counter-memory presented in "Prisoner on the Hell Planet," Vladek cannot see his son's pain but is reminded only of the grief he, Vladek, experienced at Anja's suicide. Artie remains a blank for Vladek, a blank that is both painful and empowering for the son.

Children of Holocaust survivors experience a sense of having been "too late" acutely, and it is not unusual for such children to express the insane wish, as Artie does, to have been with their parents in Auschwitz "so I could really know what they lived through" (II:16). The gap between the experience of the disaster and any mimetic or symbolic construct of it is unbridgeable. If Artie cannot make sense of his complex family relationship, he certainly cannot make sense of Auschwitz or the Holocaust (II:14). Spiegelman's oxymoronic "crystalline ambiguity" connotes that the only certainty is the state of uncertainty, ambivalence, and incompleteness in the understanding—the making sense—of disastrous history and its influence on the complexities of personal relationships. At the same time, Artie has *chosen* to witness his father's eyewitness account of the disaster; he appropriates Vladek's narrative as legacy, but he does not own it, cannot invest it with sense. No matter how hard he tries, hyperconscious Artie is left out in the cold—orphaned.

Four episodes, each involving Artie's ambivalent relation to his father and to Vladek's Holocaust experience and narration, crystallize ambivalently the orphaned self. Already the epigraph, which depicts the only incident in Maus from Artie's childhood, foreshadows the persistent failure of communication between father and son. Deserted by his friends after he falls skating, a crying Artie runs to his father to exact sympathy, but Vladek overwhelms the ten-year-old with innuendoes of disaster and diminishes his son's self (I:5). Both Vladek and Artie have their "heart of darkness" experience, but Artie's is anxiously influenced by Vladek's experience in Auschwitz. As Vladek tells Artie of the burning pits in Auschwitz, which he saw in all their horrendousness, Artie knows he cannot do justice to Vladek's experience. The minimalism of his comic book panels is a silent acknowledgment of the failure of any post-memory. Vladek survived the disastrous history of Auschwitz; Artie survived his mother's suicide, his "heart of darkness," with anger and with guilt. Artie's narration in "Prisoner on the Hell Planet" is in the fullest sense of the word an "underground comic" that Vladek is not supposed to read, that was hidden from him but somehow was found. Vladek is depressed when he reads about Anja's suicide and Artie's reaction to it, but he does not truly understand the comic and shrugs it off by saying, "It's good you got it outside your system" (I:104). Artie's final orphaning is both literal and symbolic on the epitaphic page of Maus where Vladek terminates the storytelling he began haltingly in the epigraph. Vladek, after forgetting even Artie's name, goes to sleep and leaves Artie standing silently and forlorn.

These four episodes are of course governed by the central signifier—the mouse (die Maus), the German of the title accentuating otherness as well as the inextricable relationship between victims and perpetrators, between Jews and Germans. Equally important is how the mouse image is drawn. Spiegelman, who experimented with "realistically" drawn mice in his precursors to Maus, "did not want people to be aware that [he] could draw," did not want to focus attention on his authority as an artist. His eventual choice of highly expressive but stylized mice is a "picture writing" that is so connotative that survivor readers of Maus have occasionally been unaware of the allegory (CD-ROM, "Art on Art"). The tradition of the mouse metaphor from Aesop to Disney to the "vermin" that Nazi propaganda intended to exterminate has encrusted the image with conventions that disguise in Maus the loss and pain of the orphaned self's voice. With the help of Kristeva's interpretation of allegory as it is related to loss (102), we can say that the allegorical mice both depress and depreciate the exalted/profaned significance the lost parents hold for the orphaned voice whose playfulness expresses through the infantile medium of a comic book a "melancholy jouissance" (Kristeva) that sublimates the private melancholia of the grieving and the real subject of the text—the artist. Spiegelman is indeed aware that medieval allegories frequently expressed the "too holy" in animal form (CD-ROM, "Art on Art"). Likewise, the *summum malum* as well as the all-too-personal can be defensively displaced through allegory.

The attitudes of Artie Spiegelman in *Maus* are those of a rebellious and self-pitying child who is occasionally eager to please and is almost always depressed. Behind this self-imaging there lurks that feeling of abandonment and emptiness characteristic of the unacknowledged gifted child described by Alice Miller: "They all developed the art of not experiencing feelings, for a child can only experience his feelings when there is somebody there who accepts him fully, understands and supports him" (10).

It is perhaps significant that, aside from the Rego Park incident in the epigraph, no event from Artie's childhood intrudes upon the narrative. The epigraph is outside the main narrative frame, yet it is the crucial incident that projects Artie's problematic relation to his father. This incident of emotional abandonment is presented by Spiegelman without commentary. When the ten-year-old loses his roller skate, his friends abandon him with laughter. Artie runs crying to his father, not because he fell but because he is deserted. Vladek, usefully employed with some carpentry, immediately engages Artie in holding the board, even as he asks, "Why do you cry, Artie? Hold on better to the wood." He is not interested in Artie but in the task at hand. When Artie complains that his friends skated away without him, the word *friends* triggers Vladek's memory that friends are an impossibility: "If you lock them together in a room for a week . . . "—and, ballooning out in the last panel— "*Then you should see what is, friends.*" Vladek hovers over little Artie, one knee on the workbench, while Artie is cowed and looks up submissively, fearful of his father and the hostile and friendless world. Artie's physical stature diminishes as the epigraph progresses and he is overshadowed by his father. This crucial childhood memory imprints on the narrator not only that friends are unreliable but also that his pains are unimportant and that he is insignificant in relation to Vladek and his story.

If our essentialist tradition leads us to expect an imminent revelation of meaning at the heart (the center) of darkness or light, then we neglect to consider that no narrative or imaged account of ultimate horror or joy has managed to convey more than what Conrad's nested narrative defined as "the spectral illumination of moonshine," that is, connotations generated by adjectives, images, and metaphors. The Shoah, in particular, has made the search for meaning ontologically and ethically problematic, for to interpret the Holocaust as meaningful implies a validation, if not a justification. Neither Vladek nor Artie/Art makes such implications: murderous death remains murderous death; suffering remains suffering. The crucial difference between Vladek's and Artie's accounts of the Holocaust is that Vladek was an eyewitness to the horror that permeates his memory and being, while Artie/Art is an eyewitness of his father's eyewitness testimony. As an artist and in the realization of his belatedness to disastrous history, he arranges and interprets his father's master narrative. His own center of horror, his mother's suicide, is as a disastrous event in personal relations more powerful for him than the death of millions, though he realizes that one death is not as catastrophic (CD-ROM, Maus 88/99). "Prisoner on the Hell Planet" is, then, his way of compensating for his exclusion from the facticity of the Shoah as an historical event.

The agonies of murderous deaths took many forms in the Holocaust, but in our official historical memory no image is as evocative as that of two thousand or more bodies pressed into a gas chamber. No one survived that event; all who tell about it are witness-survivors who are outside the door frame. At the end of Maus I, Vladek and Anja arrive at the gate of Auschwitz in a closed truck. Anticipating Maus II, the reader wonders how Art Spiegelman can possibly depict the center of the horror through the medium of a comix. Vladek, his eyes in a trancelike expression, begins: "You heard about the gas, but I am telling you not rumors, but only what I *saw*. For this I was an *eyewitness*" (II:69). Vladek insists on the distinction between what he has seen and what he has heard, an insistence that not only supports the credibility of the teller but also makes the "incredible" real. As eyewitness he establishes the link between the event and his own body (the eye), whereas hearing links the event to the word. What Vladek's eye has seen will be with him, whether he tells of it or not.

Vladek saw the gassing installations and heard about their operations from a fellow inmate. He is therefore able to describe in blueprint fashion, imitated by the accompanying graphics, how this engineering structure disguised itself so that people "believed really it was here a place for showers" (II:70) until he arrives at his devastating conclusion: "To such a place finished my father, my sisters, my brothers, so many" (II:71). Caught in the presentness of past recollections, Vladek recalls seeing what was worse than the gas chamber. With the mass transports of Hungarian Jews in 1944 to Auschwitz-Birkenau, the gas chambers and crematoria were operating beyond capacity. Open pits—"so like swimming pools of the Pines Hotel here"— were dug, the gassed were thrown in, and those still alive had to jump in; gasoline was poured over all and ignited. A double panel reveals several "mice," their mouths agape in agony as Vladek narrates in a slim box within the panel: "And the fat from the burning bodies they scooped and poured again so everyone could burn better" (II:72).

No hyperbole suffices to describe the horror of what Vladek *saw*. Art Spiegelman copes with that insufficiency by making recourse to a litotes that might appear to make a mockery of martyrdom: screaming mice in flames. Spiegelman admits to the difficulty of this five-by-two-inch panel by revealing to the interpreters of *Maus* several of the pre-drawings (CD-ROM, *Maus* 209/74). In this case, unlike his depiction of his parents' arrival at Auschwitz (I:157), he did not choose to leave this panel unframed; clear black lines surround the concentration of horror into dense minimalism. The silent screams of the mice—the "vermin," as the Nazis defined them—do not rise into the infinity of the cosmos as do the screams in Nelly Sachs's poem "Landscape of Screams," whose ascensions seek the ear of God. Instead, the screams are brutally choked by the parallel upper line of the panel. The gaping mouths confront the viewer in the manner of Edvard Munch's *The Scream*, with the difference that the screams in Auschwitz were not due to some interior and personal agony. The wide-open eye of the victim on the left, the only eye in the panel, perceives the horror with full consciousness as an eyewitness whose deposition will never be taken. It is an eye similar to the one Michelangelo depicts in the *Last Judgment* where one of the damned descends in the embrace of demons and places one hand over his left eye, unable to bear the sight, while the other eye is aghast at the horror that is about to consume him. Spiegelman's "damnation of mice," however, makes it inexorably clear that the Shoah had nothing to do with our paradigms of transcendent or earthly judgment but had everything to do with the willful exercise of human power that perceived itself accountable to no one and could order those who had nothing to lose to execute such murderous orders. Although the artist is separate and excluded from his father's always present past, his sympathy and rage have generated here an image that demands, no, provokes us to consider the Shoah.

"I wasn't overwhelmed by thoughts of the death camp . . . it just went into the mix," says Art Spiegelman about his childhood (CD-ROM, *Maus* 211). Unable to meet his parents' expectations, he desperately needed to separate himself from them (Weschler 60–62). The alternative for the orphaned self would have been to have no separate identity other than being the incarnation of his parents' projections of what a son ought to be. "Prisoner on the Hell Planet," in which the characters have human faces, was published separately in 1973 and reveals the orphaned self's existential isolation in conventional situations of familial intimacy. Though the comic is only four pages long, its black border forms a thin, dark line down the length of the closed book of *Maus I*. The white border of the comic's page inside the text can be perceived as framed by a black border of mourning that may also be an abyss upon which the page floats as it is held by a hand (Artie's) in the context of his narrative about his father. This "nesting" is intensified in the title panel of "Prisoner" where a hand holds a photograph of young Art with his mother on vacation in 1958, the same year as the Rego Park incident. The photo, whose top corners "bleed" slightly beyond the frame, seems to float as a euphoric family memory over the conventionally aggressive comic book title. In her analyses of the photographs in *Maus*, Marianne Hirsch points out that photos always signify the simultaneous presence of life and death, the finality of "having-been-there" (5–6). Mother and son in the picture are physically connected as Anja places her hand on Art's head in what might be seen as a protective/repressive gesture. While Artie projects the approved American stance of the smiling "boy on vacation," Anja slightly turns her head away from him and gazes beyond the situation; she is detached in spite of her physical connection with her son. In the panel next to the title panel, the narrator announces: "In 1968, when I was 20, my mother killed herself. She left no note."

Artie, or Arthur as he is called on the Hell Planet, expands the hell of Auschwitz to global proportions and at the same time shrinks the prisoner to a "case history," implying that there are other "cases." Through this internal/external hell, the narrator can include himself in history and even wear the striped concentration camp uniform that his father wore as an inmate and posed in so cockily as a survivor after the war (II:134). By definition, however, Artie's hell is a belated imitation of the historical reality of the

Holocaust. The literary and art historical allusiveness of the Hell Planet to Dante's *Inferno*, German expressionism, George Grosz, and the "Cabinet of Dr. Caligari" makes the four-page comic very much a text whose textuality is enhanced by the fact that this comic within the comic is held by Artie's hand. On the first page of "Prisoner," Artie's hand holds the photograph of himself and Anja. The nested narrative of *Maus I* intensifies itself here through the signifiers of conventional moments of intimacy where, however, no intimacy is experienced.

The narrative begins with Artie, in concentration camp uniform, emerging from the subway, the metaphor for three months of confinement in a psychiatric hospital. An unfeeling doctor, whose authority inflates to a guilt-inducing demon, announces Anja's suicide. Four narrow panels on either side of the doctor's demonic face project the incredible constriction of Artie's emotional response and his difficulty of responding in the socially approved way: one viscous tear slowly emerges and droops from his left eye, traditionally the nonrational side of the self.

Artie is orphaned by his mother's death and by his father's descent into a grief that makes him dependent on Artie but incapable of imagining Artie's grief: "He held me and moaned to himself all night. I was uncomfortable. We were scared." The next day, at the funeral home, Artie loses himself in deeper memories: he visualizes the bloated body of his naked mother floating in a tub of bloodied water. Three images are projected between the four explanations for Anja's suicide: a pile of corpses against a swastikaed wall; little Artie in bed with Anja, who is reading a bedtime story to him; Anja's hand with the Auschwitz number cutting into the wrist of her other arm. "Menopausal depression/Hitler did it/Mommy/Bitch" are the verbal explanations, beginning with the most rational—"she must have been depressed." This is followed by the historical cause, but then Artie shifts to the personal with the cry for "Mommy!" only to swerve into an angry "You put me here." The last seven panels amplify Artie's aggressive thoughts toward "Mommy."

Subtextually, *Maus* suggests that Anja might have been the dialogical partner who, unlike Vladek, would have understood her son. "Prisoner," however, is a corrective to this fantasy, for Artie's "Mommy" is a profoundly needy person who seeks in her son the kind of communication and understanding that Vladek cannot give her. In his biographical essay about Spiegelman, Weschler describes the following reaction when the artist was prompted to talk about his mother's suicide:

Spiegelman becomes quiet and measured when he talks about this period. "The way she did it, I was the one who was supposed to discover
the body, only I was late coming by, as usual, so that by the time I
arrived there was already this whole scene. . . . Was my commitment to
the mental ward the cause of her suicide? No. Was there a relation?
Sure. After the war, she'd invested her whole life in me. I was more like
a confidant than a son. She couldn't handle the separation. I didn't
want to hurt her, to hurt them. But I had to break free." (62)

Oppressive overabundance and superfluousness suggest themselves in
Spiegelman's depiction of Anja's body in the bathtub, in the frame of his
bedroom door, and at his bedside. The panels seem to burst with details
difficult to contain. The four panels about his last encounter with Anja have
the serrated edges of the photos included in Maus, thus accentuating the
moment that is always present and gone forever. In the first serrated panel,
Artie crouches in a fetal position in the corner that is bordered by a straight
line. He then moves into the memory completely in the second and third
panels, but only a third of the fourth panel is serrated as Artie synchronically
remembers the last encounter with his mother. His memory has clicked in
frame by frame: close-up of Anja, clutching her dressing gown over her
breasts, as she enters his room larger than the door frame; long shot of the
same moment as Artie distances her from his bed in his memory; medium
shot of Anja at Artie's bed as Artie turns away from her with an expression
of guilt and anger; intense close-up of Artie's horror-struck and guilt-ridden
face as Anja walks out and closes the door with a "click" that sets the memory.
Artie cannot possibly meet or compensate Anja's needs for all she has lost.
   The last three panels project an ascetic and confirming rigidity that contrasts markedly with the disorder of the preceding panels. We see rows of
prison bars that in the third panel create the effect of a well of prison cells,
an abyss around which panel after panel of prison bars frame the dark interior of cells, suggesting that the whole structure is superimposed on a black
void. In the first, a shadowy Artie is behind metaphorical prison bars; he is
experiencing the punishment for the crime of which he accuses his mother:
"Congratulations! . . . You've committed the perfect crime. . . . " In the second panel his now disembodied voice issues from a row of cells; in the third
it amplifies itself to a shouted accusation—"You murdered me, Mommy, and
you left me here to take the rap!!!"—until an unseen inmate or some absurd

voice-over of the superego responds from a lower floor of cells: "Pipe down, Mac, some of us are trying to sleep."

In *Funny Aminals*, in *Maus*, and in "Prisoner on the Hell Planet," the desire or need to go to sleep terminates communication. Repression is the order of the day for a pain for which there is no empathy. Vladek certainly does not respond to Artie's pain or to the prison that his son has constructed; he only can recall, "But for me, it brought in mind such memories of Anja" (106), and he approved Artie's getting his mother's suicide "out of his system" through the comix. If Artie is to survive on the Hell Planet, he must go beyond the indeterminacy of his emotions as these are shaped by his parents' responses to their memories of the Holocaust. He must get his father's story in all its concretistic detail; then, he must retell it and displace—reveal/repress—it through his art. The autobiographical comix of Art Spiegelman are a convincing example of what Freud has called psychopathography (35), a therapeutic expression where, in this case, the nightmare of history and familial agonies interphase and are compulsively repeated by the orphaned voice. The creation of the work of art becomes in this case similar to Vladek's exercycle, the treadmill that loosens but does not liberate the congestion of personal pain.

It is, therefore, very believable that Spiegelman had great difficulty in ending *Maus*. In commenting about the last page, he admits that he tried between fifty and sixty endings. He wanted an ending that would "anchor the entire book," "yet the book keeps ending and falls in on itself in order to get out." Furthermore, on the last page "fiction and non-fiction [crush] up against each other" in three endings (CD-ROM, *Maus* 271): the "happy end" of the reunited couple; Vladek's desiring sleep and the suspension of bedtime stories; and Anja's and Vladek's names and dates on the headstone with Art Spiegelman's signature and dates of creating *Maus* beneath it, signifying the apparent finality of I-have-done. Which is the true ending? Most likely it is congealed in the image of a forlorn Artie, standing at the foot of Vladek's bed with his tape recorder under his arm. The conversation, such as it was, is over, but the "crystalline ambiguity" remains.

Vladek, however, wants closure, and tells his son, "finally I found her. The rest I don't need to tell you, because we both were very happy" (CD-ROM, *Maus* 271/136). Spiegelman changes this to "More I don't need to tell you. We were both very happy, and lived happy, happy ever after" and encloses the lovers in a square panel centered within the iris-out of a white disk. The happy end image is deconstructed not only with the forced squaring of the circle but also by the fact that the white disk on black ground is in part the Nazi flag (which is never shown unobstructedly unfurled in *Maus*). Earlier, when Vladek returned from his military service (I:66), we find the same image, though the white disk is not yet a full circle. The image cannot be perceived as separated from the flag that looms like an aggressive moon behind the couple during the persecution of the Jews (I:33) and resonates for the viewer as such again at the end. Vladek's insistence on the happy end denies the content of *Maus*, but it is appropriate in relation to his consistent refusal to come into self-knowledge. His story, in a sense his own bedtime story, has exhausted him to the point that the unconsciousness of sleep offers the most desirable conclusion.

Turned on his side and ready to sleep, he says: "I'm tired from talking, Richieu, and it's enough stories for now . . . " The second "ending" is clearly different for father and son. Artie's existence is denied after all the hours of having listened to his father's story. It is the lost son who is present for Vladek, and Artie is blanked out. Throughout *Maus*, Artie has competed with the dead brother and at the same time acknowledged him. It is Richieu's photo that is centered on the dedicatory page of *Maus II*, though two names appear, "for Richieu and for Nadja" (Spiegelman and Françoise Mouly's daughter, whose name includes all the letters of "Anja"). Richieu was "the ideal kid, and I was a pain in the ass. I couldn't compete" (II:15). As Hirsch argues convincingly, "Richieu, or Richieu's photograph, can confirm the interminable nature of mourning in *Maus*, and the endlessness of Vladek's tale." The troubles of Vladek and Artie began long before *Maus*, and they will never end (Hirsch 23), at least as long as the orphaned self is alive. Artie is perhaps again guilty, this time for having exhausted his father by insisting on the story—and is denied by him.

The tombstone and signature that follow intensify the isolation of the narrator, who is no longer visible, but a name only that is separate from the parents and their memory. Since his signature is below the tombstone, there is also the suggestion that the heaviness of the parents' memorial/memory has buried him. It took Art Spiegelman thirteen years (1978–1991) to complete *Maus*. At the age of thirteen, a Jewish boy is acknowledged and celebrated at his bar mitzvah as a full-fledged member of the Jewish community. This ritual must have been mere ritual for the artist, for he remained unacknowledged by the two people who were so formative for his life. His signature authenticates: what I have written, I have written; what I have drawn, I have drawn. This finality, emphasized by the dates of composition, is not the same as the names and dates engraved on the headstones, for the signature is handwritten—the artist and his orphaned voice are alive with all his crystalline ambiguities of "interpersonal relationships and disastrous history."

3

Cartoons of the Self

Portrait of the Artist as a
Young Murderer—Art Spiegelman's *Maus*

Nancy K. Miller

A writer is someone who plays with his mother's body.

Roland Barthes, *The Pleasure of the Text*

Autobiography by women is said to differ from autobiography by men because of a recurrent structural feature. Historically, according to academic critics, the self of women's autobiography has required the presence of another in order to represent itself on paper: for women, identity is constructed "by way of alterity." From the Duchess of Newcastle to Gertrude Stein, the acknowledgment and "recognition of another consciousness" seems to have been the necessary and enabling condition of women's self-narrative.[1] Unlike, say, Augustine or Rousseau, the female autobiographer rarely stages herself as a unique one-woman show; as a result, her performances don't quite fit the models of individual exemplarity thought to be a defining criterion of autobiographical practice.

The number of women's autobiographies that display this construction of identity through alterity is quite remarkable. And yet several recent autobiographical performances by male authors—Art Spiegelman's *Maus*, Philip Roth's *Patrimony*, Jacques Derrida's *Circonfession*, Herb Gardner's *Conversations with My Father*—have made me wonder whether we might not more usefully extend Mary Mason's insight that "the disclosure of female self is linked to the identification of some 'other'" (22) rather than restrict it to a by now predictably bipolar account of gendered self-representation. What these male-authored works have in common is precisely the structure of self-portrayal through the relation to a privileged other that characterizes most female-authored autobiography.[2]

Self-representation in these memoirs of the other is not thematically the designated subject of disclosure. In *Maus* Spiegelman sets out to tell his father's story; his own in formal terms is therefore thematically subordinated to that purpose. But as critics have seen, the stresses of the father/son interaction prove to be as much the subject of *Maus* as the horrors of Auschwitz. In what follows I will show some of the ways in which this intergenerational paradigm operates at the heart of the *Maus* books as a form of self-narrative. I will also show that the father/son material is intertwined with, even inseparable from, two equally powerful autobiographical strands: the son's self-portrayal as an artist and his relation—both as an artist and as a son—to his (dead) mother.[3] (It may also be that along with the entanglements of gender, the project of making autobiography is always tied to this intergenerational matrix of identity.)

From the first pages of *Maus I* to the last of *Maus II*, the figuration of the father/son relation constructs the frame through which we read (and hear) the father's story. We can think of this frame as generative, in the sense that it literally—and visually—produces the material of the "survivor's tale." This frame has a powerful double effect on the reader because it mimes the production of testimony and naturalizes the experience of listening to it. In the frame of narrative time, which is the present of Rego Park, we are lured into the account of a Holocaust past through the banality of American domestic life. The father, Vladek, pedals on an exercise bike in his son's former room and asks him about the "comics business." Art answers by reminding him of his old project of drawing a book about him. Vladek protests: "It would take *many* books, my life, and no one wants anyway to hear such stories." But Art has already incorporated his resistance into his book. "*I* want to hear it. Start with Mom . . . Tell me how you met." "Better you should spend your time to make drawings," Vladek protests, "what will bring you some money" (I:12).

These opening panels announce several of the book's themes: the transformation of oral testimony into (visual) narrative, the role of the listener (and then the reader) in that production, the place of his mother, Anja, in the family imaginary (Art holds her photograph as he speaks to his father), and the failure or success of Art's work as a cartoonist. The generative frame in which these problems about art and life, life and death, and death and success are sketched out also works at allaying the anxiety of the readers and critics who may enter the *space* of the *Maus* project with misgivings about its premises: who wants to hear such stories, and as comics, no less? How could a reader fail to be captivated by such self-deprecation?

The first page of "Time Flies," the second chapter of *Maus II*, lays out the terms of Art's self-portrait as an artist. The top half of the page is divided into two symmetrical panels. On the left, Art, wearing a mouse mask, gazes at his drawing board and thinks: "Vladek died of congestive heart failure on August 18, 1982 . . . Françoise and I stayed with him in the Catskills back in August 1977." On the right, the time flies buzzing around his head, Art comments on his sketch: "Vladek started working as a tinman in Auschwitz in the spring of 1944 . . . I started working on this page at the very end of February 1987." Again, on the left, Art says: "In May 1987 Françoise and I are expecting a baby . . . Between May 16, 1944 and May 24, 1944 over 100,000 Hungarian Jews were gassed in Auschwitz . . . "; and on the right, Art looks out at the reader: "In September 1986, after 8 years of work, the first part of MAUS was published. It was a critical and commercial success." Below the matching panels is a single frame. Art, in despair, leans on his arms at his drawing board, which now is at the height of a podium. The bottom half of the panel is occupied by a flattened pyramid of mouse corpses, above which the flies continue to buzz. Art complains: "At least fifteen foreign editions are coming out. I've gotten 4 serious offers to turn my book into a T.V. special or movie. (I don't wanna.) In May 1968 my mother killed herself. (She left no note.) Lately I've been feeling depressed." And an agentless bubble of words tries to get his attention: "Alright Mr. Spiegelman . . . We're ready to shoot" (II:41).

What does it mean to make (cartoon) art out of Auschwitz, money from the Holocaust? Is it possible to visualize and then represent a world designed to confound and destroy the human imagination? These are the questions *Maus* rehearses, wrestles with, and displaces through a set of concrete choices. Spiegelman's strategy for crafting his piece of this challenge to the ethics and materials of popular culture is first to personalize the enormity without reducing it. This is done in two simultaneous gestures whose interconnectedness is essential to the aesthetic project: Spiegelman narrativizes the experience of Auschwitz as an individual's trajectory and a family's saga, but the collective horror never ceases to haunt the horizon of a singular history. In retelling that tale as a comic book, Spiegelman binds its meaning to the process of rendering that material. This process literally and metaphorically is thus tied to the father/son relation.

The deliberateness of the binding is figured for the reader on the back cover of the volumes. In *Maus I* a map of Poland at the time of World War II features an insert of a map of Rego Park and a drawing of the father/son story grid: the father in his armchair explaining to an attentive son stretched out at his feet. On the back cover of *Maus II* an insert of a New York/New Jersey map showing a detail of the Catskills is laid down on the plan of Auschwitz II (Birkenau, where Anja was imprisoned); Vladek in his striped prisoner's garb connects the two territories—his head is in New York, his body in Poland.

As Art heads uptown for a therapy session, he dwells painfully on the effects of these simultaneous geographies and temporalities on him as a son and an artist. (If his father, as Art puts it, "bleeds history," the son draws blood.) Climbing onto the chair in the body of the child whom the interview session seems to have reduced him to in his own eyes, Art complains about his creative block. (In the show about *Maus* held at the Museum of Modern Art there is a drawing placed in counterpoint to the "Time Flies" panels which literalizes that metaphoric state: a self-portrait of the artist as a slightly warped child's playing block, under which Spiegelman has written: "My projections of what others now expect of me from *Maus* have bent me out of shape . . . They're not meetable." The block looks a little the worse for wear.) This crisis has to do in part with the effects of commercial success, in part with the nature of the project itself: "Somehow," he explains, "my arguments with my father have lost a little of their urgency . . . and Auschwitz just seems too scary to think about . . . so I just lie there . . . " Pavel, the therapist, who is also a survivor of the camps, zeroes in on the father material: "It sounds like you're feeling remorse—maybe you believe you exposed your father to ridicule." "Maybe," Art replies, "but I tried to be fair and still show how angry I felt" (II:44).

In the therapy session Art rehearses the ambivalence inherent in his project: being fair and staying angry. In the therapy panels the son gets to justify his anger: "Mainly I remember arguing with him . . . and being told that I couldn't do anything as well as he could." "And now that you're becoming successful, you feel bad about proving your father wrong." "No matter what I accomplish, it doesn't seem like much compared to surviving Auschwitz." As a good therapist, Pavel works to undo that bind: "But you weren't in Auschwitz . . . you were in Rego Park. Maybe your father needed to show that he was always right—that he could always SURVIVE—because he felt GUILTY about surviving. And he took his guilt out on YOU, where it was safe . . . on the REAL survivor" (II:44). Art leaves the session cheered up, ready to work on the next panels—his father's stint as a tinman at Auschwitz—but his "maybe" lingers unresolved.

The anger Vladek inspires in his son is palpable in the narrative frames in which Vladek's post-Holocaust manias are thoroughly detailed, but it also shapes Art's representation of the Holocaust testimony itself. In "Of Mice and Menschen: Jewish Comics Come of Age," Paul Buhle makes the important point that one of the "less discussed, but more vital" reasons for the extraordinary success of Maus (beyond the brilliant decision to render the insanity of the Holocaust as a cartoon) "is the often unflattering portrait of the victim-survivor Vladek." The father, Buhle goes on to argue, "was not a nice guy, ever"; and (as he observes that Spiegelman commented to him) "the mainstream critics seem to have missed this point entirely, quite an important one to the artist. Perhaps they can't accept the implications" (16). The Nation's reviewer, Elizabeth Pochoda, flagging Buhle's review, emphasizes his "political point . . . that more sentimental critics have missed: Vladek began as a typical selfish bourgeois with no politics and no ideals" (560). In the New Yorker, Ethan Mordden offers one case of this mainstream "sentimental" reading: "Through his increasingly astonishing composure in retelling these adventures, Vladek becomes oddly heroic. . . . Perhaps this is the reason Art is so forgiving of a father who was overcritical when Art was growing up and is now, not to put too fine a point on it, a real pest" (96).

Despite these differences of interpretation, both Buhle and Mordden identify the panels I've described above as emblematic of the Maus project. Buhle chooses them to illustrate his remarks ("The reflexive work of Art Spiegelman probes the perils of success and the burden of survival" [9]), Mordden to make his point about the father/son relation and its classical pedagogies ("the son trying to learn from the father" [96]). Mordden, I think wrongly, separates "Art . . . a man wearing a mouse mask" from "Art, son of Vladek." He distinguishes between the son and "Art Spiegelman, artist, passing himself off as some kind of Jew—huddled over his drawing board on top of a heap of mouse corpses" (96). The work of a son, or the work of an artist? This question of genre played itself out in the best-seller lists of the New York Times when Spiegelman himself challenged their categories and had Maus moved from fiction to nonfiction. The man in the mouse mask is precisely the figure of the son as the artist, and nothing makes the difficulty of that dual identity more visible than his representation of Vladek as Art's father.

The success of Maus is due to a double audacity. The first is the choice to represent the Holocaust as a cartoon, the second to cast its star witness as a victimizer in his own world, a petty tyrant at home. In *Maus I*, Spiegelman, an acutely self-conscious artist, agonizes over this problem of representation in a conversation with Mala, his father's second wife. Mala and Art discuss Vladek's stinginess. While sympathizing with Mala, Art tries to exonerate his father: "I used to think the *war* made him that way . . . " "Fah!" Mala succinctly replies, "I went through the camps . . . *All* our friends went through the camps. Nobody is like him!" If Vladek's cheapness—Art tries calling it pragmatism—is unique to him and not due to the war experience, then what is its justification? "It's something that worries me about the book I'm doing about him," he says in the next panel. "In some ways he's just like the racist caricature of the miserly old jew." Art adds, "I mean, I'm just trying to portray my father accurately!" (I:131–32). But of course the relationship between accuracy and caricature for a cartoonist who works in a medium in which accuracy is *an effect of exaggeration* is a vexed one, especially if the son is still angry at his father: not a nice guy, ever.

Art then suddenly invokes his mother: "I wish I got Mom's story while she was alive. She was more sensitive . . . It would give the book some balance" (I:132). But the mother's story is doubly missing here. Although Vladek tells the parts of Anja's wartime experience that overlap with his, what's missing is her own self-narrative, her chance to refigure herself. Anja, we learned earlier, killed herself in Queens in 1968. Art has already told and published his cartoon version of her suicide as "Prisoner on the Hell Planet: A Case History" (1973) in, as Art puts it, "an obscure comic book." He reprints it thirteen years later *en abyme* in *Maus*. Why?

In the course of the frame narrative Art discovers that his father (who, Art complains, "doesn't even look at my work when I stick it under his nose" [I:104]) has just read "Prisoner." Drawn in an expressionist style resembling a primitive woodcut, the cartoon depicts in four stark pages the aftermath of his mother's suicide.[4] When we as readers of "Prisoner" return to the world of *Maus*, Mala, who says she found the "personal" material of "Prisoner" shocking when it first came out, now grants approval: "It was . . . very accurate . . . objective" (I:104). Vladek says he read it and cried because of the memories it brought him of Anja. The invocation of Anja in turn leads Art to inquire about her diaries. This exchange tells us something about why Spiegelman might have decided to reproduce the early work and what his relation to his mother and *her* story has to do with the emotional effectiveness of the full-scale memoir.

The father's narrative in *Maus I* ends with Anja's and Vladek's arrival at Auschwitz, but the framing text—the conversation between Art and Vladek—concludes the volume itself. The discussion of the couple's separation at the camp leads Art to ask again for his mother's diaries so that he could discover "what she went through while you were apart." At this point he finally learns that in a second holocaust his father has burned the notebooks: "these papers had too many memories" (I:159). Acknowledging that Anja had expressed the hope that her son would be interested in her recorded thoughts, the father blames the depression that followed Anja's suicide for his actions.[5] To his son's enraged questions he has no real answers. In the last panel of *Maus I*, Art walks off, smoking his eternal cigarette and thinking a single word: "Murderer" (I:160).

"Murderer" is the epithet Art assigns to the man who has destroyed his mother's memoirs without reading them (as Vladek puts it, he only "looked in"). But we have seen this interpellation before. At the end of "Prisoner on the Hell Planet" Art draws himself in jail, calling out to his mother: "Congratulations! . . . You've committed the perfect crime. . . . You *murdered* me, Mommy, and you left me here to take the rap!!!" Now, immediately after the scene in which Art and Vladek discuss the early comic strip, Vladek lies when asked about the diaries, claiming he couldn't find them. When Art learns the truth, he can't believe that his father, who saves everything (string, nails, matches, "tons of worthless shit"), would throw these notebooks away (in *Maus II*, when Vladek goes to return food to the grocery story, Françoise acidly remarks that Anja must have written on both sides of the pages, otherwise Vladek would never have burned the blank ones).[6] The importance of Vladek's "murder" is underlined again in the credits page of *Maus II*, where Spiegelman notes by way of summary: "Art becomes furious when he learns that his father, VLADEK, has burned Anja's wartime memoirs." The highlighting of that act not only points to the ways in which the question of Anja's story has haunted the *Maus* project from the start but also serves to guide the reading of its second installment.

Art's quest for his mother's diaries punctuates the dialogue with the father out of which Vladek's testimony is produced. The inclusion of "Prisoner on the Hell Planet" connects the enigma of the suicide—the mother left no note—to the violence of destroying the diaries. Both gestures entail the suppression of a maternal "text." Art's response, as both a son and an artist, to this erasure is complexly layered: in "Prisoner" he blames himself and his mother for her death; in *Maus* he attempts to provide a measure of reparation for "murdering" his mother by putting into images what he could know from Vladek of life during the war; throughout the volumes he indirectly links his task as an artist to her body by representing as a crucial piece of the *Maus* recovery project his own doomed and belated attempt to figure out her reality.

In the penultimate episode of "Prisoner," "Artie" turns away from his mother's plea—"Artie . . . you . . . still . . . love . . . me . . . Don't you?"—and fantasizes that this rejection makes him responsible for her suicide; the image of his mother in pained retreat locks him literally into the jail of his guilt, fed by the imagined "hostility mixed in with [the] condolences" of his father's friends. "Arthur, we're so sorry." "It's his fault, the punk." But in a single panel Spiegelman also renders the impossibility of ever knowing the answer to "why": at the top of the panel Anja lies naked in a tub, under which thick capital letters spell out "MENOPAUSAL DEPRESSION." A triangle of concentration camp iconography—barbed wire, piled-up human corpses, a swastika—under which HITLER DID IT! is scrawled separates the body in the tub from the jarring scene below in which three images are juxtaposed: a mother reads in bed with a little boy dressed in miniature prison garb by her side, MOMMY!; a forearm with concentration camp numbers on it slits a wrist with a razor blade, BITCH; and finally, diagonally across from the body in the tub, the prisoner sits on his bunk and holds his head. The mosaic of images proposes the pieces of truth to which no single answer is available.

Replaced in the *Maus* books, the mother's suicide is given not an answer but other images through which to locate it. What more would the son have learned about his mother from her memoirs? After Vladek has told the story (which inaugurates the persecutions ending in Auschwitz) of the hanging in Sosnowiec of four Jews for dealing in goods without authorization, Art asks what his mother was doing in those days: "Houseworks . . . and knitting . . . reading . . . and she was writing always in her diaries." "I used to see Polish notebooks around the house as a kid. Were those her diaries?" "Her diaries didn't survive from the war. What you saw she wrote after: Her whole story from the start." "Ohmigod! Where are they? I *need* those for this book!" (I:84). But of course the book will get made without them. In the absence of his mother's autobiography, Art writes his father's. He also writes his own; or rather, through the father's murder of the mother's texts, the son seeks to repair his own monstrosity: the fatal unseemliness of surviving the victims, but not without violence of his own.

As *Maus II* opens, Art and Françoise drive from Vermont to the Catskills where Vladek has summoned the couple to his aid. In the car Art agonizes over the presumption of doing his book: "I mean, I can't even make any sense out of my relationship with my father . . . How am I supposed to make any sense of Auschwitz? of the Holocaust?" He then asks: "When I was a kid I used to think about which of my parents I'd let the Nazis take to the ovens if I could only save one of them . . . Usually I saved my mother. Do you think that's normal?" Although Françoise replies reassuringly that "nobody's normal," the question hangs fire (II:14).

In the panels about the incredible success of Maus that appear in the next chapter, Art, the man behind the mask, puts his head down and remembers: "In May 1968 my mother killed herself. (She left no note.) Lately I've been feeling depressed" (II:41). In the Vermont frame narrative it is Françoise's question "Depressed again?" that leads to Art's reflection about the enormity of his book venture. Toward the end of the therapy session about survivor guilt, Pavel, the shrink, says, "Anyway, the victims who died can never tell their side of the story, so maybe it's better not to have any more stories." Art, reminding himself of Beckett's comment that "Every word is like an unnecessary stain on silence and nothingness" (and the fact, as he puts it to himself, that nonetheless Beckett said it!), seems to feel compelled as an artist to try to represent the words otherwise condemned to silence. It's as if at the heart of Maus's dare is the wish to save the mother by retrieving her narrative; as if the comic book version of Auschwitz were the son's normalization of another impossible reality: restoring the missing words, the Polish notebooks. Though Vladek tries to shrug off the specificity of her experience that Art pursues—"I can tell you," he gestures disparagingly, "I can tell you . . . She went through the same what me: terrible!" (I:158)—that isn't good enough for Art, who keeps the question of Anja alive from the beginning to the end of the memoir.[7]

What is the relation between creating Maus out of his father's words and restoring the maternal body? For the reader of the autobiographical collaboration at the heart of Maus, one who wants to find the place that might exceed the artist's recorded self-knowledge, there's not much to do beyond playing secondhand shrink (and he's already got a great therapist!). But if the outrageousness of comic book truth is any guide, and what you see is what you get, then we should understand the question of Anja as that which will forever escape representation and at the same time requires it: the silence of the victims. Perhaps that impossibility is what keeps Art forcing his father back into the memories he has tried to destroy. In one of the framing sections of *Maus II*, chapter 3 (which bears the heading that is the subtitle to the volume, "And Here My Troubles Began," and which narrates the final scenes at Auschwitz),[8] Art asks about a Frenchman who helped Vladek in the camps, whether he saved any of his letters. "Of course I saved. But all this I threw away together with Anja's notebooks.[9] All such things of the war, I tried to put out from my mind once for all . . . Until you *rebuild* me all this from your questions" (II:98).

For Vladek, "rebuilding" memory means reviving the link to Anja; Anja cannot be separated from the war: "Anja? What is to tell? Everywhere I look I'm seeing Anja . . . From my good eye, from my glass eye, if they're open or they're closed, always I'm thinking on Anja" (II:103). But this memory is by now the artist's material as well, and despite Vladek's protest, Art finally extracts the images he needs from his father's repertoire in order to close his narrative, including Anja's last days in Sosnowiec and their reunion: "More I don't need to tell you. We were both very happy and lived happy, happy ever after" (II:136). The tape recorder stops. Vladek begs for an end to stories and, in his exhaustion from the past brought into the present, calls Art by his dead brother's name, Richieu. The last drawing in *Maus II* is of the tombstone bearing the names of Art's parents as well as their birth and death dates; beneath the monument the artist signs the dates that mark the production of his book: 1978–1991. The dates on the tombstone give the lie to Vladek's "happy ever after," since Anja killed herself some twenty years after the war. Did she live happy ever after? Mala, Vladek's second wife, doesn't mince words: "Anja must have been a *saint!* No wonder she killed herself" (II:122). The dates also point indirectly to the fact that Art's text keeps his father as well as his mother alive: Vladek died in 1982. Both volumes of *Maus* were published—and critically acclaimed—after the death of the man who thought, after looking at some of his son's early sketches of the Jews hanged in Sosnowiec, that he might someday "be *famous*, like . . . what's-his-name?" "You know . . . the big-shot cartoonist . . . " "What cartoonist could *you* know . . . Walt Disney??" "YAH! Walt Disney" (I:133).[10]

Throughout the frame narrative to the survivor's tale, Art forces Vladek back into the past of suffering and the double loss of Anja. In the corners of the pages Art presses Vladek to continue with his narrative, and Vladek pleads: enough. Vladek dies before *seeing* himself "comically" reunited with his beloved Anja, and before seeing his words and deeds in some ways turned against himself (though given his incapacity for self-criticism and his talent for self-justification, he would probably have missed the bitter ironies of his portrait). And before seeing his son become the Walt Disney of the Holocaust.

The frame narrative displays an acute self-consciousness about what is at stake psychologically for the son in telling his father's story. The Museum of Modern Art show in turn emphasized the *work* involved in that process. Located in the "Projects" room, the exhibition illustrated the detail of the Spiegelman method. In one display case the process by which life becomes art is broken down and narrated. "An incident from V. Spiegelman's transcripted memories becomes a page of *Maus*." A typed page of the transcript describing the long march out of Auschwitz is displayed and marked. The episode involves the shooting of a prisoner, which Vladek likens to a childhood memory of a mad dog being shot by its owner: "And now I thought: 'How amazing it is that a human being reacts the same like this neighbor's dog.'" The commentary in the display case deals with Spiegelman's technical process: "The incident is broken down into key moments, first into phrases, then into visual notations and thumbnail sketches of possible page layouts." "Phrases are rewritten, condensed and distilled to fit into the panels."

The exposition of the myriad details involved in the transformation of the father's narrative of lived atrocity into the son's comic book underscores the degree of re-presentation involved in the *Maus* project and the versatility of skills required for its realization. Although the son claims that he became an artist in part to define his identity *against* his father's—"One reason I became an artist was that he thought it was impractical—just a waste of time . . . It was an area where I wouldn't have to compete with him"—the boundaries between them turn out to be more permeable than distinct. This crossover works in complicated ways. Vladek, for instance, also draws: early in *Maus*, Art reproduces Vladek's detailed sketch of the bunker he designed for hiding in Sosnowiec: "Show to me your pencil and I can explain you . . . such things it's good to know exactly how was it—just in case" (I:110). The exhibit lays bare the literal dexterity entailed in the "comics business"; it materializes the challenges posed to an artist committed to rendering what was never meant to be seen again. Art had to learn to *draw* what his father had faked in the camps—how, for instance, to be a shoemaker when you're a (fake) tinman.[11]

This is part of what Art's self-portrait in the mouse mask preparing to render Vladek's stint as a tinman also points to: the work of "rebuilding" Holocaust memories. There's also a specific issue here about the ethics involved in converting oral testimony—"the ruins of memory," to borrow

Lawrence Langer's phrase—into a written and visual document (let alone a comic strip!). This leads us to a final question about the making of *Maus:* what happens *between* the father's voice and the son's rendering of it as text?

In the exhibition, a tape of the father's voice was made available to the listener curious to know what Vladek sounded like. The desire to hear his voice is intensified by the inscription throughout the frame narrative of the tape recorder—both as the mark of their collaboration (even after Vladek's death)—"Please, Pop, the tape's on. Let's continue . . . Let's get back to Auschwitz" (II:47)—and of the testimony's authenticity. The reader of *Maus*—especially one with immigrant parents or grandparents (me)—is also made (uncomfortably) aware of the foreign turn of Vladek's English; the tape offers the possibility of hearing what one has been reading.

What surprised me when I listened to the tape was an odd disjunction between the quality of the voice and the inflections rendered in the panels. For while Vladek *on tape* regularly misuses prepositions ("I have seen on my own eyes," "they were shooting to prisoners"), mangles idioms ("and stood myself on the feet"), and "mispronounces" words ("made" as "med," "kid" as "kit"), the total *aural* effect, unlike the typically tortured *visualized* prose of the dialogue in the comic balloons, is one of extraordinary fluency.[12] It's almost as if in "distilling" his father's language to fit the comic strip, the son fractured the father's tongue. By contrast, the voice on the tape has the cadences of a storyteller: it is smooth, eloquent, seductive. Is breaking the rhythms of that voice an act of violence or restoration, or both at once?

What the show allows to happen which the text *as representation* necessarily forecloses is that the reader of *Maus* gains momentary access to the voice that survived the event, freed from the printed voice of the frame. In that moment (and listeners greedily listened to every word of the tape, unwilling to relinquish the headphones), one is tempted to say, the father performs unmediated—to the world.[13] But this would also be to miss the crucial function of the listener in the production of testimony. As Dori Laub writes in *Testimony: Crises of Witnessing in Literature, Psychoanalysis, and History,* "The listener . . . is a party to the creation of knowledge. . . . The testimony to the trauma thus includes its hearer. . . . The listener to trauma comes to be a participant and a co-owner of the traumatic event. . . . The listener, however, is also a separate human being . . . he preserves his own separate place, position and perspective; a battleground for forces raging in himself, to which he has to pay attention and respect if he is to properly carry out his task" (Felman and Laub 57–58). Paradoxically, then, the reader's experience of the father's voice returns him or her to the son's task and its realization. As "co-owner" of his father's trauma, the son cannot fail to map out those places and those wars.

By forcing Vladek to "rebuild" his memory, Art becomes both the "*addressable other*" (Felman and Laub 68) necessary to the production of testimony and the subject of his own story. In the end the man in the mouse mask moves beyond his task by fulfilling it, by turning it into art, and by replacing it in history. This is not to say that his losses, any more than those that define the survivor's life during and after Auschwitz, are erased by that gesture—Anja will not return to explain herself—but rather that by joining the murderers, he also rejoins himself. If after the Holocaust violence and reparation can no longer be separated, perhaps this is also the form postmodern forgiveness takes.

Notes

1. Mary Mason made the case over a decade ago in a pioneering essay from which I have been quoting, "The Other Voice: Autobiographies of Women Writers," and her analysis has been important to the mapping of women's traditions, so often neglected in the formulation of theories of cultural production.

2. In a revision of Mason's model, Susan Stanford Friedman has shown that women autobiographers tend to locate the self of their project not only in relation to a singular, chosen other but also—and simultaneously—in relation to the collective experience of women as gendered subjects in a variety of social contexts. Here again—with the inevitable measure of asymmetry that gender comparisons always present—the men's texts echo the female paradigms. In *Maus* (and to a lesser degree in *Patrimony*) this collective identity—the other Other—plays a crucial, indeed constitutive role in the elaboration of the autobiographical subject. This socially attributed identity, however, is not so much a generalized masculinity as specified Jewishness. It could even be argued that the father/son relation, and more broadly the familial scenario, finds meaning primarily when plotted against the cultural figures of Jewish identity. This double proximity may mean either that at the end of the twentieth century the autobiographical model is becoming feminized or that we need to reconsider the assumptions of the model itself. After all, one could easily see Augustine as constructing his autobiographical self in relation to his mother, Monica (and a collective audience of sinners), and Rousseau elaborating his in relation to the other constituted by his imagined and hostile readers.

Since the original publication of this essay, I have pursued the implications of this hypothesis in "Representing Others: Gender and the Subjects of Autobiography." I have also included an expanded version of "Cartoons of the Self" in my book *Bequest and Betrayal: Memoirs of a Parent's Death*.

3. There is from the start a tension about whose story it is. On the cover of *Maus* is the father/mother (mouse) (*couple*) whose joint destiny gets summarized in the singular "survivor's tale." Although the son clearly distinguishes the two parts of the couple by asking specifically about his mother, he is limited finally by his father's plot.

Maus also conforms to Catherine Portuges's account of recent autobiographical films by contemporary women filmmakers (primarily postwar European directors): "These films share as a common gesture . . . the desire to create an intergenerational testimonial for the benefit of parents or children and to recount a story formerly repressed, silenced, or distorted. . . . It is the desire to make restitution for pain inflicted, real or imagined, and to see the other as a whole individual with a separate identity that infuses these films, rather than the 'manic defense' more typical of the work of male autobiographical filmmakers" (343). I think we have to complicate these patterns of gender differentiation and to articulate them with the historical demands of postwar representation. See also in *Lear's* (June 1992) the striking photograph of TV news reporter Charles Stuart *with his mother* (the story is about her unsolved murder) and described as a *self-portrait taken by himself*.

4. In the upper left-hand corner of "Prisoner," in its title frame, a hand holds a summer snapshot of Anja and Art dated 1958. It's hard to make out the expression on Anja's face, but her little boy is grinning at the camera. In the lower left-hand corner of the page in *Maus* on which "Prisoner" is reproduced, Spiegelman has drawn in the same hand, as if to mark the place of his own rediscovery of the earlier work. The repetition also ties the hand as signature to the mother/son bond. In the photo, Anja rests her hand on her son's head—the hand that a few panels later will hold the razor blade.

5. The tension between obsessional saving and impulsive throwing away is rehearsed earlier in *Maus*. After a session with his father on the pre-Auschwitz days in Sosnowiec, Art looks for his coat only to discover that Vladek has thrown it away: "It's a *shame* my son would wear such a coat!" His father offers one of his old jackets as a replacement (having bought a new one for himself at Alexander's). The chapter ends with Art verifying that his coat is indeed in the garbage, and walking home alone·in shock (as in after his father's revelation): "I just can't believe it . . . " (I:69).

6. The whereabouts of the diaries are associated with the saving of junk much earlier in *Maus*. Art interrupts a conversation with Mala about the roundup of the Jews in Sosnowiec to track down a vague memory of having seen the notebooks on

Vladek's shelves in the den. He catalogs the kinds of things Vladek saved: four 1965 Dry Dock Savings calendars, menus from cruises, hotel stationery, etc. There's a question here about what part of this kind of saving can be seen as a specific effect of surviving the Holocaust and what belongs more generally to a diasporic identity. I was struck by a remark in Susan Cheever's memoir of her father, John Cheever, the ultimate chronicler of goyish sensibility: "My father never saved anything. He scorned all conservative instincts" (53). Like Vladek (and like the story of the Collier brothers that haunted many of us in the 1950s), my father always had teabags drying on the stove (the degraded transformation of the perpetual samovar and the tradition of what he called "sens"—the essence, presumably, of tea) and saved rubber bands, jars, broken pencils, old flowerpots, and plastic containers until the apartment overflowed from the hoarding. Was this the aftermath of the Depression? A way of always being prepared—the "you never know" of survivors?

7. In the scenes of Auschwitz following the therapy session, Art has his father describe Birkenau (Auschwitz II), where Anja was interned. Here Vladek relates what he managed to learn of Anja's fate, including a letter reproduced in one of the panels: "'I miss you,' she wrote to me. 'Each day I think to run into the electric wires and finish everything. But to know you are alive it gives me still to hope'" (II:53). Despite the "reproduction" of the letter—the only instance of Anja's written words—we are necessarily left as readers with the mother's voice in translation: into Vladek's English, into his idealized version of the couple, into Art's comic strip. Nonetheless, the disembodied voice delivers the message of despair that seems to have been hers from the start. At the beginning of her narrative we learn that Anja has a kind of nervous breakdown after giving birth to Richieu and is sent to a sanitarium.

8. In *Holocaust Testimonies: The Ruins of Memory*, Lawrence Langer comments on the status of this phrase in survivor interviews: "Asked to describe how he felt at the moment of liberation, one surviving victim declared: 'Then I knew my troubles were *really* about to begin,' inverting the order of conflict and resolution that we have learned to expect of traditional historical narrative" (67).

9. Toward the end of *Maus II*, Vladek presents Art with a surprise, a box of snapshots: "I thought I lost it, but you see how I saved!" This raises for the last time the matter of the memoirs: "*Mom's diaries?!*" (II:113). The snapshots—redrawn as photographs—mainly show other members of Anja's family, including a brother, a commercial artist Anja said he resembled and who, like his sister, killed himself. The photographs record what was left of her family after the war. In "Family Pictures: *Maus*, Mourning, and Post-Memory," Marianne Hirsch analyzes the role of photographs in *Maus* and their crucial role in the "aesthetic of post-memory" that Spiegel-

man elaborates. She also emphasizes the ways in which the *Maus* project represents an attempt to reconstruct the missing maternal legacy.

10. The epigraph to *Maus II* is drawn from a German newspaper article of the mid-1930s linking the "Jewish brutalization of the people!" to the miserable "Mickey Mouse . . . ideal."

11. In *Maus II* Vladek explains how in the camps he justified his boast that he had been a "shoemaker since childhood" (in reality he had watched his cousin work in the ghetto shoe shop). He describes repairing a lace-up boot in need of resoling. Art illustrates this task with a complicated drawing. In the show, above the comic drawings is mounted the technical drawing of shoemaking from which Art derived his cartoon version. Vladek draws the moral of his successful gamble: "You see? It's good to know how to do *everything*." Art's insistence on his impracticality—not knowing how to do anything—is undone by his accomplishment as an artist in figuring out how to *draw* anything. The survivor's skills honed in the camps pass on to the next generation as a matter of artistic survival.

12. A portion of the tape corresponds to the transcripted account of the march out of Auschwitz, and thus it becomes irresistible to compare the aural and written voices.

13. There's no escaping the effect of the frame, of course, since the taped passages are just as *chosen* (out of the twenty or more recorded hours) as the illustrated ones.

2
Blood Legacies

Maus and Holocaust Testimony

4
Necessary Stains

Art Spiegelman's *Maus* and
the Bleeding of History

Michael G. Levine

> In making *Maus*, I found myself drawing every panel, every figure, over
> and over—obsessively—so as to pare it down to an essence, as if each
> panel was an attempt to invent a new word, rough-hewn but stream-
> lined.
>
> Art Spiegelman, "Little Orphan Annie's Eyeballs"

The publication of Art Spiegelman's *Maus* "comix," the first volume of which
appeared in 1986, the second in 1991, has helped to mark and define an
important turning point in the history of Holocaust testimony.[1] Forty years
after the events of World War II, many survivors had reached a point in their
lives where they knew it was late, that if ever there was a time to talk, to pass
on their experience as a "legacy," it was now (Hartman, *Shadow* 133–50). It
was also a time when the children of survivors began to participate in increasing numbers in the process of bearing witness. For this second generation it was a question not only of helping to elicit their parents' stories, of
persuading them to write, speak, or agree to be interviewed, but also of coming to terms with their own implication in their parents' experiences. Indeed, many of these children had reached a point in their own lives where
they were discovering that the first generation's stories had in a sense *already*
been passed on to them, that they had themselves become the unwitting
bearers of a legacy of pain, of a trauma that had, in Spiegelman's words, in-
advertently "spilled over" from one generation to the next.

Various terms have been proposed recently to describe the situation of
this second generation of survivors in general and Spiegelman's own predica-
ment with regard to his parents' memories in particular. Referring specifically
to the photographs contained in *Maus*, Marianne Hirsch has noted that they
"connect the two levels of Spiegelman's text, the past and the present, the

story of the father and the story of the son, because these family photographs are documents both of memory (the survivor's) and of what I would like to call post-memory (that of the child of the survivor whose life is dominated by memories of what preceded his/her birth.)" For Hirsch, post-memory is not simply "beyond memory," nor is it "purely in history." It is distinguished from the former "by generational distance" and from the latter "by deep personal connection." "Post-memory," she argues, "should reflect back on memory, revealing it as equally constructed, equally mediated by the processes of narration and imagination" (8–9).

Although the post-memories of this second generation may thus be said to be more distanced and mediated than those of the first, in coming after they also have the retroactive effect of revealing things about the parents' memories that might not have been sufficiently appreciated the first time around—not just that they are "equally constructed, equally mediated by the processes of narration and imagination," but also that the overwhelmingly *immediate* impact of the Holocaust on the first generation was such that it was not fully assimilated as it occurred. It is ultimately this legacy of *un-assimilated memories* unwittingly passed on from one traumatized generation to the next that Hirsch seeks to call attention to in coining the term "post-memory" and in reading *Maus* as representative of an "aesthetic of the trauma fragment, the aesthetic of the testimonial chain." "The power of the photographs Spiegelman includes in *Maus*," she argues, "lies not in their evocation of memory, in the connection they can establish between present and past, but in their status as fragments of a history we cannot take in" (27).

While Hirsch traces the insistence of these unassimilated historical fragments in *Maus* and, in so doing, helps one to appreciate some of the ways in which the first generation's "legacy" is passed on not just in words but in silence, she also suggests that this silent mode of transmission is itself strangely double-edged: at once a way of silently and unconsciously acting out that which "we cannot take in" and a way of repeating from one generation to the next the very *act of silencing*. Thus, in addition to Spiegelman's father, who effectively silences the mother's voice when he burns the diaries she had written after the war, and who compounds the violence of this act by refusing to tell Art he had done so until much later (a moment depicted on the last page of the first volume), the son is also guilty, in Hirsch's eyes, "of banishing female voices from his narrative" (21).

The "survivor's tale" Art draws in collaboration with his father, Vladek, is seen by Hirsch as a process of masculine, Orphic creation, as an Orphic song "about the internal workings of a Hades which few have survived, and fewer still have been able to speak about." This Orphic creation, she continues (drawing heavily on Klaus Theweleit's *Buch der Könige*), results not only from such a descent into Hades but from a reemergence out of it as well; it is

> a masculine process facilitated by the encounter with the beautiful dead woman who cannot herself come out and sing her own song. Orphic creation is thus an artificial "birth" produced by men—by male couples unable to bypass the generativity of women, male couples whose bonding depends on the tragic absence of women. In this process, women play the role of "media" in Theweleit's sense, of intermediaries, not of primary creators or witnesses. In *Maus*, father and son together attempt to reconstruct the missing story of the mother, and by extension, the story of women in Auschwitz. . . . Art and Vladek perform the collaboration of the creative male couple: the difficulties that structure their relationship only serve to strengthen the ties which bind them to each other and to the labor they have undertaken. (21)

Hirsch is right to apply critical pressure to the question of creativity in *Maus*, to suggest that there is something odd and perhaps even "artificial" about its "birth." Nevertheless, her attempt to describe this "birth" in terms of a process of masculine, Orphic creation based on female absence and to link this explanation in turn to Art's "process of banishing female voices from his narrative" itself seems to domesticate a much more unwieldy connection forged in the text between birth and death trauma to which I will return below. Let it suffice for the moment to note with Hirsch the strange appearance of an umbilical cord, a figure so obviously associated with the moment of birth, in the very scene of *Maus* in which Art describes his mother's death. Not only does this cord come to figure the complex ties through which Art remains bound to the traumatic moment of his mother's suicide, but, as the figure of a certain interweaving of life- and death lines, as a figure that is itself woven through others in and around *Maus*, it makes one see the "birth" of the text in a way very different from the view outlined above.

Whereas Hirsch seeks to explain the silencing of women in this male-centered text in terms provided by Theweleit, I would urge that, rather than endeavoring *to interpret* the one through the other, we view the role of women and that of the "media" as two related *questions*, as questions so bound up with each other that in broaching the one it is impossible not to address the other. These questions surface again in James Young's essay "The Holocaust as Vicarious Past: Art Spiegelman's *Maus* and the Afterimages of History." While Young does not speak of women as "media" in Theweleit's sense, he agrees with Hirsch that Spiegelman is "an accomplice to the usurpation of his dead mother's voice" (686). In Young's account, Art is no longer paired off with his father in a male couple "whose bonding depends on the tragic absence of women" but is described instead as "the midwife to and eventual representer of his father's story" (678). The choice of terms here is no doubt telling, for in depicting Art as a midwife to his father's story Young suggests not only that the men have once again taken the place of a woman, usurping both Anja's voice and her role in the "creative process," but, moreover, that they have done so *as women*—as a father who gives birth and as a son feminized as a "midwife" who assists in the delivery. This strange crossing of gender and generational lines would hardly be worth mentioning were it not for the fact that the question of the woman's role—of the mother as a generative source—comes up again at another point in Young's essay where the birth of the father's story seems once again to overlap with that of the son's. According to Young, Art

> is on a mission, a self-quest that is also historical. "I still want to draw that book about you," Artie says to his father, who answers, "No one wants anyway to hear such stories," to which Artie answers, "*I want to hear it.*" And then he asks his father to begin, in effect, with his own implied origin: "Start with Mom . . . " he says. "Tell me how you met." He did not ask him to start with the war, deportation, or interment, but with his mother and their union—that is, his *own* origins. (669–70)[2]

Although there are other ways of reading this passage (I will propose such a reading below), at this point it is important first to underscore the insistence of birth imagery in Hirsch's and Young's essays, to remark the way it is repeatedly linked to the usurpation both of the mother's voice and of her procreative role, the way father and son, in bypassing the generativity of the mother, seek not only to engender their own stories but to do so in such a way that the son is made to assist in the birth of a paternal tale that is also in effect his own.

Both Hirsch and Young are concerned with the ways in which the first generation's traumatic tales—tales that in some fundamental sense will never have been entirely their own—have become the children's life stories as well. Yet, while Hirsch's notion of post-memory tends to stress the ways in which "a history we cannot take in" has been unconsciously passed on, Young coins the term "received history" to describe the highly self-conscious narratives produced by Spiegelman's "media-savvy generation, born after—but indelibly shaped by—the Holocaust." "This postwar generation," Young contends,

cannot remember the Holocaust as it actually occurred. All they remember, all they know of the Holocaust, is what the victims have passed down to them in their diaries, what the survivors have remembered to them in their memoirs. They remember not actual events but the countless histories, novels, and poems of the Holocaust they have read, the photographs, movies, and video testimonies they have seen over the years. They remember long days and nights in the company of survivors, listening to their harrowing tales, until their lives, loves, and losses seemed grafted indelibly onto their own life stories. (669–70)

Whereas Hirsch describes the women in *Maus* as "media," as "intermediaries" who are never permitted to play the role of "primary creators or witnesses," parts reserved in the text exclusively for men, in Young this gender distinction becomes a generational one. Working with a surprisingly linear notion of generational descent (surprising, at least, in a context where the belated structure of traumatic experience significantly complicated such notions), Young repeatedly contrasts the first generation's "immediate" knowledge of the Holocaust with the second's "hypermediated experience of the memory of events." While such an approach clearly makes sense on one level, on another it fails to account for—or even to address—those moments in *Maus* where it is a question not only of the initial trauma returning in disjointed fragments in the memory of the survivor but of time itself being "out of joint."[3]

In contrast, then, to Young's notion of "received history" that ultimately frames "the ways the events of the Holocaust are passed down to us" in very traditional terms as a movement from "painful immediacy" to "somewhat less painful mediacy" or from "trying to remember events" to recalling one's "relationship to the memory" of them, I would urge that one view Spiegelman's "survivor's tale" instead as an act of *belated witnessing*, as a text in which Art may be said to function as a second-degree witness, as a witness who is not just one step removed from the experiences of the first generation but otherwise implicated in them. In *Maus* it is this implication of the second-generation survivor in the traumas of the first that not only tangles the lines of descent but makes Art a witness to the *delayed impact* of the Holocaust.

In becoming a witness to the witness, Art elicits and records his father's testimony. Yet in doing so he also opens a space in which the impact of that testimony is given a chance to register as if for the first time, to register first on the audience and then as if by ricochet on the traumatized survivor himself. In what follows I will explore how the positions of first- and second-degree witness, of teller and listener, are reworked in the course of the text, how Vladek in *listening through* his own audience, through an audience that has in a sense been delegated the task not just of surviving but of listening on his behalf, comes to experience the belated impact of his own testimony, of testimony that will only first become his to own in the act of passing it on.

Translation and Survival

As critics have often noted, the act of transmission in *Maus* involves various processes of translation.[4] Perhaps nowhere in Spiegelman's work are questions of translation so clearly raised as in the very title of his "survivor's tale." *Maus* is, after all, a German word, a cognate of the English term *mouse*. *Maus* means "mouse."[5] Yet it is precisely the seeming transparency of this translation that the text calls into question. For only in a particular historical and ideological context, one shaped by the visual media of posters, caricatures, and Nazi propaganda films such as *Der ewige Jude* ("The Eternal Jew"), does *Maus* begin to mean not just "mouse" but "Jew," and not just "Jewish mouse" but "plague-infested vermin." As such, a Jew is not a human being who is murdered but a disease-ridden rodent that is "exterminated," and exterminated not just with poison gas but with the pesticide Zyklon-B. In addition to raising questions about the translation of terms *between* languages—about the pseudo-transparency of terms that seem to *need no translation*—*Maus* also draws attention to the deceptive sense of immediacy, the pseudo-familiarity with which one relates to one's own "mother tongue"—and *Maus*, as we will see, is very much a text about (the silence of) the mother. Whereas the dogs in *Maus* speak English, the cats German, the pigs Polish, and the frogs French, the mice speak a variety of idioms, none of which could be said to be their own "natural language." It is certainly not by chance in this regard that the cat word for mouse is used in the title. Compared to the other animals of the text, the mice seem to have a less "natural"—that is, less transparent, unmediated—relation to a particular national language. Moreover, if Spiegelman makes a point of using the German word *Maus* in the title, he perhaps does so in order to allow it to resonate with the German verb *mauscheln* and thereby to point to a particular German-Jewish, cat-mouse, *linguistic* relation. As the Czech-Jewish writer of German animal stories, Franz Kafka, once observed in a famous letter to Max Brod, *mauscheln* involves "a bumptious, tacit, or painfully self-critical appropriation of another's property. . . . It is an organic compound of bookish German and pantomime" (288; trans. modified).

Spiegelman has openly acknowledged his debt to Kafka on a number of occasions. Of particular relevance in this regard is his response to a question posed by Jonathan Rosen concerning the genesis of the text.

The real origin of *Maus* was being invited, twenty years ago, to do a three-page comic strip for an underground comic book called *Funny Aminals* [sic], the only requirement being that I use anthropomorphic characters. Fishing around for something led me toward my center. A number of things helped. One of them was sitting in on Ken Jacobs' film classes at SUNY-Binghamton where he was showing racist cartoons and at the same time cat-and-mouse chase cartoons. They conflated for me and originally steered me toward possibly doing something about racism against blacks in America. Shortly thereafter, Josephine the Singer began humming to me and told me that there was something closer to deal with and I began pursuing the logic and possibilities that that metaphoric device opened up. (11)

In what language, one wonders, did Spiegelman hear Kafka's singing mouse hum? To respond to this question one might recall the words of one Kafka critic: "Although etymologically related to the names Mauschel, Moishele, and Moses, the verb *mauscheln*—to speak German 'like a Jew'—recalls the German word for mouse. . . . In this sense the language spoken by the mice in 'Josephine'—what one might term their *Mäusedeutsch*—can be interpreted as Kafka's fictional version of *Mauscheldeutsch* and, perhaps, as a figure for his own Jewish-German language" (Anderson 205).[6] One might say in turn that Spiegelman uses the German word for mouse in the title of his book in order to allude to the ways his own text seeks to displace the dominant discourse from within, to dislocate it by speaking not only "cat" but other established languages and protocols of verbal and visual representation "like a mouse."[7]

While *Maus* may thus be said to be a text on translation, a text that invites one to begin translating precisely in those places where translation seems unnecessary, it is also one that deals with the question of Holocaust survival, the question not only of who survives as a witness to the Holocaust but of the Holocaust's own lack of closure, its way of outliving its own apparent end. Claude Lanzmann's remarks about his film *Shoah* are particularly relevant in this context.

> You know, this was a real question, the question of the end. I did not have the moral right to give a happy ending to this story. When does the Holocaust really end? Did it end the last days of the war? Did it end with the creation of the State of Israel? No. It still goes on. These events are of such magnitude, of such scope that they have never stopped developing their consequences. . . . When I really had to conclude I decided that I did not have the right to do it. . . . And I decided that the last image of the film would be a train, an endlessly rolling . . . train. (Felman and Laub 241–42)

Like Lanzmann, Spiegelman has spoken of the Shoah as an event without end, as a "cataclysmic world event the ripples of which keep seeping through the pages of *The New York Times* on a daily basis" (J. Rosen 1). Like Lanzmann's film, Spiegelman's *Maus* comix struggle with the enigma of this survival, with the overlapping questions of who survives as a witness to the trauma of the Holocaust and of who bears witness to *its survival*. In an interview Spiegelman has said that growing up his father was Auschwitz for him as much as he was its victim. When asked in a subsequent interview to comment on this statement, he responded that "for a child, a father can be a very threatening figure, and the fact that he carried so much pain with him, well, that spilled over" (J. Rosen 9). One begins to get a sense here of some of the ways in which the "cataclysmic world event" of the Shoah will have overflowed its apparent end—namely, as a dissolution of boundaries, as ripple effects seeping through the pages of the daily press, as the spilling over of unbearable suffering, as ongoing cycles of victimization. It is no doubt telling in this connection that the first volume of *Maus* bears the subtitle "My Father Bleeds History."

In *Maus* such bleeding is most obviously linked to the hemorrhaging of Vladek's left eye, an eye, the text suggests, that cannot come to terms with what it has seen, that is physically wounded by what it is forced to see over and over again in flashbacks and recurrent nightmares, so wounded in fact that it must eventually be removed by a surgeon and replaced by a glass facsimile.[8] What is perhaps less obvious, however, is the connection between this spectral presence of an unassimilated past, this bleeding of the past into the present through the very medium of vision, and the hemorrhaging of *visual images* in the text, of images that literally burst out of their pictorial frames on numerous occasions (I:30). Although such moments may be said to stage a certain hemorrhaging of history in a particularly concentrated, painful, and graphic way, they also suggest more generally that one pay close attention to the body of the text itself, to a body composed not only of multiple narrative layers but of ones that repeatedly bleed into and through one another. The question raised by the text's enigmatic subtitle is thus the following: how is one to read this *internal* bleeding of history, this palimpsest of interpenetrating narrative layers?

Cartoon Narrative as (Slow-)Motion Picture

In order to pursue the question of narrative stratification in *Maus*, it is necessary to examine what exactly it means for Spiegelman to tell a story in a medium that "mixes together words and pictures." In his introduction to *Breakdowns: From MAUS to Now*, the author's 1977 "Anthology of Strips," Spiegelman notes that his "dictionary defines *comic strip* as 'a narrative series of cartoons.' A *narrative* is defined as 'a story.' Most definitions of *story* leave me cold. Except the one that says: 'A complete horizontal division of a building . . . From Medieval Latin *historia* . . . a row of windows with pictures on them'" (*Comix* 28). These definitions are themselves situated over a row of three consecutive "picture windows," the first of which is a panel subdivided into four quadrants, each of which is in turn broken down into further subpanels. The second, central panel depicts a man viewed from behind looking out a window onto nothing but cold, inky blackness; the window facing him is itself divided into eight individual panes of glass with the man's circular hat positioned over the central horizontal-vertical axis of the window frame. The third panel depicts a repetitive series of open bathroom stalls.

Whereas the words blocked out above the images in this row of panels seem at first to define the smallest "historiographic" unit as a panel—that is, as a kind of window with a picture on it—the images themselves call this definition into question. For not only can each window be broken down into individual panes, but these subwindows can in turn be reworked into a mise-en-abîme structure of panes within panes. Through this co-mixing of words and images Spiegelman prompts one to see the panel as a picture *and* a window, as an oxymoronic "picture window" that must at once be looked at and looked through: *looked at* because its signifying surface does not simply efface itself, does not merely yield before the authority of a signified reality or become a transparent means to an end outside itself; *looked through* because such "picture windows" *do* open onto other windows, onto the abyssal depths of panes within panes. In an interview with Lawrence Weschler, Spiegelman remarks that what concerned him in *Maus* was "not so much whether my father was telling the truth, but rather, just what had he actually lived through—what did he understand of what he had experienced, what did he tell of what he understood, what did I understand of what he told, and what do I tell? The layers begin to multiply *like pane upon pane of glass*" (56).

The third panel in Spiegelman's mise-en-abîme structure provides a window onto a repetitive series of open bathroom stalls and seems at first to emphasize this movement of infinite regress. Yet its scatological, "raw" humor subtly takes the movement one small but decisive step further.[9] For as Spiegelman observes elsewhere, comics are "a gutter medium; that is, it's what takes place in the gutters between the panels that activates the medium" (*Comix* 100). Thus it is ultimately not the panel itself, whether infinitely expanded in rows or infinitesimally broken down in a series of panels within panels, that constitutes the true unit of "historiographic" analysis for the comix artist. That unit, never directly named in this series of definitions, is instead the gutter *between* frames.

Yet to call this between-space a unit is also somewhat misleading. Not only is the gutter never unitary, never one with itself, but it "activates the medium" of the comic strip precisely by setting the seemingly self-contained, intact panels in motion. What I would describe as Spiegelman's art of the "slow-motion picture" may thus be said to fall somewhere between drawing and film; that is, once the medium is activated, the individual "picture windows" are no longer read primarily as positive meaningful units but rather as links in a chain of signifiers—which is to say that each panel itself becomes a kind of gutter, an interspace, a self-different image whose relative value is determined only through its relation to other "inter-images."

Although these strips may thus be said to set seemingly static images in motion, they obviously do so at a speed much slower than that at which normal moving pictures are typically projected. Indeed, whereas in the movies the illusion of continuous motion is produced by screening images at a speed of twenty-four frames per second, a speed that effectively effaces the "gutter between the panels," the activated medium of Spiegelman's comix slows things down enough to expose just these interspaces. If, as was suggested earlier, history becomes legible in the internal bleeding of the narrative tissue in *Maus*, it may now be added that it also bleeds through the interspaces of the text, through the very gaps and gutters in the narrative that define, structure, and activate the comix medium. It must be emphasized, however, that these interspaces through which history bleeds are not merely positive breaks in the narrative but also and above all the cinematic movement of framed images repeatedly *breaking into* one another, a movement that not only splits each image from itself but, in doing so, effectively splices it into a chain of images open to and opened by the difference of the others. History bleeds, in short, through the slow-motion projection of these mutually reframing inter-images.

The formal principle of the "slow-motion picture" is introduced at the very beginning of *Maus* through the pointedly cinematic title for its first chapter. Taking its name from the silent film classic *The Sheik*, first released in 1921, the chapter highlights Vladek's own star quality—his vaunted resemblance to the film's leading man ("People always told me I looked just like Rudolf Valentino" [I:13]), his self-image as a real-life ladies' man, and finally his casting by Art as the protagonist of *Maus*. The title also implicitly draws attention to important formal similarities between Spiegelman's comix and the medium of silent film, both of which rely heavily upon captions and speech bubbles to tell their stories.

As a way of suggesting that *Maus* itself be read as a kind of silent film, Spiegelman casts his father not only as the star and narrator of "A Survivor's Tale" but also as its psycho-cinematic "projectionist." These two senses of the term are brought together in a single panel toward the beginning of the first chapter. In this frame an image of Vladek riding his exercycle is superimposed on a poster of *The Sheik* (I:13). At the bottom of the poster in the portion covered by the figure on the stationary bike one can just make out the generic subtitle "A Motion Picture." Though partially obscured by Vladek's frame, these words have a way of bleeding through; that is, the superimposition of fore- and background, of images and words, in this panel brings an altogether different kind of scenario into focus. Indeed, while

Vladek may be going nowhere on his stationary bike, his pedaling not only sets the text's own pictures in motion but, in doing so, generates a very different genre of silent "motion picture" from the one explicitly referred to in the poster behind him.

If, as Spiegelman says, "it's what takes place in the gutters between the panels that activates the medium," Vladek's pedaling here embodies this activation process. Moreover, in contrast to film, where the projectionist is little more than an appendage to the machine that screens images at a constant speed, in *Maus* the pictures set in motion through Vladek's pedaling are projected at widely varying tempos. Obviously, the speed at which Vladek pedals is determined by the condition of his body. Yet, as the very *embodiment* of the activation process, of a process that sets seemingly static images in motion, his pedaling at various speeds suggests different ways of reading these motion pictures in relation to one another. For instance, high-speed pedaling at an even pace evokes not only the cinematic illusion of continuous motion but also the continuity of a diachronic narrative read quickly row by row, from left to right, top to bottom, past to present. By contrast, a slower speed suggests frame-by-frame cinematic analysis or a breakdown of panels on the page which are to be read vertically as well as horizontally, in the time frame of the past as well as the present; a complete halt evokes the cinematic freeze-frame or photographic still and suggests in narrative terms a reading of the entire page as one static, synchronic unit.

While Vladek is in one sense a projectionist who repeatedly varies the speed of the images he sets in motion, he is in another sense one who psychologically projects a little too much of himself into the motion pictures he screens. Telling in this regard is the way mouse faces have been projected onto the typically orientalized image of Valentino and his swooning European consort in the poster of *The Sheik*. It is as though the poster bearing the subtitle "A Motion Picture" had itself somehow become a kind of motion-picture *screen*, as though an overly identified projectionist had taken over the screen and filled it with images of his girlfriend and himself. Indeed, the poster of *The Sheik* ultimately bears a closer resemblance to Vladek and his old girlfriend, Lucia Greenberg, dancing together in the adjacent panel than to the Arab chieftain (who, it turns out by the end of the film, was actually educated abroad in England) and his "liberated" English mistress (who had fled the company of her compatriots abroad only to fall into the arms of a properly domesticated version of the Other). If, according to the conceit upon which *Maus* is constructed, Jews are mice and Germans are cats, this panel of Vladek pedaling before a poster of *The Sheik* suggests that the human faces one expects to find hidden beneath the animal masks of the text are themselves less obviously but all the more irreducibly screens, masks, and projection surfaces.[10] As Spiegelman reflects elsewhere, "one thing that fascinated me, and it was a horrible fascination that I suspect I share with many non-religious Jews, was the fact that the people sent to their slaughter as Jews didn't necessarily identify themselves as/with Jews; it was up to the Nazis to decide who was a Jew. As Sartre pointed out in *Antisemite and Jew,* a Jew is someone whom others call a Jew" (*Comix* 15). It is in just this way that the "projectionist," Vladek Spiegelman, eventually has a very different, much more literal kind of "stardom" projected on him.

Framing the Testimonial Contract

While *Maus* may thus be described as a slow-motion picture, as a narrative of words and images set in motion by Vladek's pedaling, it is nevertheless one that has a hard time gearing up and getting started. "I went out to see my father in Rego Park," the first chapter begins. "I hadn't seen him in a long time—we weren't that close" (I:11). The real story, however, the story Art has really come for, must wait for the moment when Vladek first mounts his stationary bike to begin. As his father slowly starts to cycle, Art begins to circle apprehensively about the true purpose of his visit. "I still want to draw that book about you . . . ," he stammers, "the one I used to talk to you about . . . about your life in Poland, and the war" (I:12). As though Art's tentatively phrased proposition carried with it more than he could put into words—namely, an unspoken desire *to contain the other,* to draw not just a book but a frame about his father—in the next panel he effectively proceeds to do just that. He takes up a picture that had been sitting on a table and, holding it by its frame, examines it more carefully as he describes his project to his father.[11] Not only is the question of the frame quite literally taken up here, but it is one, the visual language of the text suggests, that is still very much up for grabs at this point. Moreover, as if to emphasize the purely formal aspect of the situation—the question of the relationship between the framing and the framed—the panel provides no information to help the reader determine what the content of the framed picture might actually be. Thus, faced with Art's proposition and apparently sensing all that it implies, Vladek counters that "it would take MANY books, my life, and no one wants anyway to hear such stories" (I:12). His accentuation of the word "MANY" seems to shatter the unique frame of the book Art wants to draw about him. Furthermore, as Vladek voices his objection, his arms and the handlebars of the exercycle they grasp are depicted in such a way as to contain Art. They hold his head within the contours of their frame while the framed picture once held aloft by the son is now shown sitting in its former place on the table. In a sense it is not just the picture but Art himself who is put back in his place here, a suggestion that is reinforced in this panel by a depiction of the paternal frame drawn about its would-be framer.

As the struggle over the frame continues, not only is the surrounding image of the paternal frame itself split up and spaced out in a triptych of three vertically contiguous panels, but in the lower left-hand corner of the page the son again takes up the framed picture he had just set down. The gesture suggests that Art is now once again prepared to take up the challenge of drawing his father's many stories into a single book. In the same panel he verbally draws his father back in by contesting the claim that "no one wants anyway to hear such stories" with the emphatic attestation, "I want to hear it." Vladek's fear that his testimony will fall on deaf ears, that it too may die an anonymous death, is thus met and countered by Art's desire to be an exemplary listener, a live audience of one whose presence and integrity, he presumes, will be enough to stave off the indistinct specter of "no one."[12]

At this point a compromise is apparently struck between Vladek's fears and Art's desires. Yet it is negotiated in a way that makes manifest the tenuous and provisional nature of the arrangement. Indeed, signs of its instability are legible at every point and in every position of the scene. Perhaps nowhere is this more apparent than in the place held by Art, whose "I" is itself a kind of pronominal placeholder—a displacement substitute, as Freud would call it, that only holds off the "no one" it stands in for by holding open a space for it, by having its own apparent identity compromised and haunted by the spectral anonymity of "no one." Indeed, as it turns out, Art only becomes the audience he had hoped to embody for his father's "life" stories through an act of self-division and supplementation—only by becoming a "live audience" with a hearing aid, an audience that, as it turns out, can only listen with the mechanical ear of a tape recorder on hand. "Writing things down is just too hard," Art concedes midway through the first volume (I:73). Yet what he fails to add is that the microphone he now wields is henceforth to be used not only as a writing supplement but also as a means of self-defense. Indeed, in a video appendix to the CD-ROM version of Maus, Spiegelman observes that "unlike other survivors, [Vladek] had no specific need to bear witness. What he had a need for was his son to hang out and be around, and about the only way I could arrange for that to happen was with a microphone holding him at bay."

Just as the microphone Art wields turns out to have a surprisingly double-edged quality, so too does the shift from handwriting to recording make manifest certain tensions touched on but not really played out in the scene in which the testimonial contract is first framed. Indeed, the belated introduction of the microphone, a writing supplement that seems, on the one hand, to add nothing to the testimonial dynamic and, on the other hand, to change it dramatically by highlighting its surprisingly conflictual nature, in the end leads one to reflect upon Art's own conflict-ridden status as a second-degree witness. It suggests that the struggles waged in this inaugural scene are played out not only between subjects but within them. By drawing attention to the particular way Art listens to his father's testimony, the shift from writing to recording prompts one to ask whether there might not be something uncannily and irreducibly mechanical, something strangely dead, about the live audience he wishes to embody. In other words, one is led to question whether in defending himself in the act—and with the very instruments—of listening there are not things he manages to hear only in an unconscious and automatic way, to register without really hearing, without experiencing the full force of their impact. Indeed, perhaps the most unsettling question raised by the compromising situation in which Art initially finds himself is whether that which survives of the very excess of life stories—of that which cannot be bound in a single book—and which "no one wants anyway to hear," perhaps least of all Art, will nevertheless have recorded and replayed itself—like a ghost in the machine—between the frames of *Maus*.[13]

Bearing these questions in mind, let us return to the moment in the initial negotiations where a compromise seems to be struck between the father's fears and the son's desires. For it is at this moment that Art again decides to take up the picture resting on the table. Yet this time he does so not in order to raise it as a question but simply and finally to indicate its content. He thus points a finger at the framed picture and identifies the person depicted in it as his mother. "Start with mom," he suggests to Vladek. "Tell me how you met" (I:12). In a sense the testimonial contract that the father and son negotiate in this scene is framed in the name of the mother. Like the microphone already strangely on hand, the belated introduction of this supernumerary figure seems at once superfluous and oddly necessary. Even after being identified as the person in the photograph, the mother remains invisible to the reader. Although she is now in a sense on the scene, she is still very much out of the picture.

As a supplementary witness to the inaugural scene of witnessing, as a supernumerary both in the sense of a person serving no apparent function and of an actor employed to play the part of a walk-on, the mother appears here as a kind of testimonial specter whose presence haunts the entire telling of "A Survivor's Tale." As though obeying a summons to appear at this pivotal moment in the text, the ghost of the dead mother bears witness *in her very supplementarity* not just to the start of the testimonial act per se but to the unstable limits of the scene of witnessing, to the way the testimonial contract negotiated between Art and Vladek seems to raise more questions than it settles. The name of the dead mother, one might venture to say, lives on in the very supplementarity of witnesses, in the interminability of the survivors' struggle to bear witness.

It goes without saying that Anja, Art's mother and Vladek's first wife, never bears witness in her own person in *Maus*. Although she is depicted on the cover of the first volume in an image centered over the words "A Survivor's Tale," the telling of that tale is left entirely to the husband and son who survived her. Conspicuously absent from the scene of narration, Anja, whose name first appears in a dedication placed between the title page and the opening of chapter 1, seems nevertheless to hover indefinitely at its limit precisely as the figure of a certain excess or remainder. She remains, in short, a figure of that which in "a survivor's tale" may be said to survive its telling by any or all of its more easily identifiable survivor-narrators. If Spiegelman makes a point of invoking the name of a silent film classic in the title of his opening chapter and of formally defining the text itself as a kind of slow-motion picture, it is, I would suggest, because *Maus* is itself a silent film about silence, a "motion picture" in which the speech bubbles of its garrulous star/projectionist always threaten to eclipse the mother's silence in particular and that of those who died in the Holocaust in general. The challenge for Spiegelman in drawing *Maus* is thus in a sense how to avoid silencing this silence, how to rehistoricize it by making a place for it in the telling of "A Survivor's Tale," how, in short, to let it bleed through the words and images that his comic inevitably superimpose upon it.

In the opening chapter of *Maus II*, Art directly addresses this challenge in the context of a therapy session with his "shrink," Pavel, himself a survivor of Terezin and Auschwitz. "Anyway," the latter says, "the victims who died can never tell THEIR side of the story, so maybe it's better not to have any more stories." "Uh-huh," responds Art, adding, "Samuel Beckett once said: 'Every word is like an unnecessary stain on silence and nothingness.'" There follows a wordless panel, the silence of which is only interrupted by Art's observation in the next frame, "On the other hand, he SAID it" (II:45). In pointing out the obvious irony of the situation (as well as his own un-avoidable implication in it), Art does not so much refute Beckett's dictum as draw attention to the contradictory *necessity* of its being formulated in just this way, for it seems that the words which he and Beckett cannot help but speak do not so much break the silence as make it strangely palpable. Like the preparations with which microscope slides are treated in order to make transparent structures visible, the speakers' words function here as stains marking a silence they resolutely refuse to fill in for. Indeed, far from at-tempting to fill in the silent gaps, such words tend instead to hollow them-selves out, to turn themselves into empty shells in which the "silence and nothingness" they cover may be given a chance to resonate, in which the reader, in the words of Wallace Stevens's "The Snow Man," may behold "Nothing that is not there and the nothing that is" (10).

Fatal Attachments

As in the frame narrative of *The Thousand and One Nights*, telling tales in *Maus* is literally a matter of life and death. When, for example, Art finds out that his father did not simply misplace the diaries his mother had written after the war but had in fact burned them, he experiences this revelation as an all-too-literal repetition of the Holocaust, as a brutally ironic repetition in which the Auschwitz survivor, Vladek, now finds himself cast in the role of "murderer" (I:159). The burned diaries were to have been Anja's legacy to Art. As Vladek says, "only I know that she said, 'I wish my son, when he grows up, he will be interested by this'" (I:159). If Vladek can thus be called a murderer by a son whose maternal inheritance has been lost in transmis-sion, it is presumably because the father does to these texts what his own persecutors had done to the bodies of so many of their victims. That Art can experience the incineration of his mother's writing as the burning of a hu-man being no doubt suggests his intense investment in whatever will have survived of his mother and of his relation to her. It also suggests a certain investment in the matter of burning itself, an investment, moreover, that effectively keeps the term "Holocaust" (from the Greek *holocaustos*, meaning "burnt whole") from ever establishing itself as a proper name used to designate a discrete, temporally circumscribed event. The uncanny resonance of this burning may thus be said to hold open a tenuous interspace in which the conflagrations of bodies, lives, and texts are experienced as repetitions of each other.

The psychically interchangeable conflagrations of bodies and texts is related to the notion of a smoke screen first introduced at the moment Art inquires into the fate of his mother's diaries. "I used to see Polish notebooks around the house as a kid," he says. "Were those her diaries?" "Yes," Vladek replies, "and also no. Her diaries didn't survive from the war. What you saw she wrote after: her whole story from the start." "OHMIGOD! Where are they?" Art asks. "I need those for this book!" "Coff! Please, Artie," Vladek interjects, "stop with the smoking. It makes me short with breath." "I think it's all your pedaling," Art caustically responds as he puts out his smoke. "Don't be so smart!" says Vladek. "What I was telling you? Yes . . . after the hanging I looked for another business" (I:84). Here the question of the burned diaries, which Vladek obviously wishes to avoid, is dispatched—or at least deferred—by drawing attention to Art's smoking habit.

Although Art as a character appears to be taken in by Vladek's ruse, Spiegelman the artist uses the scene to introduce the figure of a smoke screen as a key to the structural principle of displacement operative in the text. Just as the smoke from the cigarette conceals that of the incinerated notebooks, so too does the revelation of the actual fate of the diaries later on lead Art to experience their incineration as a second Holocaust, as the burning not only of his mother's written remains but also of her body, and moreover of a body that in its turn seems to stand in as a screen for countless others. All these issues come together in a panel in *Maus II* in which the mention of the mother's suicide is accompanied both by a drawing of corpses piled up at the foot of Art's drawing table and by the parenthetical mention of the fact that Anja left no suicide note (II:41). Insofar as the diaries would have been—or at least would have somehow filled in for—the note the mother never left, their burning not only returns Art to the traumatic moment of Anja's death but deprives him a second time of the explanation or exoneration he had so desperately hoped to obtain from her.

That Art calls Vladek a "murderer" when he learns what his father has done to Anja's diaries suggests not only an identification of the father with his own persecutors or a reexperiencing of the mother's suicide as a homicide but also and above all a way of seeing the mother, who is clearly no longer alive, as still somehow at this point *not yet* dead. Indeed, if we now revisit the inaugural scene in which the testimonial contract is first framed in *Maus*, a scene in which Vladek and Art fight to see who can frame whom and, in doing so, also implicitly battle over possession of the maternal frame, we may now begin to view their conflict not merely in adversarial terms but also in terms of a *joint struggle* to frame a question neither of them ever seems able to ask—the question, namely, of Anja qua specter.

Nancy Miller comes close to this view in her very perceptive essay on *Maus*, one of the few readings that even thinks to raise the question of the mother in the context of "a survivor's tale" told by the father in collaboration with his surviving son.[14] "We should . . . understand the question of Anja," Miller suggests, "as that which will forever escape representation and at the same time requires it" (49). Yet, whereas for Miller this question is primarily one of life, a question of its preservation or restoration, a matter, as she says, of keeping "the question of Anja alive," of "saving the mother by retrieving her narrative," of "restoring the maternal body," of "reviving the link to Anja," or of keeping "his father as well as his mother alive" (49–50), my own reading seeks to frame the question of Anja in terms of a more haunted notion of sur-vival, in terms, namely, of that which is more than living and more than dead, of an experience so traumatically massive that it exceeds the very opposition of life and death.

Clearly, neither Vladek nor Art is ever able to come to terms with Anja's death. Indeed, as Vladek remarks in the second volume, "Anja? What is to tell? Everywhere I look I'm seeing Anja . . . From my good eye, from my glass eye, if they're open or they're closed, always I'm thinking on Anja" (II:103). Yet, I would suggest that what *remains* to be seen in *Maus* is not only the spectral presence of Anja per se but also, through her, a host of other haunting questions and persons that, in Miller's words, escape representation and at the same time incessantly demand it. It is no doubt telling in this respect that it was the trauma of his mother's suicide in 1968 that first prompted Spiegelman to engage explicitly with the related trauma of the Holocaust. It is thus through the scene of the mother's death (whose limits remain to be defined) that one must proceed.

I begin then with the strangely corporeal terms in which Art figures his relationship with his mother in the section of *Maus* entitled "Prisoner on the Hell Planet," a section that is explicitly framed as a text within the text. Describing his last encounter—a painfully *missed* encounter—with his mother on the eve of her death, a suicide she committed by slashing her wrists in the bathtub, Art writes, "She came into my room . . . It was late at night." "Artie," Anja stammers, "you . . . still . . . love . . . me . . . don't you?" "I turned away," he says, "resentful of the way she tightened the umbilical cord."[15] Here Art literally turns his back on his mother and, in doing so, turns her away for the last time. Such turnings graphically and verbally depict Anja's abandonment, her sense of having nowhere left to turn and no one left to turn to. Not only will Art remain bound to this traumatic scene, bound to repeat its tragically missed encounter long after his mother's death, but the very figure that continues to bind him to it is tellingly described as a potentially life-threatening link to the mother's body. The umbilical cord, introduced significantly in the penultimate moment before the mother's suicide, seems to function here less like a nurturing lifeline than a tightening hangman's noose (and here it should be noted that the preceding chapter not only bears the title "The Noose Tightens" but is accompanied by a graphic image of hanging mice [I:71]). This life-threatening umbilical link to the mother's body functions in this particular scene as a tie that binds Art not only to the last fatal moments of his mother's life but also to the mother as a source of life and of death, and moreover to the mother as a *tainted* source of life-in-death.

That a mother's demand for love is described here as being so strong that it threatens to crush the very life out of her child is certainly nothing new. Yet while Art perhaps wishes the figure of the tightening cord to be understood in just this way, and perhaps only in this way, there seems to be something else going on in the knotting of life- and death lines, something else that is being transmitted through this equivocal link from mother to child that is specific to the Holocaust and the unconscious transmission of massive trauma.

In an essay entitled "Images of Absence, Voices of Silence," analyst Louise Kaplan borrows the famous oxymoron of "black milk" from Paul Celan's poem "Deathsfugue" in order to describe how a survivor's child may be said to suckle the noxious nourishment of trauma. Such a child, she observes, "relishes and absorbs this 'black milk,' cultivates its bitter taste as if it were vital sustenance—as if it were existence itself" (224). In this article Kaplan discusses the notion of "transposition" first introduced by Judith Kestenberg to describe the psychological process of unconscious cross-generational transmission of trauma, noting that until the late 1970s therapists had regularly misdiagnosed the children of Holocaust survivors because their symptoms were often no different from those of other patients: "All were plagued by dreams and fantasies of body mutilation. All were beset by fears of bodily damage and illness. All complained of an eating disorder." Yet "what made our experiences with children of survivors distinctly different," she says, "was our own uncanny sensation of speaking with the dead. Our consulting rooms," she continues,

> were filled with voices and gestures of the dead. The terrors in our patients' fantasies and dreams were only partially theirs. The children of survivors were living out and dreaming out their parents' nightmares. The children were enacting experiences and relating fantasies that could only come from a person who had actually been in a ghetto or extermination camp and actually observed the slaughters and deaths of her loved ones, her friends and neighbors, the strangers who became her cell mates—the murder of her own soul. Since the survivor parent had been unable to witness the horror, she could not remember it. And if she did remember, she remembered only fragments, and even these were rarely, if ever, put into words. The child of the survivor had been sheltered from the truth. But the child was living the nightmare. (222–23)

Spiegelman's figure of an asphyxiating umbilical cord, in which life- and death lines not only pass through but also turn into one another, exemplifies the way the "black milk" of trauma is unwittingly transmitted from mother to child.

"Well, mom," Art cries in the concluding panel of "Prisoner," "if you're listening . . . congratulations! . . . You've committed the perfect crime . . . You put me here . . . shorted all my circuits . . . cut my nerve endings . . . and crossed my wires! . . . You MURDERED me, mommy, and you left me here to take the rap!!!" In this final twist of the cord, it is now Art himself who claims to be the victim of the mother's suicide—its true victim as well as its falsely framed perpetrator. Little wonder then that Art speaks here of crossed wires and shorted circuits.

If the parameters of the scene of the mother's death are difficult to delimit (despite its all too obvious encasement in the "Case History" of "Prisoner"), it is because the pages of *Maus* are haunted not merely by the traumatic loss of the mother but by the specter of her *repeated killing*. Not only does Art's mother die more than once, each time in a different way, but she herself is cast at certain moments as a murderer. Her killing should thus be viewed simultaneously as a suicide, an infanticide ("You MURDERED me, mommy"), and a matricide ("It's his fault—the punk"); as a suicide that is repeated in the form of a homicide (Vladek's "murderous" burning of the diaries); and as a suicide that is itself the repetition or belated enactment of the Holocaust ("HITLER DID IT").

As the painful question of who murdered whom becomes increasingly difficult to settle, and as the attachments between mother and son become more complex—as though fated by a strange logic to be even more fatal *after* the mother's death than before—the single thread of the umbilical cord initially used to figure such attachments itself gives way at this point to a language of shorted circuits, severed nerve endings, and crossed wires. In short, as the questions surrounding this fatal attachment grow in complexity, they become not only harder to answer but increasingly difficult to pose—questions such as: if the mother-child attachment is destined to be even more fatal after Anja's death than before, is it perhaps because her untimely demise is also a kind of belated birth? In other words, does the introduction of the figure of the umbilicus, a figure so obviously associated with life's beginnings, at the very moment in the narrative when Anja is about to take her own life not suggest some connection between the cutting of her wrists and the severing of the cord? Would not such a connection in turn imply that Art only really comes to life belatedly at the moment of his mother's death, that Anja in a sense dies in childbirth? Does the child born in this way perhaps carry not only his mother's death but his mother as a tainted source of death-in-life within him, bearing the one who had borne him as a noxiously nourishing womb turned inside out?[16]

The difficulty of the questions raised here is such that they should be left open. In endeavoring (in Friedlander's terms) to "withstand the need for closure," one should not just leave them hanging, however, but actively tarry with them, *keep them open* through an examination of other related passages (*Memory* 132). Of particular relevance in this connection is the series of panels in which Vladek recounts the circumstances surrounding Art's "first" untimely birth in 1948. Before we turn to these frames, however, it is important to note that Spiegelman goes out of his way to interpolate them into Vladek's account of the birth of his elder brother, Richieu, a story that initially was to have been followed immediately by a description of Anja's ensuing postpartum depression. Whereas in an earlier draft of the page (included in the CD-ROM version) the narrative remains in the past and proceeds directly from the announcement of Richieu's birth in the first row of panels to a phone call Vladek receives in the second instructing him to leave everything and come back to Sosnowiec ("Anja is sick and needs you!"), in the final, published version of the text the second, third, and fourth rows are now set in the present and are marked by a series of verbal and visual disruptions.

"But wait—," Art interrupts Vladek, "if you were married in February and Richieu was born in October, was he premature?" "Yes, a little," Vladek responds. "But YOU—after the war, when you were born—it was VERY premature. The doctors thought you wouldn't live. I found a specialist what saved you . . . he had to break your ARM to take you out from Anja's belly!" (I:30). In this revised version of the scene, the two births now appear to be so closely related in Vladek's mind that the memory of the second, more violent one in which Art's arm must be broken is itself made to break through an account of the first. As always in *Maus* such sudden narrative shifts leave one to consider how the second story not only abruptly draws attention away from the first but, in doing so, becomes a screen through which to read it.[17] Moreover, the very violence of this narrative interruption suggests that the traumatic break that *is* Art's premature birth, a trauma related through the break in Vladek's account to Richieu's own untimely birth in 1937 and his premature death in 1943 ("Of course, you never knew him. He didn't come out from the war" [I:30]), is a rupture that cannot safely be contained as an object of narration.[18] Like the arm that had to be broken in order to save Art from Anja's womb, the traumatic story of his untimely birth is inscribed here in a series of narrative interruptions.

Vladek continues, "And when you were a tiny baby your arm always jumped up, like so! We joked and called you 'Heil Hitler!' Always we pushed your arm down, and you would oops!" (I:30). The account again breaks off here as Vladek spills a bottle of pills while performing the very act he is describing. Tellingly, at the moment Vladek plays himself and another, when his description of his own response to his son's "Hitler salute" is accompanied by a restaging of those gestures, the performance itself becomes a scene of involuntary repetition. As the past spills into the present, the pills Vladek knocks over fall not just onto the table but out of the visual frame of the, panel itself. Insofar as the effect of such spills is to leave neither the receptacle nor the relationship between contents and their containers intact, insofar, that is, as these spills *transform the very limits they transgress,* they turn the visual frame of the panel itself into a kind of overflowing pillbox.[19]

Underlying these visual and narrative ruptures is yet another connection to the maternal body. In his essay "Mad Youth," Spiegelman describes the Rego Park house in which he grew up as a "two-family brick pillbox" (*Comix* 21). While the pun on "pillbox" depicts the family residence as a place where drugs and the trauma of "The War" cohabited, this same house is figured elsewhere as a suffocating womb. "What happened to me the winter I flipped out was that I had gotten the bends; I had surfaced too quickly from the overheated bunker of my traumatized family . . . into the heady atmosphere of freedom" (*Comix* 23).[20] Not only is the "pillbox" now an "overheated bunker," but Spiegelman's emergence from the oceanic depths of this home is a birth trauma inseparable from the trauma of his mother's death.

If, according to the strangely twisted logic we have been tracing, the attachment between mother and son is fated to be even more fatally binding after Anja's death than before, it is because the mother, while clearly no longer alive after her suicide, is still somehow not yet dead; because her untimely end is in a certain sense also a belated beginning; because the trauma of her repeated killing is also that of an incessant birthing. It is no accident in this regard that an account of one son's premature birth is made to interrupt and displace the story of another in *Maus.* Nor is it by chance that an account of Anja's first birth-related, suicidal depression (" . . . I don't care. I JUST DON'T WANT TO LIVE" [I:31]) is placed on the page directly facing the one in which the tale of these untimely deliveries is told. Tellingly, the frame in which Anja first gives voice to this death wish is the only one on the page that visually breaks out of the horizontal-vertical grid in which the panels are plotted.

The thematic connection of the mother's suicide to her sons' premature births (and Richieu's untimely death) and the structural link tying these related traumata to a series of visual and verbal disruptions combine to suggest that *Maus* is a text more generally conceived as a story of narrative ruptures, made up of tales (or tails) that are repeatedly broken off and prolonged without ever beginning or ending. As though to signal the circularly repetitive, nonlinear, and seemingly static narrative movement of the text, *Maus* opens with an image of Vladek astride his stationary bike pedaling hard and going nowhere fast.

The Growth of a Relationship

In an audio appendix to the "Prisoner on the Hell Planet" section of *Maus*, Spiegelman stresses that "it's important in these pages to think of them as complete pages. In the book there's a black border around the whole page that actually bleeds off the page. It acts as a funereal border. When the book is closed, on the edges you actually see that as a separate section inside the book" (CD-ROM). Spiegelman's investment in having one view this text-within-the-text as a discrete, self-contained subsection of *Maus*, as a kind of crypt in which the painful story of his mother's suicide is safely and securely buried, is understandable. The preceding analysis has tried to heed Spiegelman's suggestion. Yet at the same time, the strangely twisted logic at work in this section and elsewhere in the text has made it necessary to trace the various ways in which the story told here—like the black border surrounding it—bleeds off the page. In contrast to that ink, however, whose bleeding ultimately sharpens the edges it soaks through, the traumatic story of the mother's death spreads in a more insidious manner. It so pervasively invades the narrative layers surrounding it that there is no visible point of effraction, no clearly definable break, wound, or hematoma in the text. In an attempt to trace this bloodless and inkless bleeding, the sheer imperceptibility of which is to be read less as an index of its immaculate absence than of its haunting ubiquity, it has been necessary to follow the faintest of leads, to allow oneself to be led by the highly overdetermined and unstable figure of the tightening umbilical cord, by a narrative "red thread" whose strategic importance is highlighted by its placement in the central panel of the last page of "Prisoner" and which is itself tied up with and displaced by the language of shorted circuits, severed nerve endings, and crossed wires mentioned in the panel directly below it. Following the twists and turns of this tightening cord, a trope that marks the last time Art was ever to see his mother alive, I have attempted to trace the complicated ties binding Anja, viewed here as a source of life and death, as a tainted source of life-in-death, to a series of premature births and untimely deaths, to the traumatic repetition of births *as* deaths (and vice versa).

In order to continue to stay with the open questions raised in "Prisoner on the Hell Planet," questions that tend perhaps against the author's intentions to bleed off its pages and into other layers of the narrative, I turn now from the "crossed wires" of the mother-son relationship to Spiegelman's own fatal attachment to his rodent offspring, to a work on which, as he told Lawrence Weschler, "I'd spent my life." When asked in the course of this 1986 interview "why he'd decided to publish the book version of *Maus* in its current truncated form," Spiegelman's response was "Funny you should ask."

> I'd never really had any intention of publishing the book version in two parts. But then, about a year ago, I read an interview with Steven Spielberg that he was producing an animated feature film entitled *An American Tail,* involving a family of Jewish mice living in Russia a hundred years ago named the Mousekawitzes, who were being persecuted by Katsacks, and how eventually they fled to America for shelter. He was planning to have it out for the Statue of Liberty centennial celebrations.
>
> I was appalled, shattered. . . . For about a month I went into a frenzy. I'd spent my life on this, and now here, along was coming this Goliath, the most powerful man in Hollywood, just casually trampling everything underfoot. I dashed off a letter, which was returned, unopened. I went sleepless for nights on end, and then, when I finally did sleep, I began confusing our names in my dreams: Spiegelberg, Spielman . . . I contacted lawyers. I mean, the similarities were obvious, right down to the title—their *American Tail* simply being a more blatant, pandering-to-the-mob version of my *Survivor's Tale* subtitle. Their lawyers argued that the idea of anthropomorphizing mice wasn't unique to either of us. . . . [W]hat I was saying was that the specific use of mice to sympathetically portray Jews combined with the concept of cats as anti-Semitic oppressors in a story that compares life in the Old World of Europe with life in America *was* unique—and that it was called *Maus: A Survivor's Tale.*[21] (56)

One might begin here by noting certain similarities between the publication of the book and the birth of its author. Not only were both forced to appear prematurely due to a perceived life-threatening situation, but each "delivery" was in its own curious way a violent act of salvation; for just as Art had to have his arm broken by a specialist in order "to take [him] out from Anja's belly," so too was it necessary to break the spine of *Maus* in order to bring it out into the world "in truncated form" as a book.[22]

To pursue this curious link between text and body, parent and child, author and work, I turn now from Spiegelman's description of the circumstances surrounding the publication of the first volume of *Maus* to an interview he gave upon completion of the second.[23]

> Thirteen years ago I bet I'd live long enough to finish *Maus* and by God I did. On the other hand, insofar as I can tune in to these things, there's already a slight feeling of mourning. Somehow I got used to this large carcinogenic growth attached to my body and I feel sad that it's been cut away. . . . [A]lthough it was painful and difficult work, it was, in some ways, a staving off of a certain kind of other mourning. Even though it was on the battleground of a piece of paper, I was able to keep my relationship with my father going and was even able to have the illusion of having an effect. And so that was something, even though, like I say, it was difficult to keep going. (J. Rosen 1)

Whereas the "crossed wires" of the mother-son relationship in "Prisoner on the Hell Planet" were originally figured in pointedly corporeal terms as a twisted umbilical link, here the author's attachment to his own tainted offspring appears to be associated with a different kind of bodily link—namely, with the inflamed tissue of what, for him, is not simply of the body or the text, but the very texture of his relationship to his work. If, as was suggested earlier, telling tales is a matter of life and death both for Scheherezade of *The Thousand and One Nights* and for the artist-narrator of *Maus*, a significant difference between them now becomes apparent. While the former tells stories in order *to defer* her own death, the latter seems to draw "A Survivor's Tale" precisely in order to accommodate it—or rather to make room for that which is more than living and more than dead. Spiegelman describes his relationship to his work and to what is commonly referred to as the creative process in pointedly uncreative and self-destructive terms. Indeed, in this interview the thirteen-year gestation of *Maus* is depicted as a kind of anti-pregnancy, as a time when the host body of the artist seems to accommodate itself not only to the unmourned dead who continue to inhabit it but moreover to the *monstrous vitality* of a deadly "carcinogenic growth."[24]

Through this unsettling image, Spiegelman seems to redefine the work of art and its extended labor process as a work of mourning gone awry.[25] While the "painful and difficult work" of drawing *Maus* no doubt provided a way for him to work through loss by reworking it into art (and Art), at the same time it appears to have worked against itself "in some ways," to have compromised and suspended itself in a way that made it possible to accomplish through the very work of mourning the task of "staving off a certain kind of other mourning." While this "other mourning" is presumably that which could not have been done so long as Art was able to keep his father—or rather his contentious relationship with him—alive by continuing to live it out on "the battlefield of a piece of paper," the notion of "a certain kind of other mourning" also seems to point more fundamentally to the inherent otherness of Spiegelman's *Trauerarbeit*, to the way this work of mourning may not only have worked against itself but, in so doing, have *worked open* (*aufgearbeitet*) the space for a certain kind of other survival.

What, then, is the space of this other survival? In an attempt to locate its unassimilated excess, the surplus of that which is more than body and more than text—and yet somehow (though not umbilically) linked to both the body and the text—one may be guided by excessive language employed by the artist to describe his relationship to his work. *Maus* is depicted not only as a growth attached to Spiegelman's body, as a cancer he "somehow got used to," but also as a text whose publication is experienced as an amputation that leaves him, as he says, "feeling sad." This surprisingly affectionate characterization of the text-as-tumor is, at the very least, a sign of ambivalence, an indication of Spiegelman's own potentially fatal attachment to a noxious growth attached to him. That this growth is described as being "carcinogenic" is all the more significant in light of the cartoonist's notorious nicotine habit. Indeed, I would suggest that Art's attachment to the cigarettes he so conspicuously and compulsively smokes throughout *Maus* is no less desperate or ambivalent than his relationship to the work itself. Moreover, because these relationships themselves tend, as it were, to draw on each other, each may be read as the figure or symptom of the other.

This interaction between the draftsman's work and his drawing of smoke, between activities that sustain and contaminate one another, is further complicated by the artist's portrait of himself on the rear inner flap of the first volume of *Maus*. He is shown sitting at his drawing table, cigarette in hand, while on the small shelf to his right reserved for the tools of his trade—ink, pens, correction fluid, and so forth—one notices a full ashtray and a pack of cigarettes. At first glance the cigarettes appear to be Camels, yet on closer inspection the brand turns out to be called "Cremo Lights." Where one might have expected to find a hump rising under the arch of the brand name, one discovers instead two fuming smokestacks. The cigarette pack is located in the lower left-hand corner of the self-portrait, while on the upper right one sees through the closed window of the artist's New York studio the barbed-wire fence, cat-patrolled guard tower, and smoking crematorium chimney of Auschwitz.

If one draws a line connecting the top of the chimney on the upper right to the lid of the cigarette pack on the lower left, it passes directly through the glowing tip of Art's "Cremo Light." This diagonal connecting the smoking within to the burning without suggests that with each pull on his cigarette Art in effect draws in a breath of Auschwitz.[26] In other words, every drag seems to draw together inside and out, present and past, the inflamed airways of the living and the airborne remains of the dead. With each inhaling moment of concentration Art draws in the scattered ashes of the incinerated bodies of Auschwitz and buries them within himself, only to witness their immediate disinterment and redispersion as he exhales. Each drag thus has the symbolic value of a burning desire fleetingly realized, a desire to draw two radically heterogeneous worlds together, to draw the one in with the other, and, moreover, to keep the contract of that double drawing safely encrypted within himself. While the ensuing moment of exhalation may be said to vent the crypt, to atomize all that had just come together, and, in doing so, to frustrate Art's desire just as it was being realized, it also at the same time guarantees through its very opposition the insistence of that impossible wish. In short, the cigarettes Art smokes do not so much satisfy his desire as exasperate it. Or rather they satisfy it *in its very impossibility* by frustrating and intensifying it.[27] What keeps Art's desire aflame is thus this incessant oscillation between the two mutually constitutive, mutually inhibiting moments of aspiration and expiration, concentration and atomization, a pulse Richard Klein has described as the very "rhythm of smoking, tapped out in every puff on a cigarette" (105).

Any analysis of the rhythms of Art's smoking must be considered incomplete, however, if it does not in turn include an examination of the artist's depictions of smoke. For if the self-portrait of the artist-as-draftsman suggests nothing else, it is that the drawing of smoke is really no different from the drawing of smoke. Tellingly, this highly self-reflexive image is temporally focused around a *momentary break* in the drawing process, around an interval in which Art is shown staring off into space, abstaining both from putting pen to paper and from taking a drag on his Cremo Light. Such a pointed and pregnant pause no doubt accentuates a moment of artistic reflection within the already reflexive medium of the self-portrait. Yet in making one see the suspended activities of drawing and smoking in their mutual implication, the image also suggests that whatever compels Art to light one cigarette after another is the same thing that drives him to draw and redraw himself drawing smoke. His self-portrait is thus a *draft* in the further sense in that it is but one in a series of provisional renderings, none of which constitutes the final, definitive version of himself.

In order, then, to approach this seemingly self-contained image *as a draft*, it is necessary to read it first and foremost in relation to other drawings that appear to repeat and revise it. One such image—or rather series of images— is to be found in the bottom right-hand corner of a page in *Maus II*, the very page on which Vladek begins a painstaking description of the operation of the gas chambers in Auschwitz ("For this," he says, "I was an EYEWITNESS"). As in the artist's self-portrait at the end of *Maus I*, the panel in question contains an image of a crematorium chimney with smoke coming out of it. Yet here the smoke is drawn in such a way as to appear quite literally to pour out of the past—out of a smokestack which itself appears to rise up out of its own frame and into the one above—into the present where it mingles with and loses itself in the smoke trailing out of Art's Cremo Light (II:69).[28] Whereas earlier the visual logic of the image suggested that Art drew in the airborne remains of the dead with every puff on his Cremo Light, here it seems that Auschwitz is the very air he breathes. In other words, just as smoking tends in general to make one more aware of the rhythms of one's breathing, so too does the smoke from Art's cigarette tend to act as a kind of stain on the invisible air around it. Thus, far from simply filling the surrounding atmosphere with smoke, the fumes from Art's Cremo Light function instead to screen the smoke already there. They enable one to see that which is already so much "in the air," so massively and oppressively present, that it cannot be seen as such.

While in a first moment it appeared that the rhythms of Art's smoking compulsively enacted an impossible wish to draw the past in with the present, to gather in the scattered remains of the dead and to bury them within himself, a wish whose repeated frustration was the perpetually renewed precondition for its ever-so-fleeting satisfaction, it now seems that those very same rhythms may play out another opposing yet equally impossible desire. Here the alternating movement of inhaling and exhaling, the pulse tapped out in every puff on a cigarette, may be read as the enactment of a desire to make that which is neither here nor there—a traumatic past that is all too hauntingly and pervasively present—return as if it were either here or there, now or then, present or absent. It is the coexistence of these mutually inhibiting moments of gathering in and separating out, each of which being in its turn internally contradictory, that makes the desires bound up with and compulsively played out in Art's smoking all the more impossible: both impossible to satisfy and impossible not to.

A Little Safe

The tensions inherent in such an impossible enterprise of double drawing are played out not only in the rhythms of Art's smoking (itself linked to the "carcinogenic growth" of *Maus*) or in the redrafting of scenes of him drawing himself drawing smoke but also in the rhythmic alternations of the narrative itself. Whereas *Maus* has often been referred to as a "frame story" with an external narrative "enfolding" or "surrounding" an inner one, such static descriptions rarely do justice to the dynamic beating and bleeding of the tale.[29] Like Poe's narrative "The Tell-Tale Heart," Spiegelman's "survivor's tale" repeatedly oscillates between the level of the telling and that of the tale, between a scene of narration set in the present and a dramatic restaging of events from the past.

Often these shifts between the tale and the scene of its telling are motivated by some current distraction or disturbance. For example, there is a moment early on when Vladek suddenly breaks off an account of how, as a prisoner of war, he was forced by his German captors to perform the Herculean task of cleaning a stable in an impossibly brief period of time. He interrupts this account in order to reprimand Art for dropping cigarette ashes on his living room carpet. "You want it should be like a stable HERE?" he asks (I:52). While such outbursts are clearly meant to destabilize the relationship between past and present, between the level of the telling and that of the tale, at other times the movement back and forth is more regulated and is made to accelerate in such a way that the focus gradually shifts from whatever is going on in either the past or the present to the pulsating, back-and-forth movement itself.

One such sequence significantly begins at the very point where "Prisoner on the Hell Planet" breaks off—as though it were intended to be read not simply as a new, relatively unrelated chain of events but also and above all as a continuation in displaced form of the embedded or encased narrative. In other words, even though this self-described "Case History" is clearly inserted in Maus as a text-within-the-text drawn in a distinctly different style, it is, as we have seen, anything but a self-contained piece. The mention of shorted circuits, cut nerve endings, and crossed wires in its penultimate panel suggests that the text does not so much end as reach a certain impasse. Indeed, insofar as Spiegelman's "survivor's tale" is quite explicitly a story of mice and their mutilated tails, it might be said that what *remains* to be read in Maus is precisely the way these cut-off tails, these severed nerve endings and violently interrupted narratives, are repeatedly restitched into a different kind of narrative structure—into a kind of "slow-motion picture" montage in which processes of interruption and displacement are no longer the exception but the rule.

The sequence following "Prisoner on the Hell Planet" thus tellingly begins with Art asking once again about the fate of his mother's diaries. Whereas the last time the question was raised Vladek had managed to deflect it by drawing attention to the stifling fumes coming from his son's cigarette, here, instead of trying to distract him again, the father simply lies, saying, "So far this didn't show up. I looked, but I can't find" (I:105). When pressed by his son, who insists "I've got to have that!" Vladek this time literally plays for time by looking at his watch and simultaneously announcing, "another time I'll again look. But now better we go to the bank" (I:105). The bank thus becomes another kind of smoke screen, at once an ersatz destination toward which the frame story is ineluctably drawn and a roundabout way of avoiding the inevitable question of the diaries. But the closer Art and his father come to the bank, the larger the question of the dead mother and her diaries looms.

To complicate matters even further, this tension *within* the frame story is doubled by a tension between it and the embedded narrative it is meant to frame and contain. This enframed, inner narrative recounted by Vladek on the way to the bank is itself tellingly a story of progressive containment. It is the story, namely, of German efforts to confine Vladek, Anja, and the remaining Jews of Sosnowiec within increasingly cramped and circumscribed living quarters inside the Stara section of town. At a certain point in 1943 the Germans close this ghetto inside Sosnowiec and move the remaining Jews to the nearby village of Srodula. At this point the narrative alternation between present and past, telling and told, begins to intensify as the scene of narration rendered in an image of Art and Vladek walking to the bank is superimposed on a drawing of the cat-guarded gate of the Jewish ghetto viewed from without (I:105). The ghetto is then gradually emptied out as more and more of its inhabitants are deported to Auschwitz. By the end of 1943 there is almost no one left, and those who do remain are driven to find refuge in increasingly cramped hiding places. Thus, Vladek tells of how he and his family were forced to move from a basement bunker hidden beneath a coal bin into an attic bunker, the entrance to which was hidden by a chandelier, and from there into another bunker in a shoe shop, which could be entered only by crawling through a tunnel made of shoes.

As energies and spaces become intensifyingly compressed within the en-framed story, the pulse of the narrative itself accelerates, beating with greater frequency between the story of Anja and Vladek's flight from one unsafe bunker to the next in the inner narrative and that of Art and Vladek's stroll to the local bank in the outer one. The two stories finally converge at the point where Vladek and Anja are driven from the safety of their last bunker. "It was NOWHERE we had to hide," Vladek tells Art. At this point in the frame narrative the two men, having finally reached the bank, are about to visit a safe-deposit box. "Can I help you, Mr. Spiegelman?" asks a teller. "Yes, I have here my son, Artie. I want to sign him a key. So he can go also to my safety box" (I:125). What then is the point of this narrative compression? Why is one pressured to read the two converging stories in terms of one another? What is the connection here between unsafe bunkers and bank "safety boxes"? What might it mean in the context of these interpenetrating narrative frames to be "a little safe"?

While the phrase "a little safe" is initially used by Vladek to describe the precarious sense of security he and others felt upon completing their first bunker—"and there we made a brick wall filled high with coal. Behind this wall we could be a little safe" (I:110)—it also applies to the small "safety box" in which Vladek keeps valuables from before and after the war. That this trip to the safe is staged as a kind of rehearsal for the moment of Vladek's own death is suggested by the instructions he gives Art upon entering the vault: "in case anything bad happens to me you must run RIGHT AWAY over here. Therefore I arranged for you this key. Take everything out from the safe. Otherwise it can go only to taxes or Mala will grab it" (I:126). The care with which Vladek seeks to secure the full transmission of his legacy to his surviving son stands in pointed contrast to the careless and callous way he will have allowed Art's maternal inheritance to get lost in transmission. Little wonder, then, that Vladek takes Art to the bank instead of immediately revealing what he had done to Anja's diaries. While the father once again uses one scene as a kind of smoke screen to conceal another, and perhaps even seeks through this rehearsal of his own death and his promise of an intact inheritance to compensate his son for the loss of a maternal legacy he himself had failed to transmit, in the end the "little safe" to which he has given Art a key comes to look more and more like a little coffin. Indeed, there is a striking resemblance between Spiegelman's depiction of Vladek lying prostrate over an empty safe-deposit box and crying "Anja! Anja! Anja!" (I:127) in the final frame of chapter 5 and a drawing of him sprawled across his wife's coffin screaming her name at the funeral home in "Prisoner on the Hell Planet."

Whereas the coffin in the funeral home has apparently been closed for good, the one in the bank vault has obviously been reopened and its contents have been removed. That this trip to the bank is a visit to the family *maus*-oleum is suggested not only by the visual resemblance between the depictions of Vladek in the funeral home and the bank but also by the father's instruction to his son in the vault that this is the place he should run to "in case," as he says, "anything bad happens to me." At this point one may begin to appreciate why the encased, inner story of Vladek and Anja's flight from one unsafe bunker to the next is made to dovetail with the frame story's account of a trip to the bank at the precise moment where Vladek and Anja are said to have nowhere to go and nowhere to hide. Reading the two intersecting stories through each other at this point, the little coffin in which Vladek had hoped to find his wife "a little safe" turns out to be strangely open and empty as though—like the couple starved out of its last bunker in the inner story (I:125)—she herself were now cast out in the open, unhoused, unframed, unsafe, en route with nowhere to go and "NOWHERE . . . to hide."[30]

In short, it is the very beating of this narrative rhythm back and forth between a bank safe and an unsafe bunker that in the end compels one to consider how Vladek's seemingly secure "safety box" is and is not safe, how it is a box that is at once "a little safe," a little coffin, an abandoned unsafe little bunker, and a broken heart. It should be recalled here that the trip to the bank and the story Vladek is telling on the way are themselves suddenly interrupted by a potentially fatal seizure—"when HYAAK! Mmy heart—Artie! Quick! Take from my pocket a nitrostat pill" (I:118).[31] A certain syncopation of cardiac and narrative beats thus seems to mark the location of a surprisingly unsafe little crypt in the text. In doing so, it effectively leads one back to the story of the mother's death framed by the strangely permeable "funereal border" of the "Prisoner" section as well as to rhythms of Art's smoking and the precarious little coffer located in *his* chest, one that is filled up and aired out with each puff on a Cremo Light. As was suggested earlier, this hyperventilating little vault lodged within Art should itself be viewed as the space of something *wanting*—that is, as a lack which is repeatedly, futilely, and compulsively filled in, filled only by hollowing out an even greater lack which in turn demands ever more urgently to be filled. Like the carcinogenic growth of *Maus*, this telltale little mausoleum to which Art remains so fatally attached through the chain of cigarettes he smokes is one he accommodates and maintains by putting his own life in danger. In other words, because the contents of *this* "little safe" are not just dead but deadly—as monstrously vital as a cancerous tumor—they always threaten to make over their living, breathing container in the very image of what it seeks to contain. To put it more cryptically, they always threaten to keep the keeper who seeks to keep them safe.

Maus opens by contesting the frame as container and ends by finally erecting a tombstone over Art's parents' grave (II:136). It is as though Spiegelman's "survivor's tale" had been struggling from the very outset not only to bury the dead but to find a way of keeping them safely contained, buried in little safes, in little cartoon frames that would not only stay shut but keep their deadly contents from containing their containers, from making over the living in the image of the dead. While the tombstone appearing at the end of *Maus* might lead one to conclude that the battle is finally over and won, the next-to-last frame—which has such strategic importance throughout the text—troubles such reassuring conclusions. For here Art is quite literally made over in the image of the dead when his father mistakenly calls him by the name of his deceased brother. "I'm tired from talking, Richieu," Vladek says, "and it's enough stories for now . . ." (II:136). Whereas the original three-page version of *Maus* published in 1972 is told explicitly as a bedtime story by a survivor to his little boy, Mickey, at the end of the full-length version completed nineteen years later it is still the father who tells the stories, but he does so *as a child* lying in his bed speaking to a son standing over him like a parent, whom Vladek mistakenly addresses as the other child who did not survive. Through this final slip the two brothers are made to trade places. While Art is effectively killed by his father's address, his dead brother is made to assume the role of listener to and addressee of Vladek's last words. Such role reversals suggest more generally that

Vladek's testimony will have been addressed not merely to "the living and the dead," as Hirsch contends, but rather *to the living as the dead*.

The visual language of this panel further complicates the question of address. For here Vladek is shown lying on his death bed, turning away from Art for the last time. The father's position and gesture evoke the structurally identical moment in "Prisoner on the Hell Planet" in which Art, roused by his mother's own last words, turns *his* back on her in the penultimate moment before her suicide. "I turned away," he recalls, "resentful of the way she tightened the umbilical cord." The pain of this earlier moment now bleeds through the scene of its belated reenactment as siblings, parents, and generations once again trade places, passing in this uncanny space of sur-vival through and for one another.

The thirteen-year project of drawing *Maus* was no doubt for Spiegelman a way of "coming to terms" with an all too hauntingly present and traumatic past, a way of engaging in a process Adorno referred to in a 1958 essay as one of *Aufarbeitung*. As Spiegelman himself observed in a 1986 interview,

> in order to draw *Maus*, it's necessary for me to reenact every single gesture, as well as every single location present in these flashbacks. The mouse cartoonist has to do that with his mouse parents. And the result is, for the parts of my story—of my father's story—that are just on tape or on transcripts, I have an overall idea and eventually I can fish it out of my head. But the parts that are in the book are now in neat little boxes. I know what happened by having assimilated it that fully. And that's part of my reason for this project, in fact. (Witek 101)

While Spiegelman's success at working through the past may in part be gauged in terms of his ability to bury it "in neat little boxes," to "know what happened by having assimilated it that fully," the true achievement of *Maus*, I have argued, is instead to be measured in terms of another sense of the word *Aufarbeitung*, in terms, that is, of what is *worked open (aufgearbeitet)* in the text. For it is precisely in the way that *Maus* works to open its neat little boxes—its safe little crypts—that it makes room for the very excesses of its testimony, for that which it cannot contain in words or images, for that which it cannot draft or draw together in a single, bound volume.

Working itself open in this way, *Maus* implicates the reader in an ongoing act of bearing witness. It positions such a seemingly innocent bystander as a supplementary witness, as one delegated the task of coming to terms with the very *unbound energies* of the text, of listening to the other tales that still remain to be told, of attuning oneself to the central silence of the mother's story, to a story that in crucial ways will have survived its telling by the text's explicit narrator-witnesses. In making a place not just for the reader but for the silence of those who, in the words of Art's therapist, Paul Pavel, did not survive to "tell THEIR side of the story" (II:43), *Maus* asks one to hearken to these silences and, moreover, to attune ourselves to that which is silently and unconsciously transmitted in its own testimony. As a text that "comixes" words and images, *Maus* invites one in the end to view its pictures not merely as illustrations or as visual counterparts to its verbal narrative but also and above all as the nonverbal bearer of history's silences. Staining these silences and those of his father's story with the words of his text, Spiegelman screens them in such a way as to allow them all the more powerfully and hauntingly to bleed through.

Notes

1. Here I follow the distinction Spiegelman draws between "comics" and "comix." "Rather than comics," he writes, "I prefer the word comix, to mix together, because to talk about comics is to talk about mixing together words and pictures to tell a story" ("Commix" 61).

2. Later in the essay Young makes a related point about Art's interest in knowing more about his origins and his mother (about the mother as origin). Referring to a scene in which Vladek guilts a supermarket clerk into giving him a refund on groceries he had purchased, a scene in which he trades even his story of survival for food, Young notes, "while this kind of self-interested storytelling might drive the son a little crazy, Art must face the way he too has come to the story as much to learn about his origins, his dead mother, his own *mishugas*, as he does to learn about Holocaust history" (692).

3. Being "out of joint" implies not only that past and present stand in a different relation to each other but also that the temporal and logical priority of an original over a translation, or speech over writing, of immediate over mediated experience, is being rearticulated at such moments. In contrast to Hirsch, who asserts that "*once in a while*, something breaks out of the rows of frames, or out of the frames themselves, upsetting and disturbing the structure of the entire work" (26–27, emphasis added), I view these moments of rupture not as sporadically occurring exceptions but as the general structural rule in *Maus*.

4. Alan Rosen makes the crucial observation that "Vladek's 'tortured visual-

ized prose' (the phrase is Nancy Miller's) is not only meant to represent an English-speaking 'foreigner' but is also meant to torture English into being a foreign language" (257).

5. As Hirsch observes, "*Maus* sounds like mouse but its German spelling echoes visually the recurring Nazi command 'Juden raus' ('Jews out'—come out or get out) as well as the first three letters of 'Auschwitz,' a word that in itself has become an icon of the Holocaust. Spiegelman reinforces this association when, in the second volume, he refers to the camp as 'Mauschwitz'" (11).

6. Elsewhere in his chapter entitled "'Jewish' Music? Otto Weininger and 'Josephine the Singer,'" Anderson discusses Wagner's notorious claim that "works of Jewish music often produce in us the kind of effect we would derive from hearing a poem by Goethe, for example, translated into that jargon we know as Yiddish." As Anderson comments, this "claim . . . fed on the street-level perception of recently 'emancipated' Jews as being incapable of speaking High German without a peculiar 'Yiddish' intonation, a 'hissing,' abrasive sound accompanied by aggressive gesticulation" (197).

7. As James Young notes, "Subjugated groups have long appropriated the racial epithets and stereotypes used against them in order to ironize and thereby neutralize their charge, taking them out of the oppressors' vocabulary" (690). While I agree with Young up to a point, I would still question whether the ultimate intent of Spiegelman's displacement of certain German stereotypes is merely to "neutralize their charge." I would also strongly take issue with Alan Rosen's claim that "by deploying the German word for the title, Spiegelman is asking the reader to view Jews/mice through the Germans'/cats' eyes" (261).

"The aspiring cartoonist," Spiegelman notes, "must master the conventions of picture-writing. . . . I remember looking at old cartooning books when I was a kid and learning that a Jew had a hooked line for a nose and large animated hands. . . . *Maus*, my comic book about my parents' life in Hitler's Europe that uses cats to represent Germans and mice to represent Jews, was made in collaboration with Hitler. . . . My anthropomorphized mice carry trace elements of Fips' anti-Semitic Jew-as-rat cartoons for *Der Stürmer*" (*Comix* 17). In the same letter to Max Brod cited earlier, Kafka also describes the pleasure of rummaging "with excessively lively Jewish hands."

8. In a related context, Michael Herr, writing about his work as a journalist during the Vietnam War, notes, "it took the war to teach it, that you were as responsible for everything you saw as you were for everything you did. The problem was that you didn't always know what you were seeing until later, maybe years later, that a lot of

it never made it in at all, it just stayed stored there in your eyes." Michael Herr, *Dispatches*, cited in Caruth 10.

9. "Raw" is of course also the name of the comix journal edited by Spiegelman and his wife, Françoise Mouly.

10. In "Little Orphan Annie's Eyeballs," Spiegelman describes the masks themselves as projection surfaces: "In *Maus* the mouse heads are masks, virtually blank, like Little Orphan Annie's eyeballs, a white screen the reader can project on" (*Comix* 17).

11. The repetition of "about" in three successive panels not only draws attention to this seemingly innocuous preposition but, in doing so, helps to sound out various related senses of the term. The first definition given in *Webster's* is in fact "in a circle around: around: on every side."

12. Dori Laub suggests that we can try to understand what is happening in the "testimonial interview" by viewing it as a kind of "brief treatment contract," a contract described as one "between two people, one of whom is going to engage in a narration of her trauma, through the unfolding of her life account. Implicitly, the listener says to the testifier: 'For this limited time, throughout the duration of the testimony, I'll be with you all the way, as much as I can. I want to go wherever you go, and I'll hold and protect you along this journey. Then, at the end of the journey, I shall leave you.' Bearing witness to a trauma is, in fact, a process that includes the listener. For the testimonial process to take place, there needs to be a bonding, the intimate and total presence of an *other*—in the position of one who hears. Testimonies are not monologues; they cannot take place in solitude. The witnesses are talking *to somebody*: to somebody they have been waiting for for a long time" (Felman and Laub 70–71).

13. In addition to the various senses of the word "drawing" Spiegelman plays on here and elsewhere, one might recall that the word "contract" itself derives from the Latin *contractus,* past participle of *contrahere*: to draw together.

14. Another notable exception is Marianne Hirsch's "Family Pictures" referred to earlier.

15. The centrality of this panel is underscored by its location at the degree zero of the page's horizontal-vertical axis.

16. As was suggested earlier, the language of turning plays an integral part in the penultimate scene leading up to the mother's death. The figure of the cord is introduced by Art's words "I turned away" and is accompanied by a visual depiction of him doing just that. As though to underscore the importance of this gestural language, Spiegelman uses it once again in the penultimate panel of the second volume, a scene to which we will return below.

17. In changing the topic so abruptly, Vladek may also be attempting to avoid any potentially embarrassing questions concerning the timing of Richieu's conception.

18. Speaking about the photograph of Richieu displayed in the dedication of *Maus II* and referred to by Art in a conversation with Françoise, Hirsch writes, "The parents keep it in their bedroom to refer to, Art competes with it, and we take it as the ultimately unassimilable fact that it is of a child who died unnaturally, before he had a chance to live" (23).

19. This initial scene of pill spilling should also be read in relation to another moment of rupture in the text. As Young has pointed out, "as the father recounts the days in August 1939 when he was drafted, just as he gets to the outbreak of war itself: 'and on September 1, 1939, the war came. I was on the front, one of the first to . . . Ach!' His elbow knocks two bottles of pills onto the floor. 'So. Twice I spilled my drugstore'" ("Holocaust" 684).

20. As Spiegelman notes in "Prisoner on the Hell Planet," his nervous breakdown in winter 1967–68 preceded his mother's suicide by a little more than three months.

21. Unfortunately, at the point in the story where Spiegelman presumably goes on to describe the actual publication of the first volume of *Maus*, Weschler suddenly and inexplicably breaks off the quotation and shifts to paraphrase (thereby uncannily perpetuating the movement of narrative rupture we have been tracing).

22. Throughout his work Spiegelman plays on the language of publishing and graphic art. The title of his 1977 anthology, *Breakdowns*, is a case in point. See also his "dog-eared" children's book, *Open Me . . . I'm a Dog.*

23. Spiegelman figures the publication of *Maus II* as a kind of birth when he thanks Paul Pavel, Deborah Karl, and Mala Spiegelman "for helping this volume into the world." In the German edition the phrase is translated in such a way as to foreground precisely this connection between publishing and giving birth. It should further be noted that the publication of each of the two volumes coincided roughly with the birth of Spiegelman's children. The first volume appeared in 1986; Nadja was born in 1987. Both the second volume, subtitled "And Here My Troubles Began," and his second child, Dashiell, came out in 1991. In an interview that appeared in *Forward* shortly after the completion of *Maus*, Spiegelman responds to a question concerning the recent birth of his son and the potential danger of becoming in his turn what his own father had been for him—namely, a parent who *was* Auschwitz as much as its victim. "I was terrified of having a boy child," he says. "It involved having to move carefully around and not recapitulate that particular set of problems but create new ones . . . for years my fears of having a child would be that I just didn't want anybody to think about me with the same complexity I had to think about my

father with." Rosen then proceeds to ask Spiegelman about Nadja. "Did having a daughter in the course of writing a book that takes on such a dark subject make you more hopeful?" "No," Spiegelman responds, "it probably got me more scared because now I have even a greater vested interest *in seeing this thing not all go to pieces. And that's always been a fear about having a child*" (J. Rosen 1, emphasis added). It is un-clear whether "this thing" refers to his work, his family, or both.

24. Elsewhere Spiegelman uses similarly excessive language to describe the me-dium of the comic strip itself as a monstrous offspring, as "the hunchback, half-witted bastard dwarf step-child of the graphic arts" (*Comix* 74).

25. See in this connection the passage from Shakespeare's *Richard II* and Žižek's brilliant reading of it (8–12). One portion of Busby's speech is particularly relevant here:

Each substance of a grief hath twenty shadows,
Which show life grief itself, but are not so.
For sorrow's eye, glazed with blinding tears,
Divides one thing entire to many objects;
Like perspectives, which rightly gaz'd upon
Show nothing but confusion; ey'd awry
Distinguish form; so your sweet majesty,
Looking awry upon your lord's departure,
Finds shapes of grief more than himself to wail;
Which look'd on as it is, is nought but shadows
Of what is not.

26. It might be added that the glowing tip of the cigarette occupies the same structural position in the scene as the glass in the window insofar as both mark the point at which inside and outside meet.

27. See Richard Klein's superb analysis of smoking in *Cigarettes Are Sublime,* esp. 45.

28. In a draft attached to the CD-ROM version of this page, Spiegelman makes clear that the chimney itself is to be viewed as a smoking cigarette. "Cremo = ciga-rette," he adds in a note to himself.

29. Miles Orvell describes *Maus* as a "frame story with an external narrative en-folding an inner one: in the surrounding story, Art Spiegelman, a cartoonist, is writ-ing a cartoon-fiction about his father Vladek, a refugee from Nazi Europe now living in Rego Park, Queens. The inner story is Vladek's. . . . What adds a crucial dimen-

sion to the novel is the frame surrounding that [story]—the relationship between father and son and the process of transmitting the story from one to the other, so that the book as a whole asks, what does it cost to survive?" (118).

30. It is no doubt telling in this regard that when Vladek actually burns the diaries he describes himself as having been "so DEPRESSED" that "I didn't know if I'm coming or going" (I:159).

31. It should be noted that it is on this trip to the bank that Vladek also relates the heartbreaking story of Richieu's tragic death (I:109).

5
"Happy, Happy Ever After"

Story and History in Art Spiegelman's *Maus*

Arlene Fish Wilner

Although George Santayana's injunction—to remember the past lest we be condemned to repeat it—has become a cliché, more recent students of history have observed that the study of the past does not necessarily provide insurance against its reiteration. Hayden White, for example, suggests that "[n]othing is better suited to lead to a repetition of the past than a study of it that is either reverential or convincingly objective in the way that conventional historical studies tend to be" (*Content* 82). Similarly, Cynthia Ozick argues that "'Never again' is a pointless slogan: old atrocities are models (they give permission) for new ones" ("It Takes a Great Deal" 196). Art Spiegelman's *Maus*, one effect of which is to provide historical documentation of the Holocaust, succeeds in affecting hearts and minds precisely because it is neither "reverential" nor "objective" in the common sense; rather, it is—to use a term that Ozick has applied to civilization and which cannot be applied to conventional historical narratives—"custom-built." (Garry Trudeau, in a review of Scott McCloud's *Understanding Comics*, called *Maus* an "anomaly, virtually the sole exemplar of promise fulfilled" in the comic book tradition.) The uniqueness of Spiegelman's achievement is, I would suggest, largely a function of zeugmatic strategies that yoke traditionally disjunct forms and conventions. The use of such strategies evokes the perception that the coherence encouraged by figuration—analogy, metaphor, and other sorts of juxtaposition—is simultaneously necessary and impossible. Thus readers are offered at once an illusion of comprehensibility and a constant reminder that any totalizing vision in which they may take comfort is not manifest in the events portrayed but is rather the product of moral and aesthetic choices fostered by human will and creativity.

The most obvious disjunction is, of course, between the escapism usually associated with cartoon panels[1] and the horrific realism of the subject, but *Maus* also includes many other ironic juxtapositions or tensions:

1. The psychological and relational complexity manifested by Art, Vladek, and other "characters" versus the deceptively simplistic portrayals of individuals as "stereotypical" animals. Vladek, for example, is both an individual of extraordinary heroism and a neurotic, bigoted old man; Art is the vastly gifted artist and the guilty little boy, the man immortalizing his father in history and the "cannibal" nourished by the death and memory of his ancestors.

2. Private history (e.g., Art's guilt and ambivalence with respect to his mother's suicide, the spectral presence of the brother he never knew, his father's inadequacies, and his art) versus public history (the "story" of the Holocaust). Because it can never be accommodated to a psychologically or emotionally familiar pattern, the unfolding in narrative time of the "public" history of the Holocaust cannot be considered cathartic in the classic Aristotelian sense, as telling his "story" is for Vladek and recording it is for Art. Ironically, we already "know" the public story, while the private ones are still being played out in the course of the narrative. And it is these private stories embedded within the larger public one that agitate us because we cannot predict their direction or outcome (e.g., at the end of *Maus I*, Art calls his father a "murderer"). Still, in another way, *Maus* conflates the public and the private, so that each becomes the other: Vladek resists consulting a marriage counselor to save his failing relationship with Mala because, as he tells Art, he doesn't "want that a stranger should mix into our private stories"; at the same time, he ignores the likelihood that the success of Art's book will widely publicize many intimate details of Vladek's personal life. Conversely, it is only because Vladek's private story is a Holocaust story that it demands reconstruction; the narrative of *Maus* is generated by the facts of European history from 1933 to 1944, facts to which the excruciating story of Vladek, his (mostly annihilated) family, and his ruined community bears a synecdochal relation, recapitulating in miniature the panoramic sweep of history.

3. The voice of Vladek recounting horrors in the presence of the tape

recorder versus the tradition of "normal" oral family history. Art's story is consciously an act of reconstruction (II:16) of "a reality that was worse than my darkest dreams." The fact of a reality worse than dreams inverts the "normal" processes of childhood whereby our nightmares are far worse than the reality of our everyday lives. Artie grew up with the sounds of his father's anguished sleep-cries, sounds he thought "all grown-ups made while they slept" (II:74).

4. The insufficiency of stories as sources of truth versus the power of stories to maintain, restore, and perpetuate individual, family, and group identity. At the end of *Maus II*, Vladek tells Art that after his remarkable reunion with Anja, "we were both very happy and lived happy, happy ever after," whereas readers of *Maus I* know better, having had a vivid impression of Art's anguish after Anja's suicide. Nonetheless, Vladek feels able to die after he has told his son "enough stories."

5. The juxtaposition of horror and humor. Consider, for example, the grotesque slapstick elements of the scene involving Mandelbaum in the concentration camp: with a shoe he cannot wear and pants that fall down, he loses his spoon while trying to pick up the pants, and drops his soup.

6. The use of startling analogies to "familiarize" the horrific. Consider, for instance, Vladek's observation that the mass graves dug for victims of the gas chambers "were big, so like the swimming pool of the Pines Hotel" (II:72).

7. The juxtaposition of both graphic images of the most intense human suffering, ironically portrayed by mice, and the portrayal of the petty obsessions (e.g., Vladek's pill counting) and the ordinariness of everyday life (II: 72–74) with Vladek's "objective" documentary style of testimony ("Prisoners what worked [at the mass graves] poured gasoline over the live ones and the dead ones. And the fat from the burning bodies they scooped and poured again so everyone could burn better").

The discomforting linking of heterogeneous elements works against the psychological "closure" demanded by the comic strip format (a perceptual phenomenon defined by McCloud as "observing the parts but perceiving the whole" [63]), so that the resulting text is simultaneously a complex set of coherent interlocking narratives—the story of the Holocaust as recalled by Vladek and recorded by Art, the story of how the story came to be, the story of how the artist comes to terms with the meaning of the stories he is telling—and a testament to the ultimate incomprehensibility of the Holocaust and to the impossibility of representing it within the logic of narrative structure. That is, the synecdochal relation of narrative to "reality" points to its own inadequacy: the perceivable parts encoded in stories can never be commensurate with historical events that engender them, nor do they pretend to be. Vladek can never tell enough stories to make Art—or us—understand what happened, much less why or how. Nonetheless, Vladek's narrative of his experiences during the war, and the contextualization of these experiences within a time before and a time after, does achieve a kind of internal coherence to the extent that it manifests the expected structure of retrospective biography. Maus thus enacts from a postmodern perspective the tension between the fundamental human impulse to make meaning of history and "the consciousness which is engulfed and overwhelmed by the enormity of stark actualities" (Zavarzadeh 41).

One of Spiegelman's most daring choices is his use of animals to portray ethnic groups, most prominently Germans as cats and Jews as mice. The brilliance of this decision is evident in its several simultaneous effects. First, it points to the grim moral underpinnings of the fable tradition, in which might makes right, the strong exploit the weak, and any chance for survival depends upon a combination of luck, foresight, cynicism, and resourcefulness. This artistic decision also horrifically invigorates what James E. Young, in Writing and Rewriting the Holocaust, describes as the Nazi use of "figures" as an instrument of the "final solution": Jews as "vermin," running through the Warsaw ghettos for their lives, the use of the roach gas Zyklon-B for extermination, and so forth (93). The fact that Jews are humans, not rodents, is made emphatic by the portrayal of them with mouse heads, just as the truth that Nazis are not instinctively predatory animals but human agents responsible for crimes against humanity is made more persuasive by the comparison with cats. Moreover, the figuration of prey and predator on the one hand and vermin that must be exterminated for the betterment of society on the other is intensified by the echo in maus of mauscheln (derived from the name Moishe), a "sick" language attributed by nineteenth-century Germans to Jews. Sander Gilman defines mauscheln as "the use of altered syntax and bits of Hebrew vocabulary and a specific pattern of gestures to represent the spoken language of the Jews" (Jewish Self-Hatred 139). The Yiddish-inflected English with which Vladek (who is also fluent in Polish, German, and scriptural Hebrew) tells his story stands in ironic defiance of the Nazi attempt to silence the Other.

In his use of cartoon animals, Spiegelman also suggests the paradoxical power of metaphor as an instrument of both evil and good: as Young observes, although metaphors may seem to trivialize and distort, they are "our only access to the facts, which cannot exist apart from the figures delivering them to us. . . . If carried to its literal end, an injunction against Auschwitz metaphors would place events outside of language and meaning altogether," ironically fulfilling the Nazi goal of "mystifying" events (*Writing and Rewriting* 91). Indeed, Spiegelman incorporates a critique of the power and limits of metaphor into the structure of the narrative. On the one hand, he recognizes the grim efficacy of the Nazi literalization of metaphors when Vladek recounts how he had to level huge mounds of dirt as a starving prisoner of war in the forced labor camp: "we had to move mountains" (I:56). On the other hand, he acknowledges that in ordinary times, ordinary figures of speech, even (or especially) the most hyperbolic ones, will be used unself-consciously, that is, with no fear that the figurative could be made literal. Thus, Françoise can observe during a peaceful moment with Art that "It's almost impossible to believe Auschwitz ever happened" and in the next breath Art can complain that "these damn bugs are eating me alive" (II:74). A quick whoosh of insecticide takes care of the problem; the insects drop—like flies. In context, however, the incident is itself a gruesome reminder that Auschwitz did happen; two pages earlier, Art has portrayed the suffering of Jews ("mice") burned alive, an instance of "pests" exterminated. The two scenes are retrospectively joined by the illustration that begins chapter 2, "Auschwitz (Time Flies)": a portrayal of the agony of burning "mice" in a panel being invaded by scavenging flies (II:39). In the panels that follow, the same flies hover over Art as he sits at his drafting table overlooking a mound of corpses, plagued with guilt over the success of *Maus I* as he works on *Maus II*. Here is the power of Auschwitz to make the literal horribly metaphoric, as the flies conjured up by Art's tormented mind cannot simply be swatted or sprayed away. Without Pavel's therapeutic counsel, they might indeed "eat him alive." Spiegelman's careful orchestration of these allusions reveals the artist's exquisite sensitivity to his representational choices and thus undercuts any facile response to the limitations of metaphor.

Ironically, the distancing of the reader implicit in the portrayal of cartoon animals makes the overwhelming nature of the subject more vivid. In this regard, Adam Gopnik has astutely observed that the animal heads attributed to humans in this narrative reflect "our sense that this story is too horrible to be presented unmasked" and that in this way Spiegelman's artistic "problem" was analogous to that of the medieval religious artist: "For the traditional illuminator, it is the ultimate sacred mystery that must somehow be shown without being shown; for the contemporary artist, it is the ultimate obscenity, the ultimate profanity, that must somehow be shown without being shown. . . . We want an art whose stylizations are as much a declaration of inadequacy to their subject as they are of mystical transcendence" (33–34). In a similar vein, Irving Howe speculates that Theodor Adorno's famous dictum that there could be no poetry after Auschwitz reflects a primal sense (codified in ancient religious proscriptions) that some things are too terrible to be looked at or even to be named. Such taboos, Howe suggests, are intended "not to enforce ignorance, but to regulate, or guard against the consequences of knowledge" (181). Spiegelman's "masked" presentation allows the reader to confront dreaded knowledge; paradoxically, this knowledge is made more accessible and thus more consequential by our consciousness of the artistic strategies that must mediate between us and a reality too stark to bear transparent representation.

If Spiegelman's brilliance as an iconographer is manifest in his daring decisions about graphic modes,[2] his mastery of narrative strategy is equally evident. And here, I think, Hayden White's attribution of metaphoric and metonymic processes to the construction of narrative is especially applicable. White's point is that in coping with a set of events that are "unclassified and unclassifiable," we "utilize both metaphor [a sense of similarity underlying disparate elements] and metonymy [a sense of difference underlying juxtaposed elements] in order to 'fix' it as something about which we can meaningfully discourse" (Tropics 96). Spiegelman's use of juxtaposition exploits the possibilities of metaphor and metonymy at the same time. His technique enables both analogy and distinction by drawing attention to parallels but insisting on differences. The swimming pool at the Pines Hotel is not a cremation pit, and the point of the comparison—the similarity in size—has the effect of reinforcing the horror of the numbers of murdered people by highlighting the *difference* in size between a normal grave and a mass one and thus the chasm between human behavior that recognizes the value and dignity of an individual life and human behavior that values degradation and death. In this instance, then, the annihilative capacity of the Nazi use of metaphor that transforms people into vermin and into things is resisted by the distinction-making implications of Vladek's analogy, a resistance similar to the effect of planting animal heads on human bodies. The same process is at work, I think, in Vladek's comparison of one of the Auschwitz crematoria to a "big bakery" (II:70).[3] Moreover, while the provocative use of figuration draws attention to the constructed, artifactual nature of the text, Spiegelman continues to acknowledge the reader's desire for the coherence and meaningfulness of stories. In *Maus* the human need for narrative and the power of its "truthfulness" is revealed in several ways: not only in Art's self-conscious crafting of Vladek's story (both biography and autobiography) but in his ironic use of the fairy-tale convention in the opening of *Maus II* (in which he imagines his French [frog] wife, Françoise, magically transformed by a mouse rabbi into a "beautiful mouse"); in the truncated and unassimilable anti-fairy-tale narratives of characters such as Vladek's nephew Abraham, Mandelbaum, the Belgian boy, and Spivak; and in his father's recoding of his own story (a nightmare) into a fairy tale.

The brief tale of Mandelbaum (II:29–35), swiftly told and heartbreaking in its ironic counterpoint of "miraculous" salvation and inexplicable annihilation, is both story and anti-story. The "miracle," of course, is achieved through human agency (Vladek's ability to trade his knowledge of Polish and English for special favors from a kapo) and human compassion (Vladek's willingness to take risks for a friend), but since Mandelbaum has pleaded with God for a piece of string to hold up his pants and a wooden shoe that fits, he concludes that God "sent shoes through you [Vladek]." Twice Vladek tells Art that Mandelbaum, after receiving the string and the shoes, "was so happy," the measure of happiness having been redefined by life as "prisoner on the hell planet" (to borrow Art's phrase for his own inner torment following his mother's suicide). For a moment, at least, Vladek and Mandelbaum seem to have won a victory.

In the very next panel, however, we learn that several days later Mandelbaum was "chosen" for a work detail and soon died. "Nobody could help this," Vladek says. The "nobody," of course, refers only to prisoners, since, like the "miracle" that made Mandelbaum cry with joy, Mandelbaum's death is also the effect of human agency, and its brutality is made vivid by Art's portrayal of his father's conjectures regarding how Mandelbaum might have "finished"—perhaps he was shot under the pretense that he was trying to escape, or was kicked in the head because he couldn't work fast enough, or got sick and was shoved into the oven. The horror of Mandelbaum's story, as a story, is that it is devoid of meaning; that is, it does not conform to any prior notions we have of cause and effect, the rules of war, justice and injustice, or even ironic reversal. Certainly there is irony (and, as mentioned above, even a kind of slapstick comedy) in the portrait of the once rich and powerful businessman trying to hold his pants up while retrieving his spoon and juggling a bowl of soup, but the narrative offers us no way of understanding or—to use White's term—"emplotting" this reversal of fortune. White defines emplotment as "the encodation of the facts contained in the chronicle as components of specific kinds of plot-structures, in precisely the way that Frye has suggested is the case with 'fictions' in general" (*Tropics* 83). No prior narrative structures tell us how to read Mandelbaum's story; he is a "nice" man (Vladek's term) whom we see at his lowest point, from which he is momentarily redeemed through Vladek's cleverness and goodwill—and whose meaningless murder soon thereafter we are left to imagine.

Moreover, the uncertainty of how Mandelbaum ended denies us a measure of closure we might otherwise have. Perhaps, we may think, it does not matter whether an innocent man "went up the chimney" or was shot and left to rot or was dumped in a mass grave. But Vladek's precise descriptions of the possible alternatives remind us that how someone dies does matter—not least because "when" is usually implied in "how"—and that under ordinary conditions we are particular about the ways we can be morally and legally engaged in the circumstances of death (witness, e.g., the precise justice with which rewards and punishments are meted out in folktales and the highly prescriptive practices and rituals governing the administration of capital punishment). While Mandelbaum's story, therefore, has elements of comedy, of tragedy, and of pathos, it ultimately resists encoding and remains in Art's reproduction of his father's narration a bare chronicle of a life and a death, Kafkaesque in its starkness: a "nice" man, once happy and affluent, is starved and tormented for reasons no one can express. The victim is momentarily given hope by a friend and shortly thereafter dies a terrible death.

The essentially plotless "story" of Mandelbaum can be taken as a metaphor—or more precisely a synecdoche—for the incomprehensible sequence of events called the Holocaust. Thus neither Mandelbaum's life and death nor the Holocaust as a whole is granted the coherence—and hence the dignity—of a story. A story, as Paul Ricoeur has observed, "must be more than just an enumeration of events in serial order; it must organize them into an intelligible whole, of a sort such that we can always ask what is the 'thought' of this story" (65). Emplotment thus has a transformative function, reconfiguring events into an apprehensible pattern: "To follow a story is to move forward in the midst of contingencies and peripeteia under the guidance of an expectation that finds its fulfillment in the 'conclusion' . . . [or] 'end point,' which, in turn, furnishes the point of view from which the story can be perceived as forming a whole. To understand a story is to understand how and why the successive episodes led to this conclusion, which, far from being foreseeable, must finally be acceptable, as congruent with episodes brought together by the story" (66, 67). No such fulfillment, no catharsis is possible when the "end point" of the story, the denouement of the "plot," is also the "final solution," an attempt at annihilation so complete that, if it is successful, the events (or "episodes") leading up to it will not only defy attempts to "configure" them in any way but will also deny their own existence. Such denial creates the paradox that the point of the story is that it can never be told because there will be no evidence that the sequence of events—not to mention the "characters" such as Mandelbaum—that comprised it ever existed.

Framing Mandelbaum's story is that of Vladek, the survivor, who is himself struck by the inexplicable contrast between his own fate and his friend's: "You see how they [the Nazis] did? And I had it still happy there. For me it was not yet the end." While Mandelbaum's death bears a synecdochal relationship to the web of events surrounding it, Vladek's survival—in its insistence on its difference from that with which it is compared—is metonymic: his narrative is the testimony of life against death. Equally important, it is an insistence on what it means to be human, the living proof of resistance to what can never be accepted as human behavior. Vladek's victory "against darkness in an age of darkness" (Fackenheim 96) is to write his own ending, not only by surviving but also by encoding his own stories into the structure of a fairy tale in which he is agent as much as victim and in which he and Anja live "happy, happy ever after." More than this, it is to have his life story recorded by his son, a son born after the war, the living legacy of two survivors whose wife is pregnant with a granddaughter whom Vladek will not live to see but who bears the family name.

The tension in this sort of emplotment has its source in the desire to impose meaning—moral coherence—on a set of events that always resists such attempts, and this is a tension of which Vladek and Art are keenly aware and which is thus always before the reader. If Vladek's survival is merely luck or randomness, then life and death do seem totally meaningless. But to take credit for surviving is to somehow diminish those who did not survive. Clearly, Vladek is caught in this dilemma, which is necessarily left unresolved. Judaism nonetheless (or all the more) enjoins its adherents to live lives of moral coherence. The competing pressures—to make meaning and to resist imposing meaning where none can ever reside—are portrayed exquisitely in Vladek's human—and humane—insistence on both pride and humility and in his son's tortured struggle both to commemorate and to demythologize his father's heroic stature. On a number of occasions Vladek calls himself "lucky"—he is "a lucky one" in Auschwitz when the prison uniform "fit[s] him a little"; "lucky" that the Polish kapo whom he is teaching English is capable of showing him a bit of kindness; "lucky" that he remains strong enough to carry heavy soup pots after months of privation and abuse; and "lucky" to find a piece of paper in which to wrap the extra, lice-free shirt he has "organized" in order to guarantee that he will be fed. Supporting this insistence on the role of luck is Art's therapist, Pavel, also a survivor, who cautions him against the conclusion that there is some way to explain why some lived and others did not: "It wasn't the best people who survived, nor did the best ones die. It was random!" (II:45). And, having witnessed the deaths of Mandelbaum, of Vladek's nephew Abraham, and of the Belgian boy who dreams of his wife's cooking, we know that this is so. Without luck, even with all the courage and ingenuity in the world, Vladek, like almost all of his family and Anja's, would have died. He could have been killed, for example, instead of only being beaten by the guard who caught him speaking to Anja in Birkenau, or succumbed to starvation or, as he nearly did, typhus.

Yet Art, having lived always in the shadow of his father's hellish experiences, tells his therapist that he admires Vladek's survival against all odds: "Well, sure, I know there was a lot of luck involved, but he was amazingly present-minded and resourceful" (II:45). And, as Art tells the story based on his father's recorded narrative, it is these very qualities that in fact shine through. His knowledge of languages and his skills as a craftsman gain him privileges and extra food. He scavenges and saves, "organizes," and makes deals with other prisoners, including kapos. He is willing to take calculated risks (as when he communicates with Anja through Nancie and supplies her with food packages) but is never foolhardy (he is unwilling, e.g., to join his comrades in trusting the German guards to let them escape in exchange for bribes as the war nears its end [II:83]). Vladek prides himself on his foresight and resourcefulness, telling Art, for example, that his friends always came to him for paper, a rare and valuable commodity that he "found and saved." When Art asks why others didn't save paper, Vladek replies, "Ach! You know how most people are!" Similarly, while others quickly consume their meager rations, Vladek exercises superhuman discipline, saving half of his bread against the possibility of even worse conditions to come or perhaps an opportunity to make a trade (II:49). He survives the ordeal of the sealed cattle car by rigging up a hammock on two hooks near a window, using a blanket he has managed to retain. Through the window he reaches snow on the roof, preventing dehydration and trading snow with other prisoners for sugar. Clearly, Vladek is not "most people." In the story we are offered—dictated by the father and retold by the son—he is especially capable and quick, ingenious and courageous. Thus, Vladek's physical and mental endurance, his resourcefulness and amazing self-possession, do endow him with a kind of heroic stature, Pavel's insistence to the contrary notwithstanding.

Moreover, Art's recognition of his father's "present-mindedness" points to an underlying moral theme as well as an issue of narrative representation. As the Nazi exterminators become more aggressive, survival often depends on one's ability to make snap judgments about seemingly impossible "choices." In this sense an essential element of Jewish culture—an ethically valid life lived willingly in accordance with the sacred rhythms and rituals codified historically in the commandments—becomes irrelevant because impossible: during the Nazi terror, life is lived in and for the moment, cut off from historical contexts and thus from God's holy covenant as both past and future dissolve into chaos. To think of horrors already suffered is to despair (as Anja would have done after learning of Richieu's death had not Vladek insisted that she not give up [I:122]); to entertain the specter of inevitable gas chambers and crematoria (as Tofa did) is also to despair. In the ghetto, in the prisoner-of-war camps, in Auschwitz, life and death depend on present-mindedness in situations that offer no context for informed decision making because they have no analogy to personal or historical experience. More often than not, Vladek's instincts drive him toward the lesser of two evils— as, for example, when he chooses, against the advice of other prisoners of war in 1939, to volunteer for labor assignments with the promise of "housing and abundant food" (I:54). Sometimes, however, neither of the evils seems "lesser": should the Jews of the Sosnowiec ghetto obey the order to register at the Dienst stadium, or should they try to hide in their homes? ("To go it was no good. But not to go—it was also no good" [I:88]). And on one tormenting occasion Vladek capitulates to Anja's refusal to believe that she must give up her baby son to hide with Ilzecki's Polish friend as "the noose tightens" in 1942 (I:81). A year later, feeling there is "no choice," they send Richieu for safekeeping to the Zawiercie ghetto, where his short life ends.

Yet, forced to make a series of crucial decisions in an increasingly savage world that is both arbitrary and cruelly systematic, Vladek never relinquishes his belief that he does have at least some choices, and thus he retains his moral stature. He tells, more sadly than bitterly, of both Jews and Gentiles so desperate under the Nazi terror that they descended to betraying others. (Indeed, he and his family are given up to the Gestapo by one such "rat.") He will not be among them. And, resourceful as he is, he has contempt for *kombinators*—schemers and crooks such as Haskel who are willing to take bribes but not the risks (I:116). Vladek, of course, is no saint. As noted above, he survives partly because he, too, is a schemer, but never at others' expense: when a young couple offers him all their remaining jewelry (two watches and some diamond rings) in exchange for his advice on how to escape from the Srodula ghetto, he takes the small watch but refuses the other items because "they needed these to live" (I:124). The obvious contrast with Haskel, who appears to feel no remorse when he fails to save Vladek's in-laws after gladly accepting their jewels, reveals that a struggle for moral freedom can endow with dignity a life scaled down to the bare question of existence. Vladek's moral triumph is to have been sharp-witted and pragmatic without descending to exploitation, present-minded but not a *kombinator*. His focus on the present is contextualized within a transcendent moral framework. In preserving his own life and the lives of his loved ones and yet not depriving others of a chance to survive, Vladek, raised in an observant Jewish home (we recall that he donned a prayer shawl and faithfully recited the daily prayers in the prisoner-of-war camp), enacts what has been called the basic tenet of Jewish ethics: do not do unto others what you would not have them do unto you. As Jonathan Sacks has observed, Judaism requires of its followers a dual dedication: "The covenant is more than a series of vertical commitments linking individual Jew with God. It is also a set of horizontal bonds linking Jews with one another in collective responsibility" (207). Thus, Vladek's present-mindedness, which helps to save his life, is shaped by a history and a tradition that allow him to emerge also with human dignity.

In addition, Vladek's ongoing obligation to make wrenchingly consequential choices is one aspect of the narrative that endows it with the dramatic power necessary to engage the reader relentlessly. Spiegelman thus confronts the problem of how to introduce novelistic tension in writing about the Holocaust. Irving Howe has defined the problem in this way:

> The Holocaust is not, essentially, a dramatic subject. Much before, much after, and much surrounding the mass exterminations, in which thousands of dazed and broken people were sent up each day in smoke, hardly knowing and often barely able to respond to their fate, have little of drama in them. Terribleness, yes; drama, no. . . . The basic minimum of freedom to choose and act that is a central postulate of

drama had been taken from the victims. The Nazis indulged in a peculiarly vicious parody of this freedom when they sometimes gave Jewish parents the "choice" of which child should be murdered. (189)

One must agree with Howe that it is absurd to ask what kind of freedom was available to victims of terrorism and torture. Mandelbaum, like most of Vladek's and Anja's families, like millions of others, was not given the option to survive. Instead of choosing, these victims were chosen—"selekted"—for annihilation in a gruesome Nazi parody of God's choice of the Jews to enter a sacred covenant enjoining them to faith, compassion, justice, and mutual accountability. Indeed, the ghosts of the murdered are always before us— made more haunting by Art's portrayal of them "before" as living, breathing individuals (who can forget Richieu asking his grandfather for another cookie or Tofa's determination to avoid the gas chambers even at the most horrifying price?). Yet *Maus* is a "story" in the conventional sense in that it chronicles the survival against all odds by a man whose character and choices were a factor in that survival. Vladek's narrative, while documenting powerfully the horror of the "final solution," portrays its protagonist and many of those around him as agents as well as victims, still defined by the nature of their responses. Spiegelman thus embodies the tension between the coherence of a narrative informed by a personal victory that seems at least in part to have been earned and the knowledge that this victory is only to have survived as a moral human being—with never-healing psychic wounds—unimaginable and meaningless suffering. Through this tension Spiegelman is able to tell the truth—that although no explanations, no logic, no coherence is possible, each of us seeks to impose a set of meanings on our lives, to find continuity and reason, sense and justice. And because we are constantly reminded of the impossible task of finding such meaning in a historical chronicle of horror, no complacency or trivialization is possible. Juxtaposed with Vladek's "happy, happy ever after" are the photos of parents, grandparents, brothers and sisters, aunts and uncles, and a small boy named Richieu—Vladek and Anja's firstborn—who never emerged from ghetto or concentration camp.

In the enforced silence of these witnesses, Adorno's plea not to try to represent what happened shadows the narrative. Somewhat surprisingly, the survivor/therapist Pavel is sympathetic to this position, suggesting that since "the victims who died can never tell their side of the story . . . maybe it's better not to have any more stories" (II:45). Yet Pavel's comment appears in a book whose very purpose is to tell stories, and Vladek dies only when he has told all the stories he remembers up until his remarkable reunion with Anja in 1944. "More I don't need to tell you," he says to Art, asking him to turn off the tape recorder. The tombstone memorializing Vladek and Anja merges with the last two cartoon panels, identifying the end of Vladek's testimony with the end of his life. At the close of a life of devastating, incomprehensible loss—including what he calls "a tragedy among tragedies," the murder of his "happy, beautiful" firstborn son by a desperate aunt who, rather than submit to the gas chamber, chose death by poison for herself and the children (I:109)—Vladek ends his story not with bitterness and hatred, not with a cry for revenge, but on a note of triumph: he and Anja survived, found each other, and were "happy." The names of Vladek and Anja and the birth and death dates on their joint tombstone are underscored by Art's signature and the dates (1978–1991) of the composition of Maus, the text that is itself a unique and extraordinarily eloquent monument to his parents. The double gravemarker signals their final reunion against all odds and a transcendent meaning for "happy, happy ever after"; the dates, in contrast, place the events narrated squarely within a concrete historical time, where, as Howe observes, the facts of the Holocaust must remain, lest they be abstracted and romanticized as somehow transcending history: "About this most extreme of human experiences there cannot be too much documentation, and what matters most in such material is exactitude: the sober number, the sober date" (182–83).

Maus does offer us numbers and dates, and also the specificity of photographs and of diagrams that illuminate Vladek's testimony regarding the desperate construction of ultimately doomed hiding places and the grim efficiency of gas chambers, crematoria, and chimneys. As such it bespeaks an unnatural rupture, an irreparable cleavage from the promise of faith and redemption. But because Maus is also a record of a family history passed from father to son, it addresses not only the past but also the future. It represents historical continuity, the beginning of a process through which future generations can be united and Jewish identity preserved. That such goals can be accomplished only within the boundaries of history is made clear by the commentary of modern Jewish philosophers. Martin Buber observes, for example, that in Judaism "the suprahistorical molds the historical but does not replace it" and that "Jews are a community based on memory" (129). Similarly, Yosef Yerushalmi suggests that "only in Israel and nowhere else is the injunction to remember felt as a religious imperative to an entire people" (9).

The transmission of stories is a means not only of recalling the past but also of forging connections with younger generations and with those to come, connections that are the essence of community survival. As I have suggested, *Maus* reminds us that the Holocaust mandated an eternal present, denying its victims both the manifestation of God in a historical past and the possibility of a future. Vladek's recitation is therefore a reclamation of the continuity essential to Jewish existence, or as Geoffrey Hartman has put it, a "remembering forward": "In the camps [victims] were systematically deprived of foresight: though they saw all too forcefully what was before their eyes, their ability to discern a normal pattern that could eventually be expressed in the form of a story was disrupted or disabled. . . . To remember forward—to transmit a personal story to children and grandchildren and all who should hear it—affirms a desegregation and the survivors' reentry into the human family. The story that links us to their past also links them to our future" ("Book of the Destruction" 324–25). The profound yearning for such linkage is painfully evident in the dedication of *Maus II* both to Richieu, the child whose life, like those of millions of others, was horribly truncated, and to Nadja, the grandchild who will know and remember. By acknowledging the inadequacy of stories and also the necessity of telling them, Spiegelman's painstaking memorial insists—as Emil Fackenheim maintains we must—on the "blasphemy" of seeking a *purpose* in Auschwitz and the inevitability of seeking a *response*.

However, as we analyze the complexity of Art's response, we need to acknowledge independently the nature of Vladek's. First, implicit in Vladek's amazingly detailed and coherent recitation is not only the need to bear witness to atrocities so transgressive of normal human experience that those who were there "couldn't believe even what's in front of their eyes" (II:73) but also a sense that the world has learned no lessons and that a repetition is not unlikely. It is not enough for Vladek to tell his son that Jews in the Srodula ghetto constructed hidden "bunkers" to escape summary execution or deportation to Auschwitz. He insists on drawing a detailed diagram of the cleverly concealed living space built in the cellar beneath the kitchen coal bin, a spot that resisted detection by the Nazis and their dogs: "Show to me your pencil and I can explain you . . . such things it's good to know exactly how was it—just in case" (I:110). The bunker, of course, does not save Vladek and Anja from the camps (forced to move to a different house, they are ultimately betrayed by an informer), but it kept them a "little safe" for a short time while "others, what didn't have such a good place like what I made, they kept being taken away" (I:111). This, therefore, is the sort of practical knowledge that Vladek must pass on to his only surviving son—just in case. Second, in contemplating Vladek's state of mind, we should also consider his guilt at having destroyed Anja's notebooks during a period of depression. Vladek tells Art that at the end of 1943, when Anja knew that most of her family, including Richieu, had been killed, she responded to the terror and starvation in Pesach's shoe-shop bunker by sitting "the whole day and night . . . writing into her notebook." We also know that when Anja killed herself in 1968 "she left no note." Because Art himself suffers a kind of survivor guilt after his mother's death, we can understand his anger at Vladek for ensuring that her voice will never be heard. And surely Vladek understands, too, which is why he can tolerate hearing his son curse him in a fit of rage and call him "murderer." In addition to being a chronicle of horrors, a testimonial, a fairy tale, a cautionary tale, and a gesture of belief in the future, Vladek's story is a remembrance of his dedication to Anja and an act of repentance for sinning against her in a fit of the kind of despair he presumably did not permit himself while she was alive. In burning Anja's diaries, he attempted to destroy unbearable memories, manifesting a "present-mindedness" quite different from the sort Art admires. The revelation of that destruction in *Maus*, the knowledge that her words went up in smoke like the lives to which those words would have been a testament, makes the absence of Anja's voice a vivid, ghostly presence. In the Jewish tradition, the transmission of familial and communal history from parent to child is a sacred obligation, and it is one that Anja evidently took seriously; even as he confesses what he has done, Vladek tells Art that although he remembers nothing of the journal contents, he does know that she wanted Art to have them ("I know that she said, 'I wish my son, when he grows up, he will be interested by this'" [I:159]). It is altogether fitting, therefore, that Vladek should expiate his obliteration of Anja's words with a narrative that idealizes their life together without diminishing the inexpressible torment that ultimately destroyed her.

Appropriately, this obligation to respond, and thus to represent what is inherently unrepresentable, recalls the receptiveness to contradiction inherent in the Midrash tradition of Jewish exegesis, which demands that we contend with precisely those events that in their enormity appear—and may indeed be—irreconcilable with the continuity and coherence of historical narrative. In his meditation on the survival of Judaism after Auschwitz, Fackenheim points out that the nature of Midrash (talmudic rabbinical commentary) is to embrace paradox—the most fundamental one being the bond between a perfect God and an imperfect world—through story: "Midrash does not 'grope' for 'concepts' in order to 'solve problems' and dissolve paradox. The midrashic Word is story. It remains story because it both points to and articulates a life lived with problems and paradox—the problems and paradox of a divine-human relation" (263–64). Like the "mad Midrash" that Fackenheim describes in the works of Elie Wiesel, *Maus* is an act of resistance to absurdity in an absurd world. Even as Art agonizes over his own inadequacy and laments that "reality is too complex for comics," his amazing work contradicts his own assertion. Finally, as we say good-bye to what Ozick has called "possibly the rottenest of all centuries," we are left to ponder the paradox that, perhaps more than any history book or documentary, it is a comic book of horrors that enables our children and ourselves to confront the meaning of history and our own roles in shaping it.

Notes

1. Adam Gopnik points out that the popular association of cartoons with children and with triviality reflects a lack of historical understanding. His argument is that Spiegelman's brilliant use of comics "work[s] not against the grain of the cartoon but within its richest inheritance . . . exploring the deepest possibilities unique to the form" (31).

2. For an analysis of the evolution of Spiegelman's graphic style in *Maus*, see chapter 4 of Witek, *Comic Books as History*.

3. In a cogent and provocative essay, Cynthia Ozick has argued for the moral basis of metaphor: it is the metaphoric imagination that enables us to identify the "other" with ourselves, and such an identification is the essence of morality, enabling us to understand the heart of the stranger ("Metaphor and Memory" 278–80). But, as Ozick has argued with equal passion, morality consists also in making distinctions, i.e., in the capacity not to assimilate the "other" to ourselves and to refuse to be assimilated to the "other" (e.g., the avoidance of "cannibalism," Nazis turning Jews into mice). See, e.g., "A Liberal's Auschwitz" and untitled response to "Is Our Schizophrenia Historically Important?"

6

The Language of Survival

English as Metaphor in Art Spiegelman's Maus

Alan C. Rosen

Writing on the Holocaust regularly reflects on the languages spoken by victims and perpetrators. However, English, as a primary language of neither, rarely and only marginally receives attention. Yet in Maus, Art Spiegelman emphasizes the extraordinary role English plays in aiding his father's survival. The prominence of English in the chronicle of events implicitly directs attention to the fractured English in which the survivor's story is told and, more generally, to the complex significance of language and languages in representing the Holocaust.

Maus's exceptional concern with English operates on at least three levels. First, in Vladek's biography, his knowledge of and competence in English is important both for initiating his relationship with Anja and for aiding or determining his survival while in concentration camps. Second, Spiegelman presents Vladek's narrative of survival in immigrant English, rife with errors and neologisms. In contrast to the biographical events recounted, Vladek's English here is noteworthy not because of competence but rather because of incompetence. Third, the fluent English of virtually all other characters (even those who, like the psychotherapist, Pavel, are also immigrants) frames and envelops both Vladek's biography and his Holocaust narrative, establishing English as the dominant language. These three levels interrogate the status of English as a language of the Holocaust and, consequently, as a language (un)fit to recount the Holocaust.

Maus's interrogation of English can be situated in the context of previous efforts to assess the significance of specific languages in relation to the Holocaust. While these attempts have focused primarily on Yiddish, Hebrew, and German, they have also considered other European tongues, including English. Sidra Ezrahi, for example, positions English in opposition to Yiddish and German, the major languages of the victim and persecutor, respectively (12).[1] In contrast, English, of little significance in the camps and ghettos, has a marginal standing, making it an "outsider" and marking it with "autonomy" and "purity." Moreover, Ezrahi places English in opposition in another way: as the chief language of the Allies, English came to stand for "defiance," for "a different hierarchy of values," values presumably informed by the democratic ideals associated with English-speaking countries.

Yet if this ascription of purity and legacy of defiance implies for English a certain heroic stature, Ezrahi's schema also suggests its vulnerability: because it was not vitally implicated in the events of the Holocaust, English is less qualified to represent them. This reservation has informed writing and testimony in, and commentary on, English. One of the most important English anthologies of Holocaust writing, for instance, registers the degree that English stands, as it were, in the shadow of the primary languages. "The Book of Books, out of the depths of the Sacred Martyrdom," writes the editor of that volume, Israel Knox, "will not find its first and original home in English or French or Russian, but in Hebrew and Yiddish" (xiv).[2] Even though some languages can serve testimony better than others, he continues, "no item was included or excluded [from the anthology] solely because of language." Yet when, out of a wish to be "comprehensive and represent[at]ive," Knox cites languages other than the primary ones, he does not refer to English: "There are items here from Yiddish and Hebrew but also from the French and German and Russian and Polish" (xv). To be sure, he goes on to note that the "sensitive and perceptive" reader will be able to distill the essence from an English translation. But at best, English plays only a tertiary role.

Intervening in this complex, even antithetical legacy of English as a language of the Holocaust, Spiegelman's *Maus* makes the position of English itself a theme. Indeed, this self-reflexive investigation of English begins with the title. On first hearing, the title would seem to be in English, the word "maus/mouse" paralleling the audacious animal imagery Spiegelman uses to represent the Jews. But while the title is phonetically English, Spiegelman actually writes (draws?) it in German, a gesture that not so much eliminates the English as, I would suggest, "contaminates" it, associating it with, rather than opposing it to, the essential languages of the Holocaust.

This strategy would seem to endow English with an authority that it previously lacked. There are, however, several ways that the association not only confers authority but provokes suspicion. First, the title links English with German, the language of the persecutors, a linkage that implicitly associates English with the debate regarding the fitness of German as a language of representing the Holocaust. And second, the devious German of the visualized title estranges the English, making it, for the American reader, not only curious but foreign, rendering the once familiar and comfortable into something strange and disconcerting.[3]

Spiegelman's choice of title, and choice of how to draw it, suggests the complex ways he reformulates the issue of representing the Holocaust in English. On the one hand, he challenges its legacy of purity, moving English from outside to inside the Holocaust. On another level, by positing English as foreign, he frustrates the American audience's sense of familiarity, moving the reader, in a sense, from inside to outside the Holocaust.

This essay will elaborate the strategies Spiegelman employs throughout *Maus* to effect this reformulation and revaluation of English. Admittedly, to foreground the verbal dimension of *Maus* may seem to miss what is most singular about its approach to the Holocaust: the cartoons. But, as these preliminary comments suggest, this graphic novel compels attention to its words.

English becomes a subject in the first represented conversation between Vladek and Anja. Vladek reveals to Anja that he has deciphered the private conversation in which Anja and her cousin praise Vladek (I:16). Anja and her cousin spoke in English to protect their secret; Vladek's capacity to "know" English comes as a surprise, displaying not only his hitherto hidden capacity to negotiate English but also his access to the secrets that, in this case, were conveyed within and by means of English. English thus initially takes on a number of striking associations. As a language of secrets, it signifies a language spoken to prohibit understanding, specifically, the understanding of the one who is being spoken about.

The associations around secrecy, resistance, and access also address the complex relation of Vladek and Anja as presented in *Maus*, for in this initial encounter Vladek understands (or at least in his recounting suggests an understanding of) certain information that Anja would prefer he did not.

Whereas Anja resorts to English to deflect his understanding, Vladek employs it to appropriate a sensitive cluster of thought and feeling not his own. This dynamic parallels the ongoing issue of Vladek's belief that he has full access to Anja's story, a belief put in doubt repeatedly by Art's counter-belief that Anja's memoirs would give an alternative version of the events his parents lived through.[4] In his recounting of this episode, then, Vladek has command of even that which seems most secret, most impenetrable. In essence, English on this level suggests a fantasy of complete mastery. Indeed, it is a fantasy that accumulates economic, political, and psychological associations as the story unfolds.

Tellingly, the discovery that Vladek understands English (and hence understands the appreciation Anja feels for him) steers their initial conversation to further consideration of the role of English in their lives, considerations this time dominated by economic and class issues. To Anja's question "Did you study it [English] in school?" Vladek responds, "I had to quit school at about 14 to work" (I:16), a reply that sets out sharply contrasting class assumptions and realities. In presuming that English is learned "in school," Anja is seemingly guided and constricted by her upper-class sensibility, a sensibility that takes for granted the leisure and resources required for children to attend school. Vladek's motivation for learning English—"I always dreamed of going to America" (I:16)—continues to suggest contrasting class orientations. Whereas Anja acquires her English as part of a secure life lived in a land of plenty, Vladek acquires his based on a "dream," a fantasy of life in a different land, America. The dream of America, while never spelled out, implies a society redeemed by an alternative social vision—a vision of radical social mobility and opportunity, in other words, where a child would not have to quit school in order to support a family. Such a dream also, of course, offers an alternative to the social stratification that so powerfully governs the contrasting methods by which Anja and Vladek have acquired English.

What America (and the English associated with it) stands for in *Maus* is ambiguous and complex, partaking of the associations of Vladek's dream but going beyond it as well. At this stage of *Maus*, English is not yet a language of survival.[5] Rather, this first meeting represents English as a romantic language of secrets and deciphering as well as a property that is acquired through various kinds of labor. Indeed, it is through the speaking of, and the speaking about, English that one sees class as a key factor in accounting for experience and perception in *Maus*. Moreover, English becomes the site in which fantasies of both mastery and transformation are entertained and played out. These fantasies will continue to operate when, in three remarkable episodes in Maus II, English becomes the language of survival and the language of the survivor.

Early in Maus II, English returns to the foreground, serving as a form of knowledge that can generate extraordinary transformations. In the context of the concentration camp, this power to transform can determine survival. After deportation to Auschwitz and separation from Anja upon arrival, Vladek tries simply to remain alive. Faced with little food, insufficient clothing, and a constant threat of brutal death, relief comes in an unexpected manner. The kapo of Vladek's barracks decides to find a tutor in English and, after examining the proficiency of the candidates, deems Vladek the best qualified.[6] During his three-month tenure as the kapo's tutor, Vladek is able to eat and dress well and to obtain protection. Under the eye of a Polish kapo interested in bettering his own circumstances, English becomes the key to survival.

English can have such leverage because of, in the kapo's words, its "worth." The kapo wants to learn English because it will stand him in good stead with the Allies when the war is over. In the kapo's view, language is generally a means to improve social status, and English is the specific instrument to achieve that end in the future. The kapo's reference to the worth of English indicates that English has the capacity not only to aid survival but also to secure privileged status in the society one inhabits.

This view of the worth of English suggests that English is not "pure," that it does not inhabit a place outside camp society but rather, like other commodities, is subject to the particular logic and laws of camp life. And like other simple commodities in Auschwitz for which there is great demand and little supply, its value rises astronomically.

Vladek's competence in English, and the association with the kapo that it garners, enables him to achieve a meteoric rise in status. By means of this facility he obtains not only food but also preferential clothing—"With everything fitted," says Vladek, "I looked like a million" (II:33)—and secures privileges with which he can help friends. That Vladek's rise in status is so closely associated with his competence in English is powerfully suggestive. For paradoxically, in the midst of the deprivation of Auschwitz, Vladek's success fulfills his "dream of America"—a dream of transformation that presumably centered on the acquisition of material abundance and originally motivated his own study of English.

The power of English to transform circumstances continues even as conditions worsen. The next instance in which English figures centrally occurs in the last stages of the war, after Vladek and the other prisoners in Auschwitz were compelled to endure a death march. Ending up in Germany, in the concentration camp Dachau, Vladek registers the new degree of torment he underwent: "And here, in Dachau, my troubles began" (II:91). It is this phrase, of course, that Spiegelman uses for the subtitle of *Maus II*. On one level, the phrase is clearly ironic because absurd: Vladek's troubles began significantly earlier. The clumsiness of the formulation is also emblematic of the problems involved in telling a story of this kind. By emphasizing through the subtitle an idiom that is inappropriate for the circumstances to which it refers, Art calls attention to both Vladek's foreignness—the difficulty of mastering English idioms—and to the foreignness of the experience—a degree of suffering that resists idiomatic formulation.

On another level, however, it is clear that Vladek (or Art) wishes to suggest with this phrase that a new dimension of anguish here enters the story, anguish generated by a set of conditions in Dachau at the end of the war that brings Vladek closer to death than ever before—they were, he says, "waiting only to die" (II:91). Here, then, when conditions have become most acute, English once again determines survival. On the verge of starvation, Vladek meets a Frenchman who, in a camp filled only with Eastern Europeans, is desperate to find someone to speak to. Vladek and the Frenchman discover they share a common language, English, and daily conversation relieves the Frenchman's isolation. Grateful to Vladek, the Frenchman, a non-Jew who benefits from extra rations mailed to him via the Red Cross, "insisted," says Vladek, "to share with me, and it saved me my life" (II:93).

Several aspects of this episode recall the earlier situation in Auschwitz: Vladek's interlocutor is a non-Jew, a fellow prisoner, and English is a language foreign to both speakers. Again, Vladek's ability to speak English results in his receiving abundant food in a situation where others are starving to death. The worth of English, however, is at least tacitly redefined. English here is not valued as a commodity but rather as a therapy, as a means of countering the madness of isolation that the Frenchman suffers. The salvific encounter with the Frenchman in Dachau also recalls the original English episode with Anja. As in that case, Vladek's ability to speak English provokes in the Frenchman an identical question: "How do you know English?" Vladek's response is virtually the same one he gave to Anja, foregrounding the "dream of America" as the motivating force for learning English.

Once in America, however, Vladek's dream of the future becomes trans-

formed into a nightmare about the past, and this transformation is most glar-
ingly felt when Spiegelman refers again to the French benefactor and to the
English that linked him and his father. The two corresponded after the war,
writing in English, an English that Vladek "taught him," but Vladek destroyed the letters along with Anja's memoirs.

Up to the end of the war, the English that plays such a vital role in
Vladek's story is spoken only by non-native speakers, by those for whom English is the "other tongue."[7] Although thus far in *Maus II* knowledge of English has meant the power to determine survival, "knowledge" refers to only
a relative mastery, a timely, if partial, competence among those who have
little or none. But when the American army arrives, the real masters of the
language set the standard for competence. Nevertheless, English continues to
play a vital, if altered, role in Vladek's story. Notably, Vladek's knowledge of
English no longer needs to be the key to survival that it was in the previous
episodes. Although no longer the language of survival per se, English becomes the language of the survivor. For, in response to the army's command
"Identify yourselves" (II:111), Spiegelman does not represent Vladek giving
his name or any other of the usual factual details that might well be the common response to such a command. Rather, Vladek responds by telling for the
first time his story of "how we survived to here" (II:112). Importantly, although they are still in Europe, the first telling of the story of the Holocaust
is in English, and to an American audience, a telling, moreover, that is
linked to identity.

Even while English is playing a key role in negotiating the change from
survival to survivor and in constructing Vladek's postwar identity as a witness, the encounter with the native speakers of English ushers in another,
more problematic dimension. As the liberated Vladek settles in with the
Americans and English becomes the language of daily discourse, there is
something unsettling about the relations that are mediated by the English
they speak. For as it turns out, this English is spoken as much by colonizers
as by liberators. Initially, Vladek and his friend are permitted to stay with the
Americans only on the condition that they "keep the joint clean and make
our beds" (II:112). The condition, in other words, is that Vladek and his
friend serve as domestic servants for the soldiers. This imposition of servant
status as the condition for staying under the protection of the Americans is
accentuated when the frame that Spiegelman uses to exemplify the work that
the survivors do shows Vladek receiving gifts for shining shoes and being

called "Willie" (II:112),[8] servile work and nomenclature that recall the stigmatized position imposed by white Americans on "Negroes" of this time. Although they conquer the Nazis and set free their victims, the American liberators are nevertheless primed, through gesture and language, to enact the role of colonizer, even subjecting (while liberating) those for whom, presumably, they have gone to war in the first place. In this climactic episode, then, when English as other tongue encounters English as mother tongue, English thus becomes even more deeply associated with mastery and domination.

How does this account of English as the language of survival inform the story Vladek tells in English, the story told by the survivor? How are we to understand the association of English with knowledge, with power, with transformation, and eventually with the capacity to attest to one's identity, on the one hand, and the fractured English with which Vladek testifies, on the other hand? And how does the tension between English as the competent language of survival and English as the incompetent language of the survivor address the issue of representing the Holocaust in English and the issue, more generally, of representing the Holocaust?

In one respect, the function of this "incompetence" is clear and forceful. Vladek's accented English is mimetically appropriate for a Polish Jewish immigrant to America, and critics have noted in this light that Art has a "good ear."[9] But, I want to suggest, Vladek's "tortured visualized prose" (N. K. Miller, "Cartoons of the Self" 58) is not only meant to represent an English-speaking "foreigner" but is also meant to torture English into being a foreign language. Indeed, this quality of "foreignness" is the means by which English can become a language of testimony. By fracturing Vladek's English and by making it the most foreign language in *Maus* (a point to which I will return), Spiegelman uses it to convey the foreignness of the Holocaust itself.[10]

That the torturing of Vladek's English does more than reveal Art's ear for language can be appreciated by contrasting it with the way Spiegelman represents the language of the other survivors in *Maus*. These other émigrés— Mala, Pavel, and Anja—also European-born and arriving in the United States no earlier than the end of the war, would seem to be candidates for an accent more or less equal to that of Vladek. But Spiegelman presents them as fluent in English, speaking like natives, virtually without accent. We know that these survivors are foreigners only by *what* they say and *what* is said about them, not by *how* they say it. It is for Vladek alone that Spiegelman reserves the distortions of syntax, the malapropisms, the quirky idiom—the stylistic correlatives, as it were, of an accent.[11]

Although the inflection of an individual voice, Vladek's accent also shapes the aesthetic structure of *Maus*, providing Spiegelman with the means to represent, and distinguish, present and past. For a time, says Spiegelman, he entertained the possibility of drawing the past episodes in black and white, the present episodes in color, but rejected such a blunt visual dichotomy as too simplistic ("Art on Art," *The Complete Maus*).[12] Yet what resisted visual coding yielded to an aural one: for episodes in the past, Spiegelman uses fluent, colloquial English to represent the languages of Europe as spoken by their native speakers; for episodes in the present, Vladek's broken, accented English serves as a constant marker. On the surface this strategy seems misguided; Continental languages do not deserve an English better than English itself. But within the terms *Maus* establishes, Vladek's broken English becomes the means by which Spiegelman articulates the incommensurability between present and past.

Spiegelman's decision to place a distinctive burden on Vladek's English as a vehicle to represent the Holocaust came only after experimentation with other options. The earliest publication of the *Maus* project, a three-page vignette appearing in 1972, already draws Vladek recounting his ordeal by means of a "tortured prose."[13] But, for at least two reasons, Vladek's accented narration in this earlier installment is less well defined and exceptional than it becomes in later full-length treatment. First, Vladek speaks with an accent not only when he is recounting his story but also when he is shown in his European past; the distinction that informs both *Maus I* and *Maus II* between Vladek in America and Vladek in Europe, between Vladek in the present and Vladek in the past, does not obtain. Second, and perhaps even more fundamental, is that all European Jews "speak" with an accent. "The safest thing it would be that we kill him" (2), says one of the Jews hiding in a bunker with Vladek. A decade or so later, in a revised version of this scene in *Maus I*, Spiegelman eliminates the accent, and now the Polish Jew says simply: "The safest thing would be to kill him" (I:113).

The contrast between the vignette and the books shows an evolution in Spiegelman's representational vision of English. In the earlier version, every victim speaks with an accent, a strategy that divides the linguistic world of *Maus* between native speaker and foreigner, between American and European. But the full-length later works divide up the universe of speakers differently. Whereas in the 1972 version English was twisted to link members of a group, in the books the erasure of group accent and exaggeration of Vladek's individual one make Vladek's American English singular. Paradoxically, it is not the representation of the events of the Holocaust itself that is most foreign to the American readers of *Maus*; it is rather the *telling about* the Holocaust, the testimony, that carries the burden of everything that is foreign.

That Vladek's broken English testimony is meant to carry immense authority is attested by the single instance in which Vladek speaks from a different vantage point. On the way home with Vladek from the supermarket, Art's wife, Françoise, stops to pick up a black hitchhiker, whom Spiegelman represents as speaking a highly inflected (and also visually "tortured") form of Black English. Vladek condemns Françoise's seemingly charitable gesture, using degrading racial stereotypes to justify his own admonitions. Inclusion of this unflattering view of Vladek's bigotry—he himself, according to Art, seems to have not learned the lesson of the Holocaust—is clearly meant to complicate the reader's reaction to Vladek.

But the episode is made more remarkable by Spiegelman's deployment of Vladek's language. For at the moment when the hitchhiker speaks broken English, Vladek relinquishes his own. Instead, he expresses his bigoted regrets in his native Polish (the only example of Vladek speaking Polish in either *Maus I* or *II*), represented here first in the original, then underscored with a fluent English translation. To be sure, Vladek's recourse to his native Polish allows him to vent his chauvinism without infuriating the other passengers in the car. But the movement from English to Polish also mobilizes a set of representational values. No longer telling the story of the Holocaust but rather uttering racial slurs, it is as if Vladek has foregone the right to the "tortured" English that is the vehicle for his testimony. In reverting to his native Polish, he finally regains a fluency—even the English translation has overcome the foreignness that defines his usual American voice—but that fluency comes at the expense of, and suspends, the authority his tortured English evinces. Moreover, the episode witnesses a shift of roles and voices, for the black hitchhiker, the victim of Vladek's bigotry, himself speaks an English that, in its idiosyncrasy and visual effect, approximates the foreign English that defines Vladek's authoritative voice as a survivor.

On one level, *Maus* celebrates English. By displaying its heroic capacity to transform and pacify the most adverse conditions, *Maus* conveys a sense of the unlimited power of English, of its almost magical potency, even of its harboring the secret of life and death. Seemingly, English can master anything it confronts, can dominate whatever demands subjection. This celebration would seem to authorize English as a language of testimony, investing it with the knowledge and power to chronicle the events of the Holocaust with unparalleled eloquence. This glorification of English would likely confirm what American readers of the late twentieth century believe about the language they—or their neighbors—speak.

On another level, however, Maus tells a story about limitations, and particularly about the limitations of English as a language of the Holocaust. Maus inscribes these limits ironically, designating fluency, competence, and mastery as relative and questionable accomplishments. The very capacity to use words well often becomes the ironic sign of blindness and coercion. Significantly, Maus enforces the limitations of English by representing as authoritative an English that is uniquely broken, incompetent, unmastered. Indeed, the only English by which to tell "a survivor's tale" is one that is singularly foreign. Such a repositioning of English would seem to go against expectations of an American audience, asking them, asking us, to question the fantasy—one that Maus itself rehearses—that English can know and master everything, even the Holocaust.

Notes

I am grateful to Ruth Clements, Jorg Drewitz, Nancy Harrowitz, and Herbert Levine for their reading of and comments on this manuscript at various stages.

1. Ezrahi's more recent views pertaining to language and the Holocaust can be found in several essays, including "'The Grave in the Air': Unbound Metaphors in Post-Holocaust Poetry" (in Friedlander, Probing the Limits 259–76) and "Conversation in the Cemetery: Dan Pagis and the Prosaics of Memory" (in Hartman, Holocaust Remembrance 121–33).

Ezrahi is one of a procession of critics who have ventured a taxonomy of Holocaust languages. See, e.g., Steiner; Roskies, "Scribes of the Ghetto," in Against the Apocalypse; Gilman, "The Ashes of the Holocaust and the Closure of Self-Hatred," in Jewish Self-Hatred; Levi, "Communicating," in The Drowned and the Saved; Felman, "The Return of the Voice: Claude Lanzmann's Shoah," in Felman and Laub, Testimony.

2. Although the anthology contains writing from 1942 to 1963, it was first published in 1968, with additional printings appearing regularly through the 1970s. The

anthology thus came into circulation at approximately the same time Spiegelman was working on and eventually publishing his first cartoons representing the Holocaust.

3. It is, I think, fairly clear that by deploying the German word for the title, Spiegelman is asking the reader to view the Jews/mice through the Germans'/cats' eyes, a strategy that emphasizes both Jewish weakness and vulnerability and German power and ruthlessness. The strategy of the title parallels and reinforces the visual animal metaphor. The appropriateness of this metaphor has been the subject of substantial critical contention.

That said, I believe that the reading I give the title, emphasizing the interplay between English and German, can be further supported by noting that whereas Spiegelman's choice of the singular, *Maus*, enables the play between English and German, the choice of the plural, *Mäuse*, would not. And yet it is probably more fitting that the title (like the image of the mice on the cover) be in the plural. I therefore suggest that, at least in part, Spiegelman opted for the singular to invoke the play between the two languages. I would like to thank Jorg Drewitz for drawing my attention to the singular/plural issue.

4. See, e.g., Hirsch 19–22.

5. By the phrase "language of survival" I am referring to the startling capacity of English as represented in *Maus* to determine survival during the Holocaust. This connotation is not synonymous with that of Sander Gilman in *Jewish Self-Hatred*.

6. As Vladek makes clear in the transcripts, his English was merely good enough: "And I, I was a teacher in English. Here I couldn't be, of course. But there I gave lessons." Spiegelman, "The Working Transcripts," in *The Complete Maus*.

7. See Kachru, *The Other Tongue*. The term refers to the English of non-native speakers.

8. Vladek notes in the transcripts that "Willie" properly translates the Polish "Vladek." Clearly, then, Willie was not a name chosen by the Americans simply in order to signal superiority. But since Spiegelman does not make the reader of *Maus* aware of the connection between the English and Polish names, the context, gestures, and language suggest the racial overtones.

9. As Alice Yaeger Kaplan phrases it, "One of the many extraordinary features of *Maus* is that Spiegelman gets the voices right, he gets the order of the words right, he manages to capture the intonations of Eastern Europe spoken by Queens" ("Theweleit and Spiegelman" 155).

10: To be sure, *Maus* represents a range of languages foreign to English: Hebrew, Polish, Yiddish, German, French. Whereas Vladek's Yiddish-English functions to estrange the reader, these other languages generally do not function so as to insist on their own foreignness; Spiegelman uses words so common to even non-speakers that they do not need translation, or, in the case of Vladek's Polish, he subtitles it with fluent English. The Hebrew that appears in *Maus*, to my mind, has a more ambiguous status; I hope to address its significance in a longer version of this essay.

Felman uses a similar metaphor of "foreignness" in analyzing Lanzmann's *Shoah* in "The Return of the Voice," and I am indebted to her discussion therein. Yet Spiegelman and Lanzmann pursue this notion by means of contrasting strategies. Whereas Lanzmann foregrounds the foreignness of the Holocaust by making sure multiple survivors speak in languages (native or adopted) different from one another and different from the narrative language of the film itself (French), Spiegelman makes this foreignness palpable through the voice of a single survivor whose testimony is in the same language as the narrative of the graphic novel.

11. While significant in its own right, Spiegelman's representation of Vladek's accent falls within the context and conventions of Yiddish voices in American literature, a point apparently overlooked by most critics. For a summary of this context and these conventions see Hellerstein.

12. In the early 1950s, Alain Resnais employed this strategy in his film *Night and Fog.*

13. First published as "Maus," *Funny Aminals* 1 (1972), reprinted in *Comix, Book* 2, ed. Denis Kitchen (New York: Magazine Management, 1974); included in "The Appendices" of *The Complete Maus.* In "Maus," Spiegelman also deployed accent unevenly. On the one hand, some adult Jews accent thickly ("Psst . . . You vant a potato? to buy?") while Jewish children have no accent ("Next time I want to play the cat").

3
Kitsch, "Commerz," and Cybermice

Marketing *Maus*

7

"We Were Talking Jewish"

Art Spiegelman's *Maus* as "Holocaust" Production

Michael P. Rothberg

Prologue

"He's dying, he's dying. *Look at him*. Tell them over there. *You saw it.*
Don't forget. . . . Remember this, remember this."

Jan Karski, speaking in Claude Lanzmann's *Shoah*

In the final comic set piece of Philip Roth's novelistic memoir about his relationship with his father, *Patrimony: A True Story*, Herman Roth attempts to cajole his author-son into helping one of his card-playing buddies from the Y get his memoirs of World War II published. Philip is understandably resistant—especially as his father has regularly asked him over the years to aid other aspiring authors of books about home mortgages or annuity funds. Of course, a book about the Holocaust is different, and Philip even admits that he has taught Holocaust memoirs and briefly knew Primo Levi.

The invocation of Levi and the ensuing description of his suicide hardly foreshadow a comic scene. Indeed, Philip wonders "if Primo Levi and Walter Herrmann [his father's friend] could possibly have met at Auschwitz. They would have been about the same age and able to understand each other in German—thinking that it might improve his chances of surviving, Primo had worked hard at Auschwitz to learn the language of the Master Race. In what way did Walter account for *his* survival? What had *he* learned? However amateurish or simply written the book, I expected something like that to be its subject" (*Patrimony* 212). But Walter's subject and the lesson he learned in Nazi Germany turn out to be quite different. In fact, they turn out to be comic and even obscene. According to Walter, he was "the only man left in Berlin" (212), and his memoirs are the graphic depictions of his sexual exploits with the women who hid him, quite a twist on the usual tales of heroism and betrayal. "My book is not a book like Elie Wiesel writes," Walter honestly remarks. "I couldn't write such a tragic book. Until the camps, I had a very happy war" (213). What with Katrina and Helen and Barbara, Walter's war was more a multiple orgasm than the greatest tragedy of human history.

This odd episode at the end of *Patrimony* suggests that there might be something pornographic about making images and ultimately commodities out of the Holocaust. It is as if the fundamental obscenity of the events themselves cannot be represented without a pornographic contamination of the person doing the representing. Walter seems to grasp this truth unconsciously and displaces it into farce; this is perhaps the flip side of Levi's— and many other survivors'—ultimately tragic and desperate inability to redeem their experience by working through, and representing to themselves, the meaning of the camps. I think we might gain insight into this irony and angst about the decorum of representing destruction by considering it as a particularly (although not uniquely) Jewish question. Well before what has come to be known as "the Holocaust," certain aspects of the debate surrounding the Nazi genocide and the question of representation were foregrounded in Jewish discourse.[1] The examples of Roth and Art Spiegelman demonstrate how a biblically mandated suspicion of idolatry and image making, as well as a cultural claim to "a kind of privileged relation to the very idea of textuality" (Shohat 9), come to constitute specifically Jewish parameters, or at least "themes," of even secular Jewish writing.[2]

Roth's self-consciousness about representation in general and his tragicomic recognition of the ungraspable contamination of representing the Holocaust form the background of *Patrimony*, against which Roth frames the story of his father's losing battle with cancer. Roth uses metaphors that call upon both timeless Jewish themes of memory and survivorship and historically specific evocations of the Nazis. Despite the father's obstinate "survivor" mentality, Herman's tumor, Roth writes, "would in the end be as merciless as a blind mass of anything on the march" (136). This Nazi-like image resonates uncannily with a passage from Roth's novel *The Anatomy*

Lesson. There Roth describes not his father's actual death but an imagined version of his mother's death (a death which in reality, we know from the chronology of *Patrimony*, must have prompted *The Anatomy Lesson*). But the categories of reality and imagination become here—as everywhere in Roth's writing—hopelessly confused, since the fictional version *anticipates* the memoir. Nathan Zuckerman's mother develops a brain tumor in this 1983 novel, as Herman Roth will a few years later. Admitted into the hospital for the second time, Zuckerman's mother "was able to recognize her neurologist when he came by the room, but when he asked if she would write her name for him on a piece of paper, she took the pen from his hand and instead of 'Selma' wrote the word 'Holocaust,' perfectly spelled. This was in Miami Beach in 1970, inscribed by a woman whose writings otherwise consisted of recipes on index cards, several thousand thank-you notes, and a voluminous file of knitting instructions. Zuckerman was pretty sure that before that morning she'd never even spoken the word aloud" (269). The carefully situated Jewish mother's death serves here as a metaphor for the emergence in the Jewish community of a new understanding of "the Holocaust" in the late 1960s, an understanding that testified to the spatially and temporally displaced effect on Jewish American identity of the extermination of European Jewry (even, or especially, for Jews comfortably situated "in Miami Beach in 1970"). The association of Holocaust and tumor forged by Roth in *The Anatomy Lesson* reappears in *Patrimony*, a memoir that further measures the health of the collective and individual Jewish body.

Patrimony's last line, and most frequently repeated motif, is a slogan often applied to the Nazi genocide: "You must not forget anything" (238). This line, which so closely echoes my epigraph from *Shoah* (cited in Felman and Laub), also occurs in the passage where Philip gives his father a bath and pays special attention to the signifier of Jewish manhood: "I looked at his penis. I don't believe I'd seen it since I was a small boy, and back then I used to think it was quite big. It turned out that I had been right. It was thick and substantial and the one bodily part that didn't look at all old. . . . I looked at it intently, as though for the very first time, and waited on the thoughts. But there weren't any more, except my reminding myself to fix it in my memory for when he was dead. . . . *You must not forget anything*." Here the phallic law of the father takes on the particularly Jewish imperative to "remember everything accurately" (177), a commandment metonymically linked to the contemplation of the one "substantial" organ of his father's body that resists the deterioration of time. In *The Anatomy Lesson* Roth had already connected the deterioration caused by cancer with a maternal evisceration (of body and language). In *Patrimony*—despite the holocaust of cancer and the cancer of the Holocaust—the Jewish communal body survives in and through the memory of the solidity of the father: his "substantial" penis and his "vernacular" speech, with "all its durable force" (181).

The power and ultimately the sentimentality of Roth's portrait arise from his manner of combining traditional Jewish motifs of survival, memory, and the law with a subtle evocation of the Holocaust in order to depict a Jewish life in the diaspora. Roth's text simultaneously exposes the potential for pornographic kitsch in his account of Walter Herrmann and draws upon a kind of emotional kitsch in the depiction of his father. Such a paradoxical stance constitutes a particular, and in this case gendered, configuration of contemporary Jewish American identity—one in which the abuses of the Holocaust have been made manifest by years of facile mechanical reproduction, but in which the Holocaust still serves as the dominant metaphor for collective and individual Jewish survival.

Problems of Representation

Sometimes it almost seems that "the Holocaust" is a corporation headed by Elie Wiesel, who defends his patents with articles in the Arts and Leisure section of the Sunday *Times*.
                    Philip Lopate, "Resistance to the Holocaust"

I resist becoming the Elie Wiesel of the comic book.
                    Art Spiegelman, "A Conversation with Art Spiegelman"

In moving from Philip Roth to Art Spiegelman—that is, from the comic to the comic book—the motifs of survival and suffering become radically reconfigured even as the subjects of that survival and suffering (the authors' fathers) seem so similar. Within the context of the ban on graven images and the "mystique" of the text—from which Roth derives both his pornographic ironization and his narrative sentimentalization—the two volumes of Art Spiegelman's "survivor's tale," *Maus*, come as a particular shock. *Maus* represents a new strand of Jewish American self-construction related to but significantly divergent from Roth's writings. Spiegelman transgresses the sacredness of Auschwitz by depicting in comic strip images his survivor-father's suffering and by refusing to sentimentalize the survivor. A phrase from Roth's memoir actually suits Spiegelman's depiction of this father, Vladek, better than it does that of Herman: "what goes into survival isn't always pretty" (*Patrimony* 126). Although Spiegelman is no Walter Herrmannesque comic pornographer of the Holocaust, his use of coded animal identities for the ethnic and national groups he depicts certainly strikes readers at first as somewhat "obscene." Spiegelman even admits that going into a comic book store is "a little like going into a porno store" ("Conversation"). But the power and originality of Spiegelman's effort derive quite specifically from this shock of obscenity which demands that we confront "the Holocaust" *as* visual representation, as one more commodity in the American culture industry.

For Jewish readers, the challenge of *Maus* will likely be even harder to assimilate because the experience (and the memory) of the Holocaust, even for those of us who know it only at a distance, remains, fifty years later, one of the defining moments of American Jewish identity. Although the situation is beginning to change, Jewish identity remains relatively undertheorized, if overrepresented, in contemporary culture and criticism. Those of us who occupy Jewish subject positions thus come to the task of what that most talmudic of anti-Semites, Céline, has called "reading Jewish" with an impoverished set of tools to help us to examine our being-in-America.[3] In this essay I will pursue a double-edged strategy, demystifying Céline's assumption of an essential Jewishness while at the same time demonstrating how Spiegelman brings a secular Jewish interpretive specificity to his rendering of the Holocaust.[4]

The need for an adequate discourse of Jewish identity strikes me as politically critical because of two phenomena that require, among other things, a specifically Jewish response: the worldwide reassertion of anti-Semitism and the relatively free rein American Jews have given to the often oppressive policies of the state of Israel. *Maus* assists us in this intellectual and political task because, even if it rarely addresses these issues directly, it does tell us at least as much about the contemporary situation of Jews in the North American diaspora as about "the Holocaust." Or rather, it meditates as much on the production of the concept of "the Holocaust" and of the concept of Jewishness as it does on Nazi inhumanity.

Maus critiques popular productions of Jewishness and the Holocaust not from a safe distance but from within, in an accessible vernacular form. In his "goodbye to *Maus*" comments, Spiegelman worries that his books "may also have given people an easy way to deal with the Holocaust, to feel that they've 'wrapped it up'" ("Saying Goodbye," 45). While the texts' very commodity form participates in the marketing of the Holocaust—*Maus I* and *Maus II* were first "wrapped up" together in boxed sets in the 1991 pre-Hanukkah/ Christmas season—they also simultaneously resist this "wrapping up." As Robert Storr notes, Spiegelman creates a visual pun on the back cover of *Maus II* that connects the stripes of his father's prison uniform with the stripes of the jacket's bar code. The text's very "wrapping" asks the reader to consider its implication in a system of economic entrapment. The self-conscious irony of this parallel between imprisonment and commodity production marks one of the many places where Spiegelman rebels against the terms of his success; such cleverness, however, reminds us that this very rebellion constitutes a large part of the artist's appeal. This paradox, which is foregrounded everywhere in *Maus*, can be read as a comment not only on the status of memory and history in capitalist culture but also on recent debates about the possibility and desirability of representing the Nazi genocide.

Among the last *Maus* images, two that Spiegelman contributed to *Tikkun* ("Saying Goodbye") stand out as emblematic of the dangers the artist recognizes in mass-marketing death. In the first, Spiegelman draws his characteristic "Maus" self-portrait standing in front of a smiling Mickey Mouse background and gazing mournfully at a "real" mouse that he cups in his hands. The uneasy coexistence of three levels of representation in the same pictorial space literalizes the artist's position—backed by the industry, but everywhere confronted with the detritus of the real. In the second drawing, the artist sits in front of a static-filled TV screen and plays with his baby daughter, who is holding a Mickey Mouse doll; silhouetted in the background, mouse corpses hang from nooses. This drawing transposes a frame from *Maus I* (I:84) in which Spiegelman depicts his family (Vladek, Anja, and the soon-to-be-dead Richieu) before a backdrop of Jews hung by the Germans in a Polish ghetto. This transposition, along with the drawing of the three mice, illustrates an aspect of repetition compulsion that the work as a whole enacts. The Nazi violence lives on, with the survivor son just as much the subject and object of the terror as his father.

Spiegelman's self-portrait on the jacket flap of *Maus II* also delineates this tension inherent in the relationships among the artist, his historical sources, his representational universe, and his public artworks.[5] Wearing a mouse mask, Spiegelman sits at his desk with *Raw* and *Maus* posters behind him and a Nazi prison guard outside the window. One morbid detail stands out: the picture reveals Art's ubiquitous cigarettes as "Cremo" brand. We find the key to this deadly pun when Vladek refers to the crematorium as a "cremo building" (II:70). Such black humor implies that with every cigarette, with every image—and Spiegelman seems both to smoke and to draw relentlessly—he does not just represent the Holocaust but literally brings it back to life (which is to say, death). Taken together, these disturbing portraits figure forth *Maus*'s strange relationship to the ashes of the real—simultaneously haunted by the inadequacy of representation in the face of the catastrophe of history and overconscious of the all-too-real materiality that representations take on through the intervention of the culture industry.

The impossibility of satisfactorily specifying the genre of *Maus* expresses this representational paradox. After *Maus II* came out, Spiegelman requested that his book be moved from the fiction to the nonfiction best-sellers list; but a few years earlier, in an introduction to a collection of "comix" from *Raw*, the magazine he edits with his wife, Françoise Mouly, Spiegelman remarked that he had been at work on his "comic-book novel, *Maus*" (Spiegelman and Mouly 7). While it is perhaps merely an artist's whim, I read this seeming contradiction as grounded in the specificity of the problem of representing the Holocaust, an event taken at once as *paradigmatic* of the human potential for evil and as a truly *singular* expression of that potential which frustrates and ought to forbid all comparison with other events.

On the one hand, critics such as Theodor Adorno, Maurice Blanchot, and Berel Lang have suggested that "after Auschwitz," poetry and fiction are impossible.[6] This proscription I understand as moral rather than technical—it would be unseemly, these writers imply, to fabricate in the face of the need for testimonial and witnessing. These critics have also tended to assert that the Nazi genocide constituted a radical and unprecedented break within Western culture, an absolutist position that tends to totalize and prescribe the practices of representation in the wake of the event. The impossibility of fiction is also true in another sense. After the Nazis' rationalized irrationality, no horror remains unthinkable; neither the "journey to the end of night" of a Céline nor a "theater of cruelty" à la Artaud seems fantastic or unreal any longer. On the other hand, such a historical trauma also de-realizes human experience. Accounts of the death camps in memoirs never fail to document the fictional, oneiric aura that confronted the newly arrived prisoner.[7] By situating a nonfictional story in a highly mediated, unreal, "comic" space, Spiegelman captures the hyperintensity of Auschwitz—at once more real than real and more impossible than impossible.

Yet *Maus* also replies to the debates about representation in ways that go beyond formalist subversion of generic categories and that indeed shift the terrain of the debate onto the cultural conditions, possibilities, and constraints of Holocaust representation (thus displacing the frequently prescriptive epistemologies and ontologies of the debate set by Adorno, Blanchot, and Lang). Spiegelman frankly recognizes the inevitable commodification of culture, even Holocaust culture. In *Maus*'s multimedia marketing (through magazines, exhibitions, the broadcast media, and CD-ROM) as well as through its generic identity as a (non)fiction comic strip, Spiegelman's project refuses (and indeed exposes) the sentimentality of the elite notions of culture that ground the Adornean position. Spiegelman's handling of the Holocaust denies the existence of an autonomous realm in which theoretical issues can be debated without reference to the material bases of their production. He heretically reinserts the Holocaust into the political realm by highlighting its necessary imbrication in the public sphere and in commodity production.

Voice and Authenticity

> My parents survived hell and moved to the suburbs.
>
> Art Spiegelman (sketch for *Maus*)

As a primarily visual artist, Spiegelman challenges dominant representations of the Holocaust by *drawing* attention to the pornographic effect of graven images within a Mickey Mouse industry dedicated to mechanical reproduction in the name of profit. But *Maus* also operates significantly on the level of text and, in doing so, takes part in the discursive production of contemporary Jewish identity. Spiegelman makes analogies between image and text "grammar" and claims that, unlike most of his projects, *Maus* is "a comic book driven by the word" ("Conversation"). This "word" can only refer to the words of the father, which Spiegelman renders not as mystical text but as fractured speech—what Roth calls, in the case of his father, "the vernacular" (181). As he makes clear in both volumes, Spiegelman created this comic book by taping Vladek's voice as he recounted his life and then transcribing the events with accompanying pictures into *Maus*. He makes a particular point of describing the pains he went to in order to ensure the "authenticity" of Vladek's transcribed voice. Many readers have testified that much of the power of *Maus* comes from the heavily accented cadences—the shtetl effect—of Vladek's narrative.[8] Spiegelman's staging of an exhibit on the making of *Maus* at the Museum of Modern Art (MOMA), complete with the actual tapes of Vladek from which he worked, has, for most people, tended to reinforce this aura of documentary realism.

However, in a perceptive discussion of *Maus* and the MOMA exhibit, Nancy K. Miller has pointed to the illusion that grounds this version of realism: "What surprised me when I listened to the tape was an odd disjunction between the quality of the voice and the inflections rendered in the panels. For while Vladek *on tape* regularly misuses prepositions—'I have seen on my own eyes,' 'they were shooting to prisoners,' [and] mangles idioms . . . the total *aural* effect, unlike the typically tortured *visualized* prose of the dialogue in the comic balloons, is one of extraordinary fluency" ("Cartoons of the Self" 51). A particularly good example of Spiegelman's (unconscious) tendency to overdo his father's accent comes in a passage, featured in the exhibit and broadcast on *Talk of the Nation*, in which Vladek recounts the shooting of a prisoner, a shooting that reminds him of having seen a neighbor shoot a rabid dog. In the book, Art has Vladek say, "How amazing it is that a human being reacts the same like this neighbor's dog" (II:82). But on tape, Vladek says simply and grammatically, "How amazing it is that a human being is like a dog." This passage also contradicts Spiegelman's assertion that the changes he made were dictated by the necessity of condensing Vladek's speech, since in this case he adds words. For related reasons of affect, Spiegelman occasionally alters Vladek's words to keep up with the changing language habits of contemporary English-speaking Jews, as when he renders his father's phrase "We were talking Jewish" as "We spoke Yiddish" (I:150); this subtle semantic gentrification registers the uneasiness at the heart of Jewish identities as well as their susceptibility to change over time.[9]

Spiegelman is right: the power of *Maus* does derive from his father's words and evocative accent. But a close analysis of these words demonstrates the artist's reconstruction of a marked dialect. In *Jewish Self-Hatred*, Sander Gilman discusses the perception of Jews as possessing a "hidden" and devalued language of ethnic difference called, appropriately enough for Spiegelman's work, *mauscheln*. Gilman quotes "Hitler's racial mentor, Julius Streicher" for his description of this perceived "hidden language of the Jews": "Speech takes place with a racially determined intonation: *Mauscheln*. The Hebrews speak German in a unique, singing manner. One can recognize Jews and Jewesses immediately by their language, without having seen them" (312). Arguably, an element of self-hatred exists in Spiegelman's careful "mauschelnizing" of *Maus*, displaced into aggression against the vernacular of the father. But another reading of the linguistic manipulations of the book, analogous to my reading of the images and the animal motif, would emphasize the irony, conscious or not, that uses caricature to unsettle assumptions about the "naturalness" of identities. Self-hatred and (more obviously) aggression against the father would then become not so much qualities of the work as two of its significant themes.

The source tape of the passage from *Maus II* about the shooting of the prisoner/neighbor's dog carries another level of significance for an understanding of the verbal narration of the story. As John Hockenberry remarked to Spiegelman after playing the segment of tape on NPR, during Vladek's telling of the story the barking of dogs can be heard in the background ("Conversation"). Nobody, including Vladek, I would guess, could definitively say whether the dogs simply triggered the memory of the association between the prisoner and the dog in Vladek's mind or, more radically, whether the association derived from the present circumstances of the narration. But in either case, this example points to the importance of the moment of enunciation in the construction of a narrative.[10] This narratological insight is not simply a truism of literary analysis; *Maus* everywhere thematizes the constitutive relationship between the present and different moments of the past. The importance of this temporal structure emerges in various facets of the work: in the constant movement between the tense interviews between father and son and the unrolling of the Holocaust story; in *Maus II*'s insistent self-reflexivity and thematization of writer's block; and in Spiegelman's practice—in exhibit and interview—of revealing the process of "making *Maus*."[11] Not simply a work of memory or a testimony bound for some archive of Holocaust documentation, *Maus* actively intervenes in the present, questioning the status of "memory," "testimony," and "Holocaust" even as it makes use of them.

The Discursive Body

> Pain is the most powerful aid to mnemonics.
> Friedrich Nietzsche, *On the Genealogy of Morals*

Thus far I have not differentiated between the two volumes of *Maus*, but Spiegelman's style clearly changes during the course of the thirteen years of his work on this project. While both volumes focus on the interplay of the past in the present and the present in the past, as Spiegelman has remarked ("Conversation"), *Maus: A Survivor's Tale: My Father Bleeds History* concentrates more on the woundedness and wounding of the familial body, as its title suggests. Because Spiegelman wrote much of *Maus II: And Here My Troubles Began* in the wake of widespread popular acclaim, the second volume explicitly interrogates its own status in the public sphere, reflexively commenting on its production and interrogating the staging of "the Holocaust." But given the serial nature of their publication in *Raw* over the course of many years, both volumes of *Maus* resist such easy binaries: the form and content of the comic strip's unfolding put into question the propriety of present/past and private/public distinctions.

Maus I, among its many functions, serves to catalog "the Jew's body," an important concept in emergent Jewish theorizing that has been elaborated most fully by Sander Gilman in his book of that name.[12] In focusing on multifarious "representations and the reflection of these representations in the world of those who stereotype as well as those who are stereotyped" (1), Gilman draws attention to the constitutive character of "difference," a category that need not succumb to the kind of binary ossification *Maus* resists. Spiegelman, like Gilman, anatomizes various Jewish bodies, including his parents' and his own; he draws attention to feet (I:20,83), eyes (I:40), hands (I:51), the beard (I:65), and the voice (throughout). Subtly but perhaps decisively different are the Jewish/mouse noses, understood in contrast to the upturned snouts of the Polish pigs. When Vladek and Anja walk as fugitives through Sosnowiec, Spiegelman shows them hiding their noses by wearing pig masks (as he himself will later don a mouse mask). But while Vladek is able confidently to feign Polishness, Anja's body leaks Jewishness, and her mouse tail drags behind her: "Anja—her appearance—you could see more easy she was Jewish" (I:136).

The emphasis on the body and its difference, as all commentators have noted, reinscribes the same essential ethnic differences that drove the Nazi war machine. But this discourse on the body is fundamentally destabilized by the more pressing truth about the Jewish body under Nazism that haunts Spiegelman's story: its disappearance. Richieu's and Anja's absence, and, by analogy, the absence of the millions of (Jewish and gay and Gypsy) victims underlies Spiegelman's aesthetic choice of grappling with the Holocaust as an impossible visual text. Spiegelman's story does not seek, however, to flatten out analogous differences into a morality tale of universalist pluralism, but draws its power from negativity: an intimacy with death, pain, and loss motivates *Maus*'s memory work.

In *Maus I*, the multiply disappeared story of Art's mother constitutes the primary wound around which the story turns and points to an almost erased narrative of Jewish gender relations.[13] Anja's story is absent for three reasons, all significant: her original diaries from Poland were lost in the war (indicating the ultimate destruction at the hands of the Nazis [I:84]); she cannot tell her own story because she committed suicide twenty-three years after the war (indicating the unassimilable damage to the "survivors"); and Vladek later threw out her notebooks, in which she probably reconstructed her diaries (indicating the legacy of violence reproduced in some "survivors"). *Maus I* builds toward the revelation of Vladek's crime against Anja and memory, which Art names "murder" (I:159). Anja's suicide and Vladek's inability to mourn her death radically upset the notion of "survival" that ordinarily legitimates the Holocaust memoir; as Art puts it, "in some ways [Vladek] *didn't* survive" (II:90). I don't think it would be an exaggeration to read *Maus I* as an attempt to occupy, or speak from, the impossible position of the mother's suicide; in this, Spiegelman's project resembles Claude Lanzmann's *Shoah*, which attempts "less to narrate history than to *reverse the suicide*" of many of its potential sources (Felman and Laub 216).

Spiegelman cannot literally reverse his mother's suicide, but he does question representations of Jewish women in his careful tracing of Anja's absent place of enunciation. Such a strategy takes on further significance given the relative lack of attention paid in dominant culture to the specific bodies and lives of Jewish women, a fact that emerges in the contrast between *Maus* and the respective academic and literary discourses of Sander Gilman and Philip Roth. In *The Jew's Body*, Gilman writes that "full-length studies of the actual roles of Jewish women in this world of representations [of the body] and their own complex responses are certainly needed and in fact such studies at present are in the planning or writing stages by a number of feminist critics." Gilman goes on to assert, however, that his own work "has generally focused on the nature of the male Jew and his representation in the culture of the West; it is *this* representation which I believe lies at the very heart of Western Jew-hatred" (5). Gilman points to the importance of the circumcised penis as an index of Jewishness, but, given the tendency of the last couple of generations of North Americans of all religions to circumcise their male children, perhaps this particular symbolic structure is waning. I don't find it unreasonable to assume, for example, that in a book dedicated to "the Jew's body," Orthodox women's shaved heads or the ubiquitous Jewish mother's body would merit chapters.[14]

Spiegelman, like Gilman, implicitly acknowledges the "need" for inquiry into the Jewish woman's body. But Spiegelman goes further in structuring his story around just such a lack and in repeatedly drawing attention to the gendered violence that has produced this empty space in his family's history: Art's mother has had her voice forcibly removed by Vladek's stubborn annihilation of her diaries. The fictional and nonfictional writings of Philip Roth, which (I have already argued) also mobilize family stories and historical motifs to reconfigure Jewish American identity, similarly foreground the gender asymmetry of those very stories. But—in contrast to Spiegelman's portrait of Anja—Roth renders his fictional mother, Selma Zuckerman, as essentially and eternally without language: her writing, for example, is belittled as consisting only of recipes, thank-you notes, and knitting instructions. In *Patrimony* he depicts his real mother not as a producer of language but as an archive; this "quietly efficient" woman was "the repository of our family past, the historian of our childhood and growing up" (36). There are, in the memoir, suggestions of a kind of patriarchal violence analogous to that enacted by Vladek—Bessie Roth's "once spirited, housewifely independence had been all but extinguished by [Herman's] anxious, overbearing bossiness" (36)—but, unlike Anja, Bessie is never granted an autonomous voice that transcends the domestic sphere. Although she presided within what Roth calls "her single-handed establishment of a first-class domestic-management and mothering company" (37), the mother's restriction to this limited space by a patriarchal Jewish culture never becomes thematized, since *Patrimony*, as its title suggests, is first and foremost the story of "the male line, unimpaired and happy, ascending from nascency to maturity" (230). The mother is notably absent from (although one wonders if she has taken) the family photograph that inspires this last formulation and which adorns *Patrimony*'s cover.

Both Roth and Spiegelman present narratives in which a certain version of history, the family, and the Holocaust implicitly disappears with the mother in the late 1960s and early 1970s. Selma Zuckerman dies after substituting "Holocaust" for her own name; Bessie Roth, the family "repository" and "historian," is "extinguished" upon Herman's retirement in the mid-1960s; and Anja takes her Holocaust testimony to the grave in 1968. In their wake, the history of the family and the "race" devolves into the hands of what Paul Breines, in a recent attempt to characterize post-1960s Jewish maleness, has called a "tough Jew." These three "tough" figures—Nathan, Herman Roth, and Vladek—are all equally well described by what Roth calls "obsessive stubbornness" (*Patrimony* 36). The quality is indeed ambiguous, seeming to provide at once the means for survival in difficult situations (whether historical or medical) and the resources for self- and other-directed violence in domestic and public spheres. While Roth's writing certainly produces ambivalent feelings about the "tough Jew," only Spiegelman foregrounds the ways in which this new Jewish subject has emerged through the repression (in two senses) of Jewish women's bodies and texts and the ways in which it can initiate new tales of violence.

The insertion into *Maus I* of the previously published "Prisoner on the Hell Planet"—the story of Anja's death—not only presents an expressionist stylistic rupture with the rest of the work but reopens the wound of his mother's suicide by documenting the "raw" desperation of the twenty-year-old Art. We should not read "Prisoner," however, as a less mediated expression of angst, despite its "human" characters and the reality-effect of the inserted 1958 photograph of Anja and Art. Rather, the "presence" of the maternal body here vainly attempts to compensate for what, many years later, remain the unmournable losses of Anja's suicide and of the years of psychic and political suffering that her life represents for Art. "Prisoner" draws attention to itself as at once *in excess* of the rest of *Maus*—a "realistic" supplement framed in black—and *less than* the mother (and the history) it seeks to resuscitate. With artist's signature and date (1972) following the last frame, "Prisoner" also complicates *Maus's* moment of enunciation—it simultaneously stands apart temporally and spatially from the rest of the work and yet is integrated into it. Like Art in this segment and throughout *Maus*, "Prisoner" cannot hide its difference from the totality of the family romance, but neither can it fully separate from the mother's story.

The Politics of Memory

By highlighting once again the complexity of the moment of enunciation in *Maus*, "Prisoner on the Hell Planet" points to the possibility of reading the work as part of a historical process that Spiegelman has focalized through the family but which opens into questions of public culture and politics. The moment of Anja's suicide—May 1968—serves as a touchstone for the countercultural rebellion that obviously informs Spiegelman's work. The same year "Prisoner" appeared in an underground comics magazine, for example, Spiegelman edited an (explicitly) pornographic and psychedelic book of quotations, *Whole Grains*. This book, dedicated to his mother, foreshadows some of the irreverence, eclecticism, and black humor of *Maus* (and even contains the Samuel Beckett quotation he cites in *Maus II* [II:45]), but it serves more as a marker of the cultural material of Spiegelman's life/career than as a developmental stage on the road to his masterpiece. The 1960s cemented Spiegelman's identity as an artist, putting him in touch, through the underground comics scene, with other "damned intellectuals"; in *Maus* and in the pages of *Raw* he continues this tradition of underground comics-with-a-message, even after "what had seemed like a revolution simply deflated into a lifestyle" (Spiegelman and Mouly 6).[15]

Besides constituting a moment of general cultural upheaval, the late 1960s inaugurated a new era for Jews in North America, one that would provide the sociological setting in which and against which Spiegelman would create *Maus*. Around this time, "the Holocaust" took on its central articulated importance in Jewish life—and it did so in a particular context. As Jewish liberation theologian Marc Ellis writes, "It is in light of the 1967 war that Jews articulated for the first time both the extent of Jewish suffering during the Holocaust and the significance of Jewish empowerment in Israel. Before 1967, neither was central to Jewish consciousness; the Jewish community carried on with a haunting memory of the European experience and a charitable attitude toward the fledgling state. After the war, both Holocaust and Israel are seen as central points around which the boundaries of Jewish commitment are defined" (3). For Ellis, it is imperative that Jewish people of conscience pass beyond the now problematic dialectic of innocence and redemption that poses all Jews as innocent victims and sees the state of Israel as a messianic redemption. Theology—indeed all discourse—that partakes of the innocence/redemption dialectic ultimately serves as a legitimating apparatus for Jewish chauvinism and for the Jewish state, since, within its terms, we cannot acknowledge Jews as themselves victimizers, either as individuals or as a collective.

Spiegelman's *Maus* operates precisely in this troubled space "beyond innocence and redemption." The Jewish subjects he produces are certainly not innocent (they're barely likable), nor have they found redemption in Rego Park, the Catskills, Soho, or indeed anywhere. The depiction of Vladek—a survivor—as a purveyor of violence in his own home, especially against his second wife, Mala, raises the crucial question of how a people with such a long history of suffering (which continues to the present) can avoid becoming agents of violence and torture themselves.[16] While neither volume of this comic strip addresses the question of Israel/Palestine (except for one ironic aside in *Maus II* [II:42]), in an interview Spiegelman makes a rather interesting comment which I believe invites this contextualization. During the discussion of *Maus* on NPR, Spiegelman alludes to the newscast that had opened the show. The top three stories, he notes, were on Pat Buchanan, South Africa, and an Israeli invasion of southern Lebanon in which Israeli tanks crushed UN peacekeeping vehicles. Spiegelman calls these three disturbing news stories evidence of the "constant reverb" of the past into the present which *Maus* seeks to illuminate, "if you dig my drift." The drift is that for post-1967 diasporic and Jewish communities, any text that explicitly challenges sentimental renderings of the Holocaust also implicitly challenges that tragedy's dialectical double—the legitimacy of Israeli incursions into Arab land.[17]

In the United States today, for Jews to speak out against the policies of the state of Israel or to question the uses to which the Holocaust has been put almost guarantees them unofficial excommunication from the Jewish community.[18] Although it carefully and provocatively explores the specificity of different generations of Jewish American identity, *Maus* does not explicitly raise the question of American Jews' relation to the policies of Israel. To do so would have been (in my opinion) to lose the mass audience so important to the book's effect among Jews and non-Jews. Revealing Jewish racism against African Americans, as Spiegelman does (II:98–100), falls within the mainstream realm of possibility and might be considered part of a coded effort to demystify Jewish American complicity with the state-sponsored crimes of Israel.

In any case, the true strength of Spiegelman's critique comes from his presentation of a people situated "beyond innocence and redemption," in that implausible ethical space which Jews must occupy in relation to their troubled history. In this sense, I believe, Spiegelman avoids what Edward Said has justly called "a *trahison des clercs* of massive proportions," the "silence, indifference, or pleas of ignorance and non-involvement [on the part of Jewish intellectuals that] perpetuate the sufferings of [the Palestinian] people who have not deserved such a long agony" (xxi). To remember genocide without abusing its memory, to confront Jewish violence while acknowledging the ever-present filter of self-hatred—these are the difficult intellectual tasks that mark the minefield of identity explored in *Maus* through the "lowbrow" medium of comics.

Maus as a whole works through the desacralizing and secularization of Jewish experience, but *Maus II* in particular marks a further crisis in Jewish identity. Through a staging of his own anguish at the success of *Maus I*, Spiegelman interrogates the ambivalent concept of Jewish power, especially the cultural capital won through the re-presentation of the Holocaust. Spiegelman condenses in one frame (which has attracted the attention of nearly all commentators) the various forces that unsettlingly intersect in *Maus*. At the bottom of the first page of the chapter "Auschwitz: Time Flies" (II:41), Spiegelman draws Art seated at his drawing board on top of a pile of mouse corpses. Outside his window stands the concentration camp guard tower which also figures in his "about the author" self-portrait; around the man in the mouse mask buzz the "time flies." Art's thought bubbles read, "At least fifteen foreign editions [of *Maus*] are coming out. I've gotten 4 serious offers to turn my book into a T.V. special or movie (I don't wanna.) In May 1968 my mother killed herself. (She left no note.) Lately I've been feeling depressed." Meanwhile, a voice-over—revealed in the next frame as a camera crew—calls ambiguously, "Alright Mr. Spiegelman . . . We're ready to shoot!" Among other meanings hovering, like the flies, in this frame, the overlay of positions and temporalities communicates an important fact about anti-Semitism: its effects persist across time and situation; someone is always "ready to shoot," even when no Nazis are visible and the media is under your control.

Art's guilt and depression, as thematized here, arise from his inability to make his mother reappear or the corpses (past and present) disappear. Instead, he finds himself unwillingly positioned as a willing victim of the culture industry. This industry—against which Spiegelman constantly defines himself—underwent its own crisis in the years between the publication of the two volumes of *Maus*. Articles proliferated on the deterioration of American publishing, and Spiegelman's own publisher, Pantheon, underwent a change in direction that caused an uproar among intellectuals concerned about the disappearance of nonmainstream work. In *Maus II*, Art finds that he can actively resist such commodification only through the contradictory gesture of directly addressing his audience and thus assuring that his success—based in the first place on such self-consciousness—will continue. Art's subsequent conversation with his shrink, Paul Pavel (who died in 1992), carries this double bind to its logical (in)conclusion. Pavel, a survivor, wonders whether, since "the victims who died can never tell THEIR side of the story . . . maybe it's better not to have any more stories." Art agrees and cites the aforementioned Beckett quotation—"Uh huh. Samuel Beckett once said: 'Every word is like an unnecessary stain on silence and nothingness'"—but then realizes the bind: "On the other hand, he SAID it" (II:45).

The impossibility of staying silent—which Spiegelman's ceaseless work on

Maus embodies—entails what Marianne Hirsch, following psychiatrist Dori Laub, has called "the aesthetic of the testimonial chain—an aesthetic that is indistinguishable from the documentary" (26) and which calls the reader into the story. The most striking example of this process, as Hirsch notes, comes at the end of *Maus II* when Spiegelman includes a photograph of his father taken just after his escape from the Nazis. This picture, sent to Anja as proof of his survival, was taken under strange circumstances: "I passed once a photo place what had a *camp* uniform—a new and clean one—to make *souvenir* photos" (II:134). This photo, which could have been taken of anyone, survivor or not, "dangerously relativizes the identity of the survivor" (Hirsch 25). Taken out of the context of Vladek's message to Anja, it also marks the becoming-kitsch of the Holocaust. Thanks to the miracle of mechanical reproduction, anybody can be a survivor! Philip Roth draws on a similar iconography, but, at least in *Patrimony*, he leaves out Spiegelman's self-conscious ironization. Roth seeks to wrap his father simultaneously in the uniforms of sentimentality and "tough" Jewish survivorhood, a strategy that, we have seen, works through the abjection, or at least forgetting, of the mother's experience.

Spiegelman's relationship to the photograph is more complicated. He clearly recognizes the sentimental tradition it inaugurates, *but he also has to use it:* "I need that photo in my book," he exclaims (II:134). In a gesture worthy of Beckett, *Maus* "stains" the "clean" uniform of Jewish suffering in the Holocaust; it reveals the impure basis of all Auschwitz *souvenirs*. Spiegelman "needs" to offer us this uniform because it figures the act of reading: for those living "after Auschwitz" (even those who, like Vladek and Anja, lived through Auschwitz), the uniform provides a kind of access, albeit highly mediated, to the events themselves. As a "site of memory" (see Nora), the photograph—and by extension the book that contains it—creates the space of identification upon which Spiegelman relies for affective and artistic success.

But identifications are always multiple, unforeseeable, and tinged with repudiation; readers are at least as likely to refuse to empathize with Vladek and instead to occupy Art's trademark vest—offered as a souvenir by an entrepreneurial "dog" (II:42). The vest, as opposed to the uniform, represents the power and risk of writing (and drawing): the ability and the need of those raised in what Hirsch calls "post-memory" (8) to reconfigure their parents' stories without escaping either their failure to revive the dead or their recuperation by a dominant non-Jewish culture. Between the vest and the uniform, *Maus* unravels as "a survivor's tale" of "crystalline ambiguity."[19] Spiegelman demonstrates how "the Holocaust" ultimately resists representation, but he uses this knowledge as authorization for *multiplying* the forms of portraiture. In this mongrelized, highbrow/lowbrow animal tale, ethnic and familial identities hover between a painful present and an even more painful past, between futile documentary and effective fiction. Simultaneously reproducing and recasting Holocaust history, *Maus* partakes of the melancholy pleasures of reading, writing, and talking "Jewish."

Notes

This essay is dedicated to the memory of three Jewish Americans: Nina Chasen, Benjamin Chasen, and Helene Rosenzweig. I am very grateful to Nancy K. Miller and Lucia Russett for insightful readings of earlier drafts. Thanks also to Karen Winkler for providing me with the NPR interview.

1. A word on terminology: the proper name "the Holocaust" is problematic for a number of reasons. As Art Spiegelman remarks, "Holocaust" (and another alternative, "the Shoah") has religious associations which imply that those who died were a sacrifice or burnt offering, a clear mystification of senseless violence ("Conversation"). The word "Holocaust" also has a specific history and, according to Berel Lang, emerged as the term to describe the destruction of European Jews by the Nazis only in the late 1960s. I will be arguing that this moment is extremely significant for Jews in general and for *Maus* in particular. Lang proposes the more neutral "Nazi genocide" (xxi). I, however, am suspicious as a rule of the concept of neutrality, and even though I do not like the term "Holocaust" I would rather contest its production and meaning than ignore its power in popular imagination.

2. But see also Daniel Boyarin's subtle consideration of the complexities of Jewish relations to the image. Boyarin demystifies the "commonplace of critical discourse that Judaism is the religion in which God is heard but not seen" (532), and his essay has implications that go beyond this religious context and are important to secular Jewish representations as well.

3. In a 1937 anti-Semitic pamphlet, Céline wrote, "J'espère qu'à présent vous savez lire 'juif' [I hope that you now know how to read 'Jewish']." Cited in Kaplan, "Rélévé" 25.

4. Apart from work cited elsewhere in this essay, two critics stand out for their theoretical sophistication in attempting to understand the Holocaust and Jewishness in an American context. On the Holocaust, see James E. Young, *Writing and*

Rewriting the Holocaust and *The Texture of Memory*. On Jewish identity, see Jonathan Boyarin, *Storm from Paradise: The Politics of Jewish Memory*. See also my review essay of Boyarin's book, "Sites of Memory."

5. See also Hirsch's discussion of this self-portrait.

6. See Adorno 361–65; Blanchot 66–69; Lang 144–45. On Lang, see White, "Historical Emplotment," 44–48.

7. See, e.g., Levi, *Survival in Auschwitz;* and Antelme. For more on this, see Rothberg.

8. Alice Y. Kaplan wrote, e.g., "Spiegelman gets the voices right, he gets the order of the words right, he manages to capture the intonations of Eastern Europe spoken by Queens" ("Theweleit and Spiegelman" 155).

9. The evidence for this alteration comes from the exhibit "Art Spiegelman: The Road to *Maus*" at the Galerie St. Etienne, 17 November 1992–9 January 1993. The phrase "talking Jewish" is one I heard my grandmother use but which makes me (and, I would guess, Spiegelman) uncomfortable to hear. I suspect that the Jewish/Yiddish difference figures a generational divide.

10. Maurice Anthony Samuels, in a fine unpublished essay, makes a similar point about the interplay between past and present in *Maus* and reads Art as "a parody of the traditional historian in what amounts to a parody of realist historiographic methods" (49–50).

11. This practice of revealing the creation of *Maus* has reached new heights (or depths) with the production of a CD-ROM version entitled *The Complete Maus*. In addition to the complete text of both volumes, the CD contains interviews with Spiegelman, writings and sketches by the author, tapes and transcriptions of Vladek, and even a family tree that allows viewers to "access" pictures of the protagonists. Although it is a valuable resource, especially with the inclusion of Vladek's original testimony, I remain doubtful whether "*Maus* in cyberspace" (as I am tempted to call it) represents a qualitative artistic advance. Rather, it seems to me another step on the road to the Spielbergization of the Holocaust, something Spiegelman generally resists.

12. Despite anatomizing a wide range of texts on Jewish themes, Gilman surprisingly makes no mention in *The Jew's Body* of Spiegelman or *Maus*.

13. See Nancy K. Miller's ("Cartoons of the Self") and Marianne Hirsch's essays for readings of Anja's absence that have influenced my own.

14. In her 1992 performance piece about the struggles in Crown Heights between Hasidic Jews and Caribbean and African Americans, *Fires in the Mirror*, Anna Deavere Smith included a perceptive monologue on Hasidic women's wigs that

she immediately contrasted with the Reverend Al Sharpton discussing his "James Brown" coiffure.

I do not mean to imply that circumcision and the wearing of wigs are parallel phenomena, since only the former derives from a biblical injunction and since it holds more fully for different types of Jews (although Gilman does point out that assimilated German Jews in the nineteenth century questioned the need for circumcision [*The Jew's Body* 91]). Rather, I think more emphasis needs to be placed on the *heterogeneity* of Jewish bodies across various lines of sociosexual demarcation: not "the Jew's body," then, but Jewish bodies. A full treatment of this question of Jewish women's bodies in *Maus* would need to consider the role of Art's wife, Françoise, and Mala, Vladek's second wife, whose marginalizations are not always treated as self-consciously as the question of Anja (see Hirsch on this topic).

A broader account of gender politics in Spiegelman's work would also consider his controversial Valentine's Day cover for the *New Yorker* (15 February 1993), which featured a painting of a Hasidic man kissing a black woman. A fairly direct reference to the same tensions explored by Smith in her performance, this "Valentine card" succeeded only in enraging black and Jewish communities. Spiegelman's avowedly utopian wish that "West Indians and Hasidic Jews . . . could somehow just 'kiss and make up'" (qtd. in "Editors' Note" 6) was directed at racial tensions but did not take account of the intersection of race with gender and sexuality. The image of a white man with a black woman connotes a whole history of sexual exploitation grounded in racial domination, while, on the other hand, a Hasidic man (as Spiegelman does acknowledge) is forbidden to touch a non-Jewish woman. With respect to the present context, I would also note the (not) accidental erasure of the Jewish woman (as well as the presumably threatening black man) from this vision of reconciliation. The scenario effectively points to an ambiguity of Jewish "ethnicity": Jews will, depending on the context, appear as white, as other than white, or as both simultaneously (as here).

15. For an essay that situates *Maus* within a tradition of Jewish comics, see Buhle. For a consideration of *Maus* as part of the emergent genre of the comic-novel, see Orvell.

16. For information on Israeli torture in the Occupied Territories, see the report by the Israeli human rights group B'Tselem.

17. For a memoir by a Palestinian living in Lebanon that movingly addresses the latter side of this dialectic (among other issues), see Makdisi.

18. Unfortunately, this situation seems to remain true even after the recent mutual recognition of the Palestine Liberation Organization and Israel. I would hy-

pothesize that this event will in the long run produce major changes in the parameters of Jewish identity configurations; however, it remains too early to tell what those realignments will look like (or what the political ramifications of this flawed agreement will be for Palestinians).

19. Spiegelman claims that the phrase "crystalline ambiguity" was his favorite description by a critic of *Maus* ("Conversation"). The only other place I've seen the phrase is in Spiegelman's own comments in *Tikkun*, where it appears unattributed. Talk about taking self-reflexivity seriously!

8

Read Only Memory

Maus and Its Marginalia on CD-ROM

John C. Anderson and Bradley Katz

It would take *many* books, my life . . .
Vladek, *Maus*

But this isn't like other comics.
Mala, *Maus*

In 1994, Voyager[1] (then the multimedia industry's premier publisher) released a CD-ROM of Art Spiegelman's much heralded *Maus*, entitled *The Complete Maus*.[2] From serial publication in the pages of *Raw*, to hardcover and then softcover book editions, including a two-volume slipcased edition, and finally to the CD-ROM, *Maus* has retained in the structure of its panels and pages the archaeology of its own composition, despite the increasing polish of its presentation.[3]

In addition to the text of the comic book, the disc includes video and audio clips, early sketches, examples of Spiegelman's post-*Maus* work, and his comments about the process of adapting *Maus* to the new medium. The materials it puts onto one's screen, if not into one's hands, are key texts and images crucial to tracking *Maus*'s development and reception, material hitherto available only to those willing to do the work of ferreting it out.[4] For example, if you weren't fortunate enough to have caught the exhibition at the Museum of Modern Art (MOMA) or to have bought *Funny Aminals*, in which Spiegelman's proto-*Maus* appeared, now you can see them. The overall effect is to gather these elements together without fully amalgamating them; the disc assembles a *Maus* that can be both read in sequence and taken apart. Yet unlike the growing number of directors' cuts of films[5] or the unexpurgated Anne Frank diary, the "uncut" *Maus* does not actually offer a more whole version of the object.

Since the actual text is unchanged (other than its renumbering as a single electronic book), one might ask if the CD-ROM is truly the "complete" *Maus* or just a highly annotated and illuminated one. Further, is the disc's claim to completeness a serious one, or is it mere hype, an information-age version of "new and improved"?

In our view, the CD-ROM version of *Maus* is not repackaging, the exploitation of a new medium as a means of cashing in on an established title. The new content stands in relation to the pages of *Maus* as marginalia and appendices, not additions or reconstructions. These materials highlight the work's fundamental incompleteness and reinforce a number of tendencies already embedded in *Maus*: an awareness of its own constructedness and self-reflexivity, an uneasy positioning vis-à-vis the history of the Holocaust, and a tense and elegiac representation of Spiegelman's family history. Some of the materials document Spiegelman's professional and personal engagement with the project. Others attempt to provide more of Vladek's own words. And still others evoke the memory of his mother, whose words are inaccessible—were, in fact, destroyed. Voyager's effort may perhaps be more complete in terms of an exploration of the production and reception of the comic and as a profile of Art Spiegelman, but by definition it is incapable of completing the gestures in *Maus* that indicate how incomplete Spiegelman's project must remain.

The Complete Maus CD-ROM, available for the Macintosh and Windows operating systems, employs a graphical user interface of windows and icons. The layout of the screen preserves the integrity of the comic book page while adding supplementary information beside it: whenever there is material to access, icons appear to the left of the comic. These can be used to call up text, still images, audio, or video akin to multimedia footnotes. However, these additional resources are presented quite literally as marginalia, outside the frame of the comic book page; they simultaneously reveal new information yet remain marginal (or at least supplementary) to the "finished" text of *Maus*. In fact, the CD-ROM allows the reader the option of removing the icons from the screen, and the User's Guide encourages new readers to "experience" the book before "exploring" the other resources.

In both ways of viewing the CD-ROM *Maus*, screens are equivalent to pages, and a reader advances in virtually the same way one would through the book. There are some difficulties, however: for one thing, the screen size and ratio do not permit comfortable viewing of an entire page on the screen at one time. Using the cursor, a reader can move the page up or down to see a particular panel.[6] Entire pages are available, one at a time, and although the resolution is legible, it is a bit like reading a reduced photocopy. Both modes (indicated by a plus or minus icon in the margin) are deficient in some respect: the magnified view disrupts the familiar experience of the narrative from the books, and the reduced version sacrifices detail for the visual integrity of the page (yet still does not allow the viewing of the two-page spread).

The icons (and what they represent) give readers a better sense of how to handle each page by providing information about the interface itself. The reader's current location is indicated by a "You are here" icon, flanked by navigational arrows.[7] An additional button allows one to switch between a reduced view of the whole page and a larger but partial one: the magnified view shows about half of the page in very clear, backlit detail. These basic navigational tools are the only icons in the "stripped down" version of the "hyped up" *Maus*—little more than a digitally scanned version of the books. The "complete" version is more complicated, even in terms of "turning" pages. The limited size of the window necessitates an additional icon that indicates what area of the page is onscreen: though fundamentally the same throughout, this icon changes from page to page as the layout of panels varies. This feature tends to disturb the more fluid reading someone using the books might have, focusing their attention more microscopically. A mock-up of each page, the icon leaves the actual panels blank and exposes elements of Spiegelman's visual syntax likely obscured on the crowded page.[8]

Not just a map, this layout icon combines annotation with navigation by being the access point for the preliminary sketches from the MOMA exhibit.[9] Yellow panels (as opposed to blank white ones) are themselves icons, and clicking on them reveals the sketches. Not just earlier, rejected versions, they are often rough and drawn in a variety of colors that reveal them, Spiegelman explains, as palimpsests of his process: the different colors indicate the refinement of the drawing over time. By revealing the progressive development of each panel, the "complete" *Maus* establishes itself instead as a "completed" *Maus*.

While the page layout icon is present on each screen, other icons appear only when there is something to add to that specific page. Some relate to the historical record: the icon of a photograph and map indicates a photo, document, or graphic from some source other than Spiegelman—for example, the arrest warrant issued for his parents is included at one point. Others relate to the production of *Maus*: directly above the page layout and the directional arrows, an icon of a pencil with sketch pad over the word "Drafts" appears when there is a preliminary version of that particular page (although these are usually earlier versions than the sketches called up by the yellow panels). When there is an icon of Art's face in a mouse mask, there is a taped audio comment by Spiegelman. And finally, two icons demonstrate how the historical record and the construction of Maus are intertwined: a film projector calls up Quicktime movies taken from videotapes of Spiegelman's trip to Poland, and a tape recorder with Vladek's mouse face appearing in a word balloon serves as the link to Vladek's testimony.

These excerpts of Vladek's own words are actual audio samples and include the option of displaying the written transcript with them. However, they are fragments of the larger body of interviews that Art conducted. Voyager packages a more complete transcription of them in a separate file entirely outside of Maus. Presented as text, the incredibly lengthy document does not follow the narrative as it appears in the books and of course does not include the portions of the story that relate more specifically to Art's own autobiographical narrative.[10] It is one of the more interesting additions on the disc, but it can be considered a work unto itself; it does not really "complete" Maus.

Before the reader gains access to the comic pages, however, the CD-ROM opens with a somewhat disorienting performance. Actually, there are three "beginning" sequences, each with its own sound track and "credits": the beginning of the CD-ROM itself, the beginning of Part I ("My Father Bleeds History"), and the beginning of Part II ("And Here My Troubles Began"). Displaying the dedications, title pages, and cover art, these sections behave more like films or slide shows than books, and the pace is out of the reader's control. This introduction of cinematic devices into an otherwise booklike structure is a bit jarring: significant elements from the books move by too quickly and cannot be recalled or stopped. Moreover, the music playing during each sequence goes uncredited on the CD-ROM, a minor but irritating omission.[11] These sequences can be skipped by clicking the mouse button, but the pages are then lost.

What all of the new components of the CD-ROM have in common is that they are in a marginal relation to the text of Maus itself. This relationship is direct and spatial: the icons that one clicks to summon new information—a sketch, a recording, and so forth—are next to the comic's page, outside the frame of the window. The usefulness of these supplementary sources varies widely depending on the reader's familiarity with both the historical facts of the Holocaust and those of Spiegelman's life. But even the parts of the CD-ROM that function as new "chapters" of this electronic book (e.g., Spiegelman's *New Yorker* cartoon "A Jew in Rostock")[12] are placed beside (or outside) *Maus*, conceptually and spatially. Though new, they do not add to the text: they augment interpretation and clarify reception but do not alter the content or frames of the pages and panels. Both the seasoned reader already familiar with *Maus* before "exploring" the CD-ROM version and the novice reader "experiencing" it for the first time will find the same *Maus* from beginning to end—albeit a variorum edition.[13] The additional texts, graphics, and images function as commentary rather than revision.

As one might expect, this wide range of material runs the gamut from illuminating and otherwise unavailable to incidental and tangential. The additional materials generally reveal the painstaking effort that went into producing the printed text. Displaying the progressive steps of its completion as narrative and as visual art, the disc rejects any notion that the work sprang fully formed from the head (and hands) of its maker or its primary source.

One example of the strange relationship between some of this material and the primary text is the videotape Spiegelman shot during his "pilgrimage" to Poland and Auschwitz. Contextualized almost as research footage, part of the documentary record, its presence illuminates something in *Maus* that can get lost: though Vladek's Holocaust tale is the most vivid and lengthy portion of the narrative, *Maus* is really Art Spiegelman's story. It opens and closes with Art, and fundamental and problematic portions of *Maus* (e.g., "Prisoner on the Hell Planet") are primarily about him. That is not to say that those two narratives actively compete against each other, but the multiple incarnations of Art (both real and fictional) are magnified in the CD-ROM. We get more of the "real" Art pursuing his project—interviewing his father, visiting sites important not only to the narrative but to Art personally and as a Jew, and responding to the reception of *Maus*.

One could argue that the new emphasis on his autobiographical narrative breaks the established frame of *Maus* and that *The Complete Maus* is different. The last image in the books is the headstone of Vladek and Anja, but that is followed by a marker for the project (Art Spiegelman 1978–1991); much of the extraneous material on the disc challenges that lifespan. Much like the signature and date in the bottom right-hand corner of "Prisoner on the Hell Planet" that marks that comic as an artifact or quotation, the date at the end of *Maus* could be seen as serving that same function for the larger text on the CD-ROM. What is missing is a narrative framework similar to the one that supports that reading of "Prisoner." *The Complete Maus* is clearly not intended to absorb *Maus* that particular way, as a book-within-a-book. In fact, such a reading would fundamentally subvert Spiegelman's design of the ending. The audio clip linked to the last page describes how the funereal image of the final panel is "crushed" against the back of the book without even a blank page, just the endpaper. The CD-ROM version of *Maus* is by no means as definite; the narrative impact of the ending may actually be lessened by the lack of a cover and by the addition of *Maus* miscellany.

These structural and formal issues are perhaps the strongest arguments one can make to support the idea that the CD-ROM is the "complete" *Maus*: it is the only form of *Maus* that combines the two parts and connects them with anything more evocative than a slipcase.[14] Only on the table of contents screen are the two parts identified side by side, emphasizing the ambiguity of the titles: "my father bleeds history/and here my troubles began." Although the second is taken from Vladek's comment about his arrival at Dachau,[15] it can also be read as Art's comment on his own documentary situation: his troubles begin with his attempt to record his father's story, or with his attempt to finish *Maus* (the second chapter of *Maus II* records his struggle with writer's block).

Even if one is not willing to map the book exactly onto Spiegelman's own life, it is at the very least a highly autobiographical narrative. That it was written and published as a serial over an extended period of time would also support speculation that the intent of the work may have changed subtly. For example, the first part starts by establishing Art's separateness from the community of survivors to which Mala and his father both belong, while the second begins with his discussion of anti-Semitism and the problem of representing Françoise as a mouse—a more complex reflection on his own Jewish identity. Moreover, Art's projection of himself as a concentration camp inmate in the pre-*Maus* "Prisoner on the Hell Planet" in 1972 is a very different representation of himself than the vest-clad investigator who not only appears in *Maus* but creates it. And the walking, talking Art Spiegelman tour guide of *The Complete Maus* is a different character than the one accessible only in mouse drag in the books.

But perhaps it is a good thing that questions of completeness, *Maus*, and memory cannot be so quickly resolved. The additional materials change our reading of the story, giving us more information about its production and reception. However, *Maus* remains *Maus*; its pages and panels and their contents remain intact. Perhaps what this contradictory state of affairs demonstrates most clearly is how "completely incomplete" *Maus* has been in its design from the very beginning. Its combinations of personal narrative and historical documentation, comic book form and survivor testimony, remain fundamentally open-ended and unresolvable.

If the marginalia surround *Maus* with a great deal of autobiographical documentation, they also serve more global documentary ends as well: the *Maus* CD-ROM is a small digital archive of Holocaust evidence and testimony. These documentary gestures are interconnected and provide both corroboration and commentary for the represented "documentation" within the narrative of *Maus*. The transcripts of Spiegelman's interviews with his father are the largest example, including 706 pages of material collected over seven years; these transcripts can be searched, annotated, and cross-referenced—an electronic notebook for the interested reader. And there are many other examples stored in the marginalia linked to *Maus*'s pages: architectural drawings of Auschwitz, drawings made by concentration camp inmates, photographs, video clips of Spiegelman's visit to the camp and of him having his parents' arrest document translated. While the User's Guide is careful to point out that these materials are intended to provide insight into Spiegelman's project rather than a comprehensive record of the Holocaust, their presence requires interpretation.

These documentary materials can be read as documents not only of the Holocaust but also of the desire to provide documentation, to establish the authenticity of *Maus*. In *Writing and Rewriting the Holocaust,* James Young describes how Holocaust diarists and memoirists are moved by the desire to make their books become "material fragments of experiences": "in asking literature to establish the facts of the Holocaust—or evidence of events—they are demanding not just that words signify experiences, but that they become—like the writers themselves—traces of their experiences" (23). The inclusion of documentary materials on the CD-ROM of *Maus* indicates this desire in two related ways. First, the working transcripts and the documentary record of Spiegelman's own research try to make *Maus* a more authentic memoir by providing more links between the text of *Maus* and the words of the transcripts—including the audio clips, which intensify the CD-ROM's authenticity by presenting the words in Vladek's own voice. Second, Spiegelman's own direct contact with the history of the Holocaust—the documents, the sites of the camps—is documented by the photographs, video clips, and sketches, making it a more authentic record of his own project.[16]

Sometimes the two overlap in interesting ways, and the CD-ROM encourages us to make connections. For example, when *Maus* shows Vladek sketching a diagram of the false-walled bunker they constructed to hide from the Nazis in the Srodula ghetto, Spiegelman's drawings include the notation that the original drawing was lost, indicating the onetime existence of a real sketch made by Vladek (*The Complete Maus* 99). The story of the bunker and the events that happened there are already preserved, but Spiegelman also documents an event that happened during the process of making *Maus*. Even when the actual document cannot be produced, the digitized sketch of the page attests to the documentary *impulse* that motivates Vladek to tell how things happened, and Spiegelman to account for the steps of transforming his father's testimony into the narrative of *Maus*. There is a complex ironic dynamic operating here: despite the missing "fact," the gesture to provide documentation gives the represented drawing an authenticity even greater than testimony alone; Art and Vladek are shown cooperating in its construction.

That the documentary impulse is something Vladek and Art share is made clear by the section of *Maus* that deals with Vladek's account of the gas chambers and crematoria. The process of investigation seems to require both direct witness and corroboration; Vladek takes pains to point out that when he tells Art about the gas chambers he is revealing what he saw himself: "You *heard* about the gas, but I'm telling not *rumors*, but only what I really *saw*" (69). The next panels (II:70–71 in the print version; 207–8 in the CD-ROM) are of the gas chambers and the crematorium. No people occupy the drawings; labels and arrows define its parts, dotted lines extend underground to show where the buried parts of the complex were, and an even more schematic diagram of the crematorium itself appears superimposed over the top two panels. These panels are among the most "documentary" in *Maus*, illustrations of Vladek's testimony rather than fully integrated parts of the narrative; they are empty of human (or animal) figures and have almost the stark quality of black-and-white photographs. Just as Vladek himself says he wants to tell only what he saw as a tinsmith assigned to help dismantle the gas chambers, Spiegelman also adopts an extremely restrained style, focusing on the building itself, its parts, and the actions his father took part in.

Both the writer and the storyteller seem to want to add even more information and to bring in other sources to help them do so. Vladek includes the words of a crematorium worker who describes the process of killing and burning that went on: at one point Vladek even states that "I didn't want more to hear, but anyway he told me" (II:71). Even a character in the narrative is driven to comment on the difficulty of hearing testimony from

Auschwitz, another index of the desire to testify and to continue placing markers that indicate the authenticity, the eyewitness authenticity, of the narrative. In the next panels, perhaps the most graphic representations of suffering in all of *Maus*, the testimony of two prisoners, Vladek and the crematorium worker, are combined. The other man starts telling the story: "It started in May and went on all summer. They brought Jews from Hungary—too many for their ovens, so they dug those big cremation pits" (II:72). Vladek continues in the present, saying, "The holes were big, so like the swimming pool of the Pines Hotel here. And train after train of Hungarians came." The rest of the panels' captions are not attributed to a speaker, although they are in Vladek's "voice." But while it is not clear whether these are part of Vladek's eyewitness account or part of the testimony he heard from the other worker, it actually seems as if the two are present and combined in the captions, corroborating testimony of the mass burnings at Auschwitz: "And those what finished in the gas chambers before they got pushed in these graves, it was the *lucky* ones. The others had to jump in the graves while still they were alive" (II:72). On the CD-ROM these pages are among the most densely populated with marginalia: the available materials include a long video clip of Art looking at the site of the Auschwitz crematorium (207), eight photographs or diagrams (207),[17] and seventeen separate sketches of the frightening drawing of the burning bodies (209). A prisoner's drawing of a corpse being dragged to the pyre is also included (209).

The documentary materials on the CD-ROM reinforce *Maus*'s status as both a survivor narrative and as the record of an artist's engagement with the history of the Holocaust, especially his own parents' histories. But there is, perhaps, a danger that the marginalia—working transcripts and other materials—might become more than marginal and deemphasize that which makes *Maus* unique among survivor narratives and records of intellectual engagement with the Holocaust: its comic book form. However, the CD-ROM highlights one of the primary *differences* between the panels of *Maus* and the pages of Vladek's testimony, thereby emphasizing the constructedness of the narrative, its hybrid status somewhere between nonfiction memoir and fictionalized narrative. While *Maus* is not a fiction (as Spiegelman has taken pains to point out),[18] it is fictionalized.

Comparing the transcript of Vladek's testimony with the dialogue on the page, one immediately perceives that Spiegelman has changed the wording while producing a faithful representation of content *and* verbal style. This is not to say that the Vladek of *Maus*'s panels and the Vladek whose testimony appears in the transcripts and recordings do not often say exactly the same thing: they do. But the passages that are *different* demonstrate the extent to which Spiegelman has adapted Vladek's voice, artistically reshaping it to meet the needs of the comic book form. For example, the working transcripts offer the following version of Vladek's story of the mass burnings (from a 1972 interview):

> But uh, the work in Birkenau, at the gas chambers, and at the ovens, they were working prisoners, Jewish prisoners. But they didn't let them longer than thirty days. Every thirty days, they burned this people; they pushed them in in the gas chamber and they burned them, and they took another section of thirty people to do the work. Not longer, because they have seen too much, and they didn't want that something will come out. In spite of it, it came out everything, because, because everything what I have seen, I was an eyewitness and everything, I knew before, but I didn't see it, but I knew also talking about it. ("Working Transcripts" 118)

The following selection from the audio clip accompanying this page of *Maus* on the CD-ROM offers a slightly different version of the same story: "I have heard much about it but now I have seen everything. I am telling you only this what I have seen, what I went through. Not this what people were talking, rumors and other things" (*The Complete Maus* 207).

Despite the differences between the transcript and the finished panels of *Maus*, the latter retain the sense of a survivor's voice speaking as well as the most important points Vladek makes: that he was an eyewitness to the events he describes and that he had heard other eyewitness accounts as well. The changes Spiegelman made to fit the transcript to the panels of *Maus* emphasize the characteristics that make Vladek's voice recognizable—that make it, in other words, a style—and moreover imbue *Maus*'s representations of memory and of the past with authenticity.[19] The "voice" succeeds not just despite Spiegelman's artistic reshaping but because of it, something the CD-ROM allows a reader to examine in detail.

In *The Complete Maus*, one can see many such attempts by Spiegelman—and Voyager—to boost the documentary sense of *Maus*. We would argue that while the CD-ROM provides a wealth of documentary evidence that would be useful to a researcher investigating either the Holocaust or the construction of *Maus*, these materials remain *secondary* sources to the text of

Maus itself: documents of its reception as much as its creation, more useful in figuring out how we have read and continue to read *Maus* than as factual evidence, despite their considerable detail and acknowledged facticity. The one potential exception to this is the aforementioned collection of working transcripts; as Vladek's testimony, they are a primary source in their own right. But even here we can see the shaping influence of two media: the tape recording and the hypermedia structure of which it is now a part. In the CD-ROM's introduction, Spiegelman describes his attempts to interview his father as similar to playing pinball, trying to get the conversational ball to go where he wanted without the machine tilting ("Interviewing Vladek"). The transcripts provide documentation of this process as well: the interplay between the "voices" of father and son are familiar to any reader of *Maus*. Vladek's original testimony is ultimately presented by the CD-ROM as an adjunct to the reading of *Maus*: what functioned as source material for Spiegelman now functions as commentary for Spiegelman's readers.

While Vladek's words and recorded voice populate the marginalia and constitute the primary source for Spiegelman's project,[20] there is also a significant silence that resonates in the screens of the CD-ROM as it did in the pages of *Maus*. This is the silence of Spiegelman's mother, Anja, and the absence of her direct testimony.[21] Here the "complete" *Maus* confronts its own incompleteness most poignantly. If Vladek's voice has been silenced by his death, a version of it persists in *Maus*—a "read-only memory" that can no longer be added to but is at least preserved from destruction. Anja's memories are unavailable; the memories of her persist only through Vladek and Art and in the photographic images left behind; these memories are incomplete fragments. Art's interviews with Vladek have been rewritten; Anja's destroyed diaries cannot be, and can never be read.

Marianne Hirsch's article, "Family Pictures: *Maus*, Mourning, and Post-Memory," deals with both the significance of Anja's absence in *Maus* and the impact of photographic images on the narrative. Hirsch concludes that both generate moments of trauma, of loss, that *cannot* be assimilated. There are three moments that "break the frame" of the printed *Maus*'s panels: the photo of Art and his mother in "Prisoner on the Hell Planet" in the first volume, and the photographs of Richieu and Vladek in the second volume. According to Hirsch, these moments draw our attention to *Maus*'s combination of the "documentary and the aesthetic" (11). She argues that "their power lies not in their evocation of memory, in the connection they can establish between present and past, but in their status as fragments of a history we cannot take in" (27). While the digital format would seem to diminish the shock of mixed media by providing an underlying common denominator, and while a computer screen's windows can accommodate photographs (or representations of photographs) more comfortably than the panels of a comic book,[22] the three drawings Hirsch singles out retain their force. One possible exception, as mentioned above, would be the photograph of Richieu in the dedication to *Maus II*, which cannot be viewed except as part of the slide show; it is possibly less disturbing because less accessible or because it stands outside a narrative context which encourages that interpretation of trauma.

Hirsch's observations raise interesting questions for multimedia, in particular about the effects of the multiplication of photographic images in the CD-ROM of *Maus*. We have already discussed the role of the new images in amplifying the documentary impulses of the project, as well as the disc's overall design. The specific significance of Anja's photographs is more complex and perhaps more painful. "Anja is recollected by others, she remains a visual and not a verbal presence," Hirsch explains (19). The disc includes many more images of Anja and other Spiegelman/Zylberberg family members and thus intensifies the sense of absence or loss Hirsch describes by multiplying reminders of it. A specific example would be the photograph of Art and Anja that accompanies Spiegelman's essay "Mad Youth." This color photograph not only appears at the head of the essay (itself an interesting meditation on Spiegelman's memories of Anja) but appears in a vivid full-screen version as a digital memento mori, part of the excerpt from the MOMA interview "Art on Art."[23] While the print *Maus* demands attention to Anja's absence, her silence in the narrative process, *The Complete Maus* does succeed in both representing her more frequently and making her absence felt that much more deeply.

The last example of "reading memory" in *Maus* is also deeply concerned with death and is an example of how the marginalia continue to illuminate and complicate the book. Spiegelman's comments from the CD-ROM regarding the interplay of the three narrative threads seem quite cynical: the highly romanticized representation of Vladek's reunion with Anja at the Jewish organization, the image of his father mistaking him for the long-dead Richieu and so appearing to be lost in a reverie of the past, and the headstone of Vladek and Anja, reunited as "dirt" (audio, 271). The drafts of this page offer alternative versions that are much darker: Art unable to remove his mouse mask; Art sitting on his parents' gravestone at his drawing table.

There are also sketches and notes regarding a Yahrzeit memorial candle. But while the commentary provided by the marginalia may alert us to the presence of a tension between these narrative threads, both cynical and romantic readings of the ending remain possible: our knowledge of Anja's future suicide does undercut the "happy ever after" promised by the reunion in 1945, and Spiegelman's critique of narratives that end happily seems partially justified, but the tone of *Maus* itself remains indeterminate and somewhat subdued. The presence of the headstone denotes the ending—or completion—of *Maus* like an inscription; *Maus* stands as a marker for his father's testimony and his mother's missing testimony, the final trace of their passage. In the end, does a "completed" *Maus* matter? The assertion of "completeness" in the title is potentially both misleading and a bit manipulative, since it seems to imply "authoritative" and Spiegelman himself convincingly argues that the CD-ROM explicitly fails to replace the printed version as the thing to "read." And yet, although the book is not supplanted, some aspects of the CD-ROM—the historical documentation, the interview recordings and transcripts, the artistic artifacts, its interface, its structuring metaphors, even its packaging and promotional materials—might still fuse elements of "mauscellany" in the user's memory as privileged, forcing the text of *Maus* away from center stage, un-completing what is already a finished work. Moreover, having been presented with the immense and unalterable collection of images, sounds, and graphics, the reader/viewer may be tempted to assume a more passive role, "exploring" rather than shaping. At best, Voyager's product allows access to the rich context for the work's historical import and artistic construction. At worst it becomes a high-speed gallery tour, associating related elements without necessarily provoking thought.

Voyager does an admirable job of physically connecting *Maus* to its marginalia; the drafts, sketches, and transcripts are all useful tools in understanding the process of producing *Maus*. And it does a remarkable job of gathering a wide range of sources, artifacts, commentary, and details of reception, presenting them in a coherent and aesthetically pleasing way. Where the CD-ROM stumbles, though, is on the more esoteric level of the theoretical relation of those materials to *Maus*. In the print version, Art Spiegelman fashioned an amazing representation—and analysis—of memory. However, in the last analysis, the CD-ROM version demonstrates an understanding of memory that remains primarily functional rather than transformative. The book is about Vladek and Art; in expanding its attention encyclopedically beyond the narrative of Vladek's telling and Art's retelling, *The Complete Maus* winds up being about *Maus*.

Notes

1. In December 1997, Voyager was purchased by Learn Technologies Interactive, L.L.C. ("LTI"). LTI acquired the Voyager brand name as well as forty-two titles, including *Maus*.

2. The disc was prominently displayed in Voyager's fall 1994 catalog ($49); it is likely that *Maus* added as much prestige to the medium of CD-ROM publishing as it did to the often misunderstood and much maligned "graphic novel."

3. The slipcovered edition introduced more elaborate endpapers and covers; the CD-ROM mimics many aspects of the books' design.

4. That audience would most likely be limited to academics, comic collectors, or freelance fetishists of the arcane, the rare, or the hip.

5. Many of these have been distributed on laser disc and DVD by Criterion, formerly a Voyager sister company. The recent trend in the production of films on DVD is to include features such as expert commentary on audio tracks, production notes, and other framing material much like those found on the *Maus* CD-ROM.

6. We examined a Macintosh-only version of the CD-ROM using an Apple PowerMac 7 100/66 with a 15-inch color monitor.

7. The locator icon gives the page number in relation to the whole work (i.e., page n of 271).

8. Namely, the role of panels as a basic constituent element of sequential storytelling and Spiegelman's manipulation and variation of them. He addresses this very subject in the introductory comments, discussing the basic four-tier layout and his variations on it. For a further explanation of Spiegelman's "syntax" of panels, addressing their narrative functions as well as the design of the page, see McCloud 77.

9. This explains in part why this icon is not present in the "View Page Only" mode of *Maus*.

10. Spiegelman points out in the introductory video clips on the CD-ROM that his father's testimony was repetitious and circular and that he had to streamline it for the purposes of publication. The transcript Voyager presents is rough, but there are features that make plowing through its massive length somewhat easier, such as a word search function that can find one or all appearances of a specific term.

11. It's a German swing tune: "Mickey Mouse."

12. Voyager categorizes the items on the disc that are not *Maus* as follows:

The Introduction: A step-by-step tour of the process involved in creating a single
page of the book with commentary by the author.

Art on Art: Audio of the author discussing a wide range of topics, accompanied
by previously unpublished artwork and photographs.

Appendices: MAUS-related miscellany, including the original three-page version
of MAUS (published in 1972) on which the Pulitzer-prize winning books are
based; speeches; articles; and a letter to the editor of the *New York Times Book
Review* by Art Spiegelman.

Supplements: Reference materials on the people and places encountered in MAUS.
Includes maps of Auschwitz/Birkenau and WWII Poland, and family trees for
the author's mother and father.

The Working Transcripts: The rough transcripts of Art's interviews with his father
Vladek, in Voyager's Expanded Book format. This is the primary source material for MAUS. (User's Guide 5)

13. After spending some time working with the CD-ROM (and reviewing Spiegelman's own complaints about the limitations of the computer screen), we have
concluded that the CD-ROM is really not the best place to read *Maus.*

14. According to the guide, "page numbers in *The Complete* MAUS are consecutive from the beginning of Part I to the end of Part II. Therefore, printed page numbers in *The Complete* MAUS do not match those of the printed books" (7). This indicates a conceptual decision to read *Maus* as a single book with two parts rather
than as two books, and it indicates a conscious rejection of seeing the CD-ROM as
supplementary to the books, keyed to them.

15. Some critics (e.g., Marianne Hirsch) have misread the passage as referring to
the arrival at Auschwitz, which of course occurs at the very end of *Maus I.* However,
in the text of *Maus* proper, the chapter titled " . . . and here my troubles began . . . "
clearly refers to Vladek's arrival at Dachau. The substitution of Auschwitz is perhaps
a logical mistake, but it is nonetheless another example of how slippery the "here"
can become when reading this title; Hirsch notes: "Reading *Maus II* we realize not
only that [Vladek's] troubles began long before, but that they (and his son's) never
end" (23).

16. In spite of the best intentions and a desire to present a firsthand record, these
clips often seem strained. Stock photographs, even, could serve the same purpose in
some cases.

17. Nine are listed, but one (an aerial photograph of Auschwitz) is mistakenly
repeated.

18. The CD-ROM includes Spiegelman's letter to the *New York Times* in which he protests the presence of *Maus* on their fiction best-seller list. *Maus* has presented problems of classification since its first publication; a separate category of Pulitzer was created for its award.

19. James Young addresses a more problematic example of such a style: D. M. Thomas's use of survivor testimony in *The White Hotel*—testimony, moreover, that had already been novelized in Anatoli Kuznetsov's *Babi Yar*. Young's comment explains both what constitutes a "style" of testimony—one we can see operating in *Maus*—and why Thomas's "stylings" are likely to make one much more uneasy than Spiegelman's: "[Thomas] loses track, it seems, of whose voice is whose. For is the 'appropriate voice' here that of Dina, the eyewitness, or is it the more figurative 'voice' of his eyewitness style? If it is a voice that is like a recording camera, it is a style; if it is the literal voice of a person who was there, it is Dina's. For Thomas, however, this voice is both a style and Dina's actual voice, for Thomas has appropriated Dina's voice *as a style*, a rhetorical move by which he would impute to his fiction the authority of testimony without the authenticity of actual testimony" (*Writing and Rewriting* 56). In *Maus*, Vladek's voice is likewise both a style and a real person's words, but we are not likely to accuse Spiegelman of appropriation—the text attempts to combine both authority *and* authenticity. However, that does not make the "voices" of either Vladek or Art (as characters) any less *styles*.

20. The editor of the transcripts does indicate that there are gaps when Art forgot to tape a session or accidentally taped over earlier sessions.

21. As Marianne Hirsch puts it, "Much of the text rests on her absence and the destruction of her papers, deriving from her silence its momentum and much of its energy. Through her picture and her missing voice Anja haunts the story told in both volumes" (20)—and, we would add, the CD-ROM.

22. For a discussion of the relationship between photographs and comics, especially in their representation of the human face, see McCloud 24–59.

23. The fact that it is a color photograph adds to its poignancy: less durable and more susceptible to fading and decay than black-and-white images, it can be said to have been "rescued" by its translation to a digital format. Of note is the fact that Art is holding a copy of *Mad* magazine, not necessarily a turning point in his professional career as cartoonist, but at least a significant source.

Works Cited

Adorno, Theodor. *Negative Dialectics*. Trans. E. B. Ashton. New York: Continuum, 1973.

Anderson, Mark. *Kafka's Clothes: Ornament and Aestheticism in the Habsburg Fin du Siècle*. Oxford: Clarendon P, 1992.

Antelme, Robert. *L'éspèce humaine*. Paris: Gallimard, 1957.

Bal, Mieke. *Narratology: Introduction to the Theory of Narrative*. Trans. Christine Van Boheemen. Toronto: U of Toronto P, 1985.

Blanchot, Maurice. *Vicious Circles: Two Fictions and "After the Fact."* Trans. Paul Auster. Tarrytown, NY: Station Hill, 1985.

Bosmajian, Hamida. *Metaphors of Evil: Contemporary German Literature and the Shadow of Nazism*. Iowa City: U of Iowa P, 1979.

Boyarin, Daniel. "The Eye in the Torah: Ocular Desire in Midrashic Hermeneutic." *Critical Inquiry* 16 (1990): 532–50.

Boyarin, Jonathan. *Storm from Paradise: The Politics of Jewish Memory*. Minneapolis: U of Minnesota P, 1992.

Breines, Paul. *Tough Jews: Political Fantasies and the Moral Dilemma of American Jewry*. New York: Basic Books, 1990.

B'Tselem. "The Wrong Arm of the Law: Torture Disclosed and Deflected in Israeli Politics." *Tikkun* Sept.–Oct. 1991: 13–14+.

Buber, Martin. "Judaism and Civilization and Thoughts on Jewish Existence." *Modern Jewish Thought: A Source Reader*. Ed. Nahum M. Glatzer. New York: Schocken, 1977. 123–36.

Buhle, Paul. "Of Mice and Menschen: Jewish Comics Come of Age." *Tikkun* Mar.–Apr. 1992: 9–16.

Caruth, Cathy. *Unclaimed Experience: Literature, Trauma, and History.* Baltimore: Johns Hopkins UP, 1996.

Cheever, Susan. *Home Before Dark.* Boston: Houghton Mifflin, 1984.

Cothias, Patrick, and Paul Gillon. *Au nom de tous les miens.* Paris. Rpt./trans. as *Der Schrei nach Leben.* Hamburg, 1988.

Daniels, Les. *Marvel: Five Fabulous Decades of the World's Greatest Comics.* New York: Harry Abrams, 1991.

DeHaven, Tom. "Comics." *New York.Times Book Review* 31 May 1998: 9, 16.

Des Pres, Terrence. "Holocaust Laughter?" *Writing and the Holocaust.* Ed. Berel Lang. New York and London: Holmes and Meier, 1988. 216–33.

"Editor's Note." *New Yorker* 15 Feb. 1993: 6.

Eisner, Will. *Comics and Sequential Art.* Tamarac, FL: Poorhouse P, 1985.

Ellis, Marc H. *Beyond Innocence and Redemption: Confronting the Holocaust and Israeli Power.* San Francisco: Harper, 1990.

Epstein, Helen. *Children of the Holocaust: Conversations with Sons and Daughters of Survivors.* New York: Putnam, 1979–80.

Ezrahi, Sidra DeKoven. *By Words Alone: The Holocaust in Literature.* Chicago: U of Chicago P, 1980.

Fackenheim, Emil L. *The Jewish Return into History: Reflections in the Age of Auschwitz and a New Jerusalem.* New York: Schocken, 1978.

Felman, Shoshana, and Dori Laub. *Testimony: Crises of Witnessing in Literature, Psychoanalysis, and History.* New York: Routledge, 1992.

Freud, Sigmund. *Character and Culture.* Trans. J. Strachey, intro. P. Rieff. New York: MacMillan, 1963.

Friedlander, Saul. *Memory, History, and the Extermination of the Jews of Europe.* Bloomington: Indiana UP, 1993.

———, ed. *Probing the Limits of Representation: Nazism and the "Final Solution."* Cambridge: Harvard UP, 1992.

Friedman, Susan Stanford. "Women's Autobiographical Selves: Theory and Practice." *The Private Self.* Ed. Shari Benstock. Chapel Hill: U of North Carolina P, 1988. 34–62.

Gilman, Sander. *Jewish Self-Hatred: Anti-Semitism and the Hidden Language of the Jews.* Baltimore: Johns Hopkins UP, 1986.

———. *The Jew's Body.* New York and London: Routledge, 1991.

Gopnik, Adam. "Comics and Catastrophe." *New Republic* 22 June 1987: 29–34.

Grossman, David. *See Under: Love.* Trans. Betsy Rosenberg. New York: Washington Square P, 1989.

Groth, Gary. "Art Spiegelman Interview." *Comics Journal* Sept. 1995: 52–114.

———. "Art Spiegelman, Part II." *Comics Journal* Oct. 1995: 97–139.

Hartman, Geoffrey H. "The Book of the Destruction." *Probing the Limits of Representation: Nazism and the "Final Solution."* Ed. Saul Friedlander. Cambridge: Harvard UP, 1992. 318–34.

———, ed. *Holocaust Remembrance: The Shapes of Memory*. Cambridge, MA: Blackwell, 1994.

———. *The Longest Shadow*. Bloomington: Indiana UP, 1996.

Harvey, Robert C. *The Art of the Comic Book*. Jackson: UP of Mississippi, 1996.

Hellerstein, Kathryn. "Yiddish Voices in American English." *The State of the Language*. Ed. Leonard Michaels and Christopher Ricks. Berkeley: U of California P, 1980. 182–201.

Hirsch, Marianne. "Family Pictures: *Maus*, Mourning, and Post-Memory." *Discourse: A Journal for Theoretical Studies in Media and Culture* 15.2 (1992–93): 3–29.

Horowitz, Elliott. Review of *The Singular Beast: Jews, Christians, and the Pig*, by Claudine Fabre-Vassas. *New Republic* 8 June 1998: 44–45.

Howe, Irving. "Writing and the Holocaust." *Writing and the Holocaust*. Ed. Berel Lang. New York: Holmes & Meier, 1988. 175–99.

Jackson, Jack. *God's Bosom and Other Stories*. Seattle: Fantagraphics, 1995.

Juno, Andrea. *Dangerous Drawings*. New York: Juno Books, 1997.

Kachru, Braj B., ed. *The Other Tongue: English across Cultures*. Urbana: U of Illinois P, 1992.

Kafka, Franz. *Letters to Friends, Family, and Editors*. Trans. Richard Winston and Clara Winston. New York: Schocken, 1977.

Kaplan, Alice Yaeger. "Rélévé des sources et citations dans 'Bagatelles pour un massacre.'" Tusson: Editions du Lerot, 1987.

———. "Theweleit and Spiegelman: Of Men and Mice." *Remaking History*. Ed. Barbara Kruger and Phil Mariani. Dia Art Foundation Discussions in Contemporary Culture 4. Seattle: Bay, 1989. 151–72.

Kaplan, Louise J. *No Voice Is Ever Wholly Lost*. New York: Simon and Schuster, 1995.

Kaps, Joachim, ed. *Comic Almanach 1993*. Wimmelbach, Germany: Comic P Verlag, 1993.

Klein, Richard. *Cigarettes Are Sublime*. Durham, NC: Duke UP, 1993.

Knox, Israel. Introduction. *Anthology of Holocaust Literature*. Ed. Jacob Glatstein, Israel Knox, and Samuel Margoshes. New York: Atheneum, 1973. i–xxiii.

Kristeva, Julia. *Black Sun: Depression and Melancholia*. Trans. Leon S. Roudiez. New York: Columbia UP, 1989.

Lang, Berel. *Act and Idea in the Nazi Genocide*. Chicago: U of Chicago P, 1990.

Langer, Lawrence. *Holocaust Testimonies: The Ruins of Memory*. New Haven: Yale UP, 1991.

———. *Versions of Survival: The Holocaust and the Human Spirit*. Albany: SUNY P, 1982.

Lanzmann, Claude. Panel Discussion of *Shoah*. Yale U, 5 May 1986. Transcript, 51–52. Cited in Shoshana Felman and Dori Laub. *Testimony: Crises of Witnessing in Literature, Psychoanalysis, and History*. New York: Routledge, 1992.

———. *Shoah: An Oral History of the Holocaust*. New York: Pantheon, 1985.

Levi, Primo. *The Drowned and the Saved*. New York: Summit, 1988.

———. *Survival in Auschwitz*. Trans. Stuart Woolf. New York: Collier, 1961.

Lipman, Steve. *Laughter in Hell: The Use of Humor during the Holocaust*. Northvale, NJ: Jason Aronson, 1991.

Lopate, Philip. "Resistance to the Holocaust." *Tikkun* May–June 1989: 55–65.

Loshitzky, Yosefa, ed. *Spielberg's Holocaust: Critical Perspectives on* Schindler's List. Bloomington: Indiana UP, 1997.

Lyotard, Jean-François. *The Postmodern Condition*. Trans. Geoff Bennington and Brian Massumi. Minneapolis: U of Minnesota P, 1984.

Makdisi, Jean Said. *Beirut Fragments: A War Memoir*. New York: Persea, 1990.

March, Joseph Moncure. *The Wild Party*. Illustrations by Art Spiegelman. New York: Pantheon, 1994.

Margulies, Donald. *The Model Apartment*. Sight Unseen, and Other Plays. New York: TCG, 1995. 141–95.

Mason, Mary. "The Other Voice: Autobiographies of Women Writers." *Life/Lines: Theorizing Women's Autobiography*. Ed. Bella Brodzki and Celeste Schenck. Ithaca: Cornell UP, 1988. 19–44.

McCloud, Scott. *Understanding Comics*. 2nd ed. New York: HarperCollins, 1993.

Miller, Alice. *The Drama of the Gifted Child: The Search for the True Self*. Trans. Ruth Ward. New York: Basic Books, 1981.

Miller, Nancy K. *Bequest and Betrayal: Memoirs of a Parent's Death*. New York: Oxford, 1996.

———. "Cartoons of the Self: Portrait of the Artist as a Young Murderer—Art Spiegelman's *Maus*." M/E/A/N/I/N/G 12 (1992): 43–54.

———. "Representing Others: Gender and the Subjects of Autobiography." *differences* 6.1 (1994): 1–27.

Moore, Terry. *Strangers in Paradise*. Intro. Diana Schutz. Houston: Abstract Studios, 1996.

Mordden, Ethan. "Kat and Maus." *New Yorker* 6 April 1992: 96.

Nakazawa, Keiji. *Barefoot Gen: The Day After*. Philadelphia: New Society, 1988.

Nietzsche, Friedrich. *On the Genealogy of Morals*. Ed. Walter Kaufmann. New York: Vintage, 1969.

Nora, Pierre. "Between Memory and History: *Les Lieux de Mémoire*." *Representations* 26 (1989): 7–25.

Orvell, Miles. "Writing Posthistorically: *Krazy Kat*, *Maus*, and the Contemporary Fiction Cartoon." *American Literary History* 4 (1992): 110–28. Rpt. in *After the Machine: Visual Arts and the Erasing of Cultural Boundaries*. Jackson: UP of Mississippi, 1995. 129–46.

Ozick, Cynthia. "It Takes a Great Deal of History to Produce a Little Literature." *Partisan Review* 60.2 (1993): 195–200.

———. "A Liberal's Auschwitz." *The Pushcart Prize*. New York: Avon, 1976. 149–53.

———. "Metaphor and Memory." *Metaphor and Memory*. New York: Vintage, 1991. 265–83.

———. "Roundtable Discussion." *Writing and the Holocaust*. Ed. Berel Lang. New York: Holmes and Meier, 1988. 277–84.

———. Untitled response to "Is Our Schizophrenia Historically Important?" *Response: A Contemporary Jewish Review* 6 (Fall 1972): 87–93. Rpt. as "On Living in the Gentile World." *Modern Jewish Thought: A Source Book*. Ed. Nahum N. Glatzer. New York: Schocken, 1977. 167–74.

Pochoda, Elizabeth. "Reading Around." *Nation* 27 April 1992: 560.

Portugues, Catherine. "Seeing Subjects: Women Directors and Cinematic Autobiography." *Life/Lines: Theorizing Women's Autobiography*. Ed. Bella Brodzki and Celeste Schenck. Ithaca: Cornell UP, 1988. 338–50.

Ricoeur, Paul. *Time and Narrative*. Trans. Kathleen McLaughlin and David Pallauer. Chicago: U of Chicago P, 1984.

Rosen, Alan. "The Language of Survival: English as Metaphor in Spiegelman's *Maus*." *Prooftexts* 15.3 (1995): 249–62.

Rosen, Jonathan. "Spiegelman: The Man behind the *Maus* That Roared." *Forward* 17 Jan. 1992: 1–11.

Roskies, David. *Against the Apocalypse: Responses to Catastrophe in Modern Jewish Culture*. Cambridge: Harvard UP, 1984.

Roth, Philip. *The Anatomy Lesson. Zuckerman Bound: A Trilogy and Epilogue*. New York: Fawcett, 1986. 246–420.

———. *Patrimony: A True Story*. New York: Simon and Schuster, 1991.

Rothberg, Michael. "Sites of Memory, Sites of Forgetting: Jewishness and Cultural Studies." *Found Object* 2 (1993): 111–18.

Sabin, Roger. *Adult Comics: An Introduction*. New York: Routledge, 1993.

Sachs, Nelly. *O the Chimneys*. Trans. Michael Hamburger. New York: Farrar, Straus and Giroux, 1969.

Sack, Leeny. *The Survivor and the Translator. Out from Under: Texts by Women Performance Artists*. Ed. Lenora Champagne. New York: Theatre Communications Group, 1990. 123–51.

Sacks, Jonathan. *One People? Tradition, Modernity, and Jewish Unity*. London: Littman Library of Jewish Civilization, 1993.

Said, Edward. *The Question of Palestine*. New York: Vintage, 1992.

Samuels, Maurice Anthony. "Representing the Holocaust: Art Spiegelman's *Maus* and the Postmodern Challenge." Unpublished essay, 1990.

Sarna, Nahum. *Understanding Genesis*. New York: Schocken, 1970.

Schafer, Roy. *Retelling a Life: Narration and Dialogue in Psychoanalysis*. New York: HarperCollins, 1992.

Shohat, Ella. *Israeli Cinema: East/West and the Politics of Representation*. Austin: U of Texas P, 1989.

Smith, Anna Deavere. *Fires in the Mirror*. New York: Anchor, 1993.

Sokoloff, Naomi. "Childhood Lost: Children's Voices in Holocaust Literature." *Infant Tongues: The Voice of the Child in Literature*. Ed. Elizabeth Goodenough, Mark Heberle, and Naomi Sokoloff. Detroit: Wayne State UP, 1994. 259–73.

Spiegelman, Art. *Breakdowns: From MAUS to Now*. New York: Belier P, 1977.

——. "Comix 101: Forms Stretched to Their Limits." *New Yorker* 19 April 1999: 76–85.

——. *Comix, Essays, Graphics, and Scraps: From MAUS to Now to MAUS to Now*. New York: Raw Books, 1998.

——. "Commix: An Idiosyncratic Historical and Aesthetic Overview." *Print* 42.6 (Nov./Dec. 1988): 61–73, 95–196.

——. *The Complete Maus*. CD-ROM. New York: The Voyager Company, 1994.

——. "A Conversation with Art Spiegelman." With John Hockenberry. *Talk of the Nation*. National Public Radio, 20 Feb. 1992.

——. Cover painting. *New Yorker* 15 Feb. 1993.

——. *Dead Dick*. In *1980–1990: The Best Comics of the Decade*, vol. 1. Seattle: Fantagraphics, 1990.

——. "An Examination of *Master Race*." With John Benson and David Kasakove. *Squa Trout* no. 6 (1975): 41–47.

——. Interview with Joey Cavalieri. "Jewish Mice, Bubblegum Cards, Comics Art, and Raw Possibilities." *Comics Journal* 65 (Aug. 1981): 98–125.

——. Introduction to Keiji Nakazawa, *Barefoot Gen: Out of the Ashes*. Philadelphia: New Society, 1994.

——. *Maus: A Survivor's Tale I: My Father Bleeds History*. New York: Pantheon, 1986.

——. *Maus: A Survivor's Tale II: And Here My Troubles Began*. New York: Pantheon, 1991.

——. *Maus I* [German version]. Trans. Christine Brinck and Josef Joffe. Reinbeck bei Hamburg: Rowolt Verlag, 1999.

——. "Mein Kampf." *New York Times Magazine* 12 May 1996: 36–37.

——. *Open Me I'm a Dog*. New York: Joanna Cotler, 1997.

——. "Saying Goodbye to *Maus*." *Tikkun* Sept.–Oct. 1992: 44–45.

Spiegelman, Art, and Françoise Mouly. Interview. *The New Comics*. Ed. Gary Groth and Robert Fiore. New York: Berkley, 1988.

——, eds. *Read Yourself Raw*. New York: Pantheon, 1987.

Steiner, George. *Language and Silence: Essays on Language, Literature, and The Inhuman*. Harmondsworth: Penguin, 1969.

Stevens, Wallace. *Collected Poems*. London: Faber and Faber, 1971.

Storr, Robert. "Making *Maus*" [Exhibit Notes]. *Projects 32: Art Spiegelman*. Museum of Modern Art, New York City. 17 Dec.–28 Jan. 1992.

Trudeau, Garry. Rev. of *Understanding Comics* by Scott McCloud. *New York Times* 13 Feb. 1994: 7.14.

Weschler, Lawrence. *Shapinki's Karma, Bogg's Bills, and Other True-Life Tales*. San Francisco: Northpoint P, 1988.

White, Hayden. *The Content of the Form: Narrative Discourse and Historical Representation*. Baltimore: Johns Hopkins UP, 1987.

———. "Historical Emplotment and the Problem of Truth." *Probing the Limits of Representation: Nazism and the "Final Solution."* Ed. Saul Friedlander. Cambridge: Harvard UP, 1992. 37–53.

———. *Tropics of Discourse: Essays in Cultural Criticism*. Baltimore: Johns Hopkins UP, 1978.

Wiesel, Elie. *Night*. Trans. Stella Rodway. New York: Avon Books, 1971.

Williams, Patricia. "Talking about Race, Talking about Gender, Talking about How We Talk." *Antifeminism in the Academy*. Ed. Vèvè Clark, Shirley Nelson Garner, Margaret Higonnet, and Ketu H. Katrak. New York: Routledge, 1996. 69–94.

Witek, Joseph. *Comic Books as History: The Narrative Art of Jack Jackson, Art Spiegelman, and Harvey Pekar*. Jackson: UP of Mississippi, 1989.

Yerushalmi, Yosef Hayim. *Zakhor: Jewish History and Jewish Memory*. Seattle: U of Washington P, 1982.

Young, James E. "The Holocaust as Vicarious Past: Art Spiegelman's *Maus* and the Afterimages of History." *Critical Inquiry* 24 (Spring 1998): 670–97.

———. *The Texture of Memory*. New Haven: Yale UP, 1993.

———. *Writing and Rewriting the Holocaust: Narrative and the Consequences of Interpretation*. Bloomington: Indiana UP, 1988, rpt. 1990.

Zavarzadeh, Mas'ud. *The Mythopoeic Reality: The Postwar American Nonfiction Novel*. Urbana: U of Illinois P, 1976.

Žižek, Slavoj. *Looking Awry: An Introduction to Jacques Lacan through Popular Culture*. Cambridge: MIT P, 1991.

Contributors

JOHN C. ANDERSON is a Lecturer in the Writing Program at Northwestern University. He also serves as Instructional Technology Coordinator for Engineering Design and Communication, an innovative program for first-year engineering students at Northwestern.

HAMIDA BOSMAJIAN is Professor of English at Seattle University. She is the author of *Metaphors of Evil: Contemporary German Literature and the Shadow of Nazism* (University of Iowa Press), *Sparing the Child: Grief and the Unspeakable in Youth Literature about Nazism and the Holocaust* (Routledge), and many essays about children's literature, Nazism, and the Holocaust.

DEBORAH R. GEIS is Associate Professor of English at DePauw University and has taught at Oberlin College, the University of Tennessee, and Queens College, CUNY. She is the author of *Postmodern Theatric(k)s: Monologue in Contemporary American Drama* and coeditor (with Steven F. Kruger) of *Approaching the Millennium: Essays on Angels in America* (both University of Michigan Press), as well as a book in progress, *Female Parts: Identity Politics in American Feminist Drama and Performance.* Her publications include articles on ethnicity in contemporary drama and other topics.

BRADLEY KATZ has extensive professional experience in information architecture, instructional design, and content development. He lives in Chicago.

MICHAEL G. LEVINE is Associate Professor and Chair of German and Comparative Literature at Barnard College. He is the author of *Writing Through Repression: Literature, Censorship, Psychoanalysis* (Johns Hopkins University Press), *The Belated Witness: Literature, Testimony, and the Question of Holocaust Survival* (forthcoming, Stanford University Press), and articles on comparative literature, psychoanalysis, and contemporary critical theory.

DAVID MIKICS is Associate Professor of English at the University of Houston and author of *The Limits of Moralizing: Pathos and Subjectivity in Spenser and Milton* (Bucknell University Press) and *The Romance of Individualism in Emerson and Nietzsche* (Ohio University Press), as well as articles on postmodern literature, cultural studies, and film.

NANCY K. MILLER is Distinguished Professor of English and Comparative Literature at the Graduate Center of the City University of New York. Her most recent books are *But Enough about Me: Why We Read Other People's Lives* (Columbia University Press) and *Extremities: Trauma, Testimony, and Community* (University of Illinois Press), an anthology coedited with Jason Tougaw. She is writing a memoir about Paris in the 1960s.

ALAN C. ROSEN lives in Jerusalem and teaches at Bar-Ilan University. He writes on Holocaust literature and early modern drama. He is the author of a monograph on representing catastrophe and editor of a collection of essays entitled *Celebrating Elie Wiesel*. He is currently completing a book on the Holocaust and multilingualism.

MICHAEL P. ROTHBERG is Associate Professor of English and Comparative Literature at the University of Illinois, Urbana-Champaign. He is the author of *Traumatic Realism: The Demands of Holocaust Representation* (University of Minnesota Press) and coeditor, with Neil Levi, of *The Holocaust: Theoretical Readings* (Edinburgh University Press).

ARLENE FISH WILNER is Professor of English and American Studies at Rider University and a Fellow of the Carnegie Academy for the Scholarship of

Teaching and Learning. Her articles include "The Jewish-American Woman as Artist: Cynthia Ozick and the 'Paleface' Tradition" (*College Literature*), "Limning the Cannibal Galaxy: Cynthia Ozick's Moral Imagination" (*Criticism*), and essays in eighteenth-century literature, writing pedagogy, and children's literature. She currently directs RiderBRIDGE, a university-wide faculty development project.

Index

Queens. *See* Rego Park

racism, 69, 129, 131, 133n. 8, 152,
  157n. 14
Rashi, 21
Raw, 5, 6, 24n. 2, 142, 143, 147, 151
Red Cross, 127
Rego Park, 35, 38, 45, 47, 75, 86,
  103n. 29, 151
Richieu, 23, 27, 30, 33, 42, 53, 58n. 7,
  85, 86, 97, 102n. 18, 104n. 31, 115,
  117, 119, 120, 142, 147, 169, 170
Ricoeur, Paul, 112
Rosen, Alan C., 9, 99–100nn. 4, 7 .
Rosen, Jonathan, 69, 70, 89, 103n. 23
Rosen, Norma, 5
Roth, Philip, 144, 148, 150; *Anatomy
  Lesson*, 138–39; *Patrimony*, 44,
  56n. 2, 137–40, 149, 154
Rothberg, Michael P., 9, 10, 11n. 6,
  156n. 4
Rousseau, Henri, 44, 56n. 2

Sachs, Nelly, 37
Sack, Leeny, 3
Sacks, Jonathan, 116
Said, Edward, 152
Sandlin, David, 2
Santayana, George, 105
Sartre, Jean-Paul, 75
Schafer, Roy, 32
Scheherezade, 89
Schutz, Diana, 16, 17
second generation (after Holocaust), 3, 4,
  8, 30, 33, 35, 38, 39, 41–43, 47, 52,
  63, 64, 67, 68, 82–83, 98, 107, 119,
  120, 153, 154, 167
Shakespeare, William, 103n. 25
Shoah (film). *See* Lanzmann, Claude
Shohat, Ella, 138
Smith, Anna Deavere, 156–57n. 14
smoking, 50, 80, 90–94, 96–97,
  103nn. 26, 27, 28, 142–43

Sokoloff, Naomi, 28
Sosnowiec, 51, 53, 54, 57n. 5, 85, 94,
  115, 147
Spider-Man, 17
Spiegelman, Anja. *See* Anja
Spiegelman, Art, works by: *Breakdowns*,
  15, 16, 19, 21, 71, 102n. 22; "Commix," 99n. 1; "An Examination of
  Master Race," 24n. 7; *Funny Aminals*,
  5, 11n. 6, 29, 41, 69, 134n. 13, 159;
  "Little Orphan Annie's Eyeballs," 63,
  101n. 10; "Mad Youth," 86, 170;
  "Mein Kampf," 6; *Open Me . . . I'm
  a Dog*, 102n. 22; "Prisoner on the
  Hell Planet," 18, 21, 22, 30, 33, 34,
  36, 38, 39, 41, 49–51, 57n. 4, 82–84,
  87–89, 93, 94, 96–98, 102n. 20, 150,
  163, 164; "Saying Goodbye to *Maus*,"
  26, 142; *Whole Grains*, 150; *Wild
  Party, The*, 7, 15. *See also* Art/Artie;
  Complete Maus, The; *Maus*
Spiegelman, Mala. *See* Mala
Spiegelman, Nadja, 23, 42, 102–03n. 23,
  119
Spiegelman, Richieu. *See* Richieu
Spiegelman, Vladek. *See* Vladek
Spielberg, Steven, 156n. 11; *An American
  Tail*, 88; *Jurassic Park*, 4; *Schindler's
  List*, 3, 4, 9, 11n. 5
Srodula, 94, 116, 119, 166
Stara, 94
Stein, Gertrude, 44
Stevens, Wallace, 79
Storr, Robert, 142
Streicher, Julius, 145
superheroes, 16–18
Superman, 17
survivors. *See* second generation

Tenniel, Sir John, 19
Terezin, 79
testimony, 3, 4, 8, 9, 28, 29, 36, 48, 52,
  55, 63, 67, 68, 70, 77, 78, 81, 98, 99,